For Ray,

The Thing of It Is

The Gospel According
To Callaway!

John H. Callaway

THE THING OF IT IS

With Reflections on Chicago and the Problem Society

John D. Callaway

~

Jameson Books, Inc. ■ Ottawa, Illinois

Jameson Books are available at special discounts for bulk purchases for sales promotions, premiums, fund raising or educational use. Special condensed or excerpted editions can also be created to customer specification.

For information and catalog requests write:

Jameson Books, Inc.
P.O. Box 738
Ottawa, IL 61350

5 4 3 2 1   97 96 95 94

Printed in the United States of America.

Distributed to the book trade by
National Book Network, 4720 Boston Way, Lanham, MD 20706

ISBN: 0-915463-65-2

For my parents,
Dorothy Garwood Callaway and Charles Ernest Callaway.

And my daughters,
Ann Hampton Callaway and Liz Callaway Foster.

And my grandson,
Nicholas Callaway Foster.

Contents

Christmas Isn't Easy

The Thing of It Is (and Other Gripes)

Words and Pictures

Over There

Foreword

In one of this book's essays, John Callaway confesses that he once devoured an entire box of chocolates at one sitting. This admission is characteristic of the sensibility that flows like a current of electricity through these essays, infusing them with human energy that is direct and unself-conscious, providing both light and warmth. In the presence of such a generous spirit, the reader will be tempted, as the author was with the candy, to consume all these pieces without pause.

Why is this so when in so many collections of writings a very different temptation invades the soul of the reader, that is, to sample the chapters warily, to skim without guilt, and to skip without hesitation?

The answer is found in the author who, without striving for such an effect—indeed it is ever a by-product and never a goal—transforms the reader into a companion on a series of walks during which, as in friendship, defenses are unnecessary because there is no attack or manipulation to ward off, time is suspended, and the wonders embedded in familiar territory are seen freshly in a new play of light. In short, John Callaway burdens us with none of the strain, so obvious in so many other writers, caused by forcing the will, as Coleridge put it, to do the work of the imagination.

It is for just such graceful experiences that we turn to books. It is all the more remarkable that a journalist who has spent so much of his career on radio and television should be able to affirm the intrinsic power of words, to show how a real writer can bring life, its ambiguities embraced rather than over-simplified, to a blank page.

In an instructive anecdote, for example, John Callaway seats us next to the suave David Niven, at New York's Hotel Pierre for an interview about the actor's book of Hollywood recollections. In an accommodation that preserves his own journalistic principles but allows Niven to answer a question that would not otherwise have been placed, our interviewer asks him what he did at lunch the previous day. This allows the actor to tell us how he would really like to be recognized, "Yesterday, I had lunch with my publisher."

This response defined the Academy Award winner as he longed to be known, not as a famous actor but first and foremost as a writer. This story is a wonderful illustration of John Callaway at work. He is dutiful, prepared, mindful of his own integrity, and yet extraordinarily sensitive to the person with whom he is speaking. He fulfills his assignment in the only way he can, by listening not only to the subject but to his own inner self, by integrating his professional assignment with his personal sensitivity, pulling off the most difficult challenge of a writer's calling and coming up with a good writer's prize, a revealing snapshot in a silver frame.

That John Callaway may, after a career of great achievement spent in the dizzying excitements of other media, be understood fundamentally as a writer happiest and most himself in the utter silence of the loneliest of callings, will be one of the felicitous outcomes of this book's publication. No matter what else John Callaway has been doing since he first arrived next to penniless in Chicago in 1956, he has always been, first and foremost, a writer.

He does not claim this but neither can he conceal it for this truth is evident on every one of these pages. The author possesses that capacity which is the blessing and burden of authentic writers. He feels everything that is going on around him. There is no real writing without this sensitivity, this gift and curse that never shuts down, so that the writer is, in a sense, at the mercy of life every moment.

Because of this sensibility the writer misses little of the pain and struggle of being human. There is no casual bus or boat ride for men and women whose inner emotional radar constantly scans the environment. Against their will, they sense the emotional radiations that lift off everyone around them: the future for the happy young couple across the way and the past of the shawled and bent old woman down the aisle. Life is forever thrusting itself on them, challenging them to put it into words, to make its mysteries less harsh and its joys more accessible for others.

That is the kind of relationship with life that John Callaway has had ever since he sat "learning," as he puts it, "to listen" under the cataract of bold and arresting parental conversation. In autobiographical snatches he brings us beneath the roof of that small town West Virginia home, recalling himself as a mediator of arguments, a boy who learned, because of difficult family circumstances, to listen very carefully to what everyone had to say. His ability to listen, to hear both sides of almost any matter, to interview skillfully later in his career: all this he attributes to others, never self-consciously naming the artist inside himself, that infinitely sensitive boy who has heard life so well precisely because of a responsiveness already sown inside his personality.

This is the fine, easily torn lining in every writer's soul. The reader will sense this quality in the writer on every page and in every adventure. If the words had not been so debased by their cheap and easy modern usage, one would describe John Callaway as compassionate and vulnerable. These essays, I think, operationally clarify these terms for they cannot be passive endowments for writers who must abjure self-pity and actively transform these, at whatever spiritual cost, into the sturdy footings of their craft.

It is no accident, then, that John Callaway adverts to his chronic nervousness as he prepares again for what he has done a thousand times, interview a statesman or a star. Because he cannot take these as other than tests of his chronicler's soul, each is like an opening night for him. That is why his essays and reflections are so remarkably devoid of cliches. Take, for example, his extraordinary piece on the raucous street theater that surrounded the 1968 Democratic National Convention in Chicago, which remains fresh, provocative testimony from an eyewitness.

This same artistry may be detected in his chapters on America as a "Problem Society." John Callaway gives us what only a true writer can, a new and stimulating way of appraising the events of our times. These essays are informed with intelligence, learning, and a great feeling for the human condition. Here, then, is a revelation of the practical compassion which is not some all-purpose, mildly guilty feeling at the plight of others, but the carefully achieved balance of a man tightrope walking us across the chasm of modern events and allowing us to look with understanding at humankind's best hopes and worst tragedies without concluding that Apocalypse is upon us.

That distinctive writer's vision delivers both the truth of history and hope for the future. Such a supportive effect does not arise from some calculated evangelization on the writer's part. It is the by-product of the intense concentration he employs when he is processing his sensitivity to the human condition by matching it with the words that throw light rather than shadows onto its surfaces.

John Callaway frequently attempts to describe himself as one of the old Chicago tough reporter school, an alumnus of the famed City News Bureau, ready to carouse and curse with the best of them. Indeed, he is so obsessive about naming his faults and confessing his shortcomings that he could be as Catholic in religion as he is catholic in his interests. He cannot, of course, convince us that he is just like the gang from *The Front Page*. His sensitivity, that piebald blessing he cannot disown, keeps asserting itself, often tenderly, as in remembering his mother and his first childhood gift of five cent soup bowls to her, and always, accurately, as in recreating the sounds of jazz and ribaldry drifting on the night air of lost Chicago.

Henry James once wrote of what genuine artists do, describing their instinctive need to be "insistent," by which they "throw the whole weight of the mind" into what they are doing. He continued of true artists: "They feel unsafe, uncertain, exposed, unless the spirit, such as it is, be at the point in question 'all there.'"

This, then, is how you will find John Callaway in this thoroughly enlightening and enjoyable book. He confesses how unsafe and uncertain he feels until his spirit is in the midst of what he is doing, and then, as the results demonstrate, he is "all there." How refreshing to discover the true John Callaway at last: that reporter, hardened by the sights of murder and venality that perhaps only Chicago could display so lavishly, who has never become hardhearted but has managed to view it all and tell us about it with an artist's soul and sensibility.

—Eugene Kennedy
Chicago, December 24, 1993

Acknowledgments

Most of the shorter essays in this book were first published as columns in *Eleven* magazine, the monthly subscriber publication of WTTW, Chicago's Public Television station. The "Street of Dreams" piece is reprinted by permission of the *Chicago Tribune* Sunday magazine. Two other pieces, "Light Up for Rights" and "America's Fuzziest Hotel Room Videos," appeared first on the op-ed pages of the *Chicago Tribune*. The essay on Chicago streets appeared as the Foreword to *Streetwise Chicago* by Don Hayner and Tom McNamee and published by Loyola University (Chicago) Press. The essay "The New Colonialism" appeared as the Foreword to *Reclaiming Our Schools,* by Maribeth Vander Weele, also published by Loyola.

I am a man of many friends and families and so permit me to thank and acknowledge all who have been so nurturing and helpful over the years. My family at WTTW and particularly my colleagues in the "Chicago Tonight" production unit at WTTW provide me with one of the great privileged franchises in American journalism. My many thanks to Bill McCarter, WTTW's president and CEO, and his superb executive and management colleagues for all their hard work in establishing and nourishing the "Chicago Tonight" programs over the past ten years (and all of my other public affairs programs over the nine years prior to "Chicago Tonight"). Much of what I learn from what I read and from the guests who are per-

suaded to sit at the "Chicago Tonight" table each night is a result of
the very diligent, skilled work of V.J. McAleer, Phil Ponce, Kay Weibel,
Jay Smith, Andrea Guthmann, Royal Kennedy, Laura Washington,
Elizabeth Brackett, Rich Samuels, Mary Crisanti, Susan Godfrey,
Michelle McKenzie-Voigt, Jack Ginay, Tim Ward, Dick Carter and
an army of wonderful interns. Ms. Crisanti, my research guru, is
responsible for much of what I read; thank you very much. Ms.
Godfrey, our assignments manager and my main personal assistant
over the years, has kept my broadcast life in some kind of relative
order. To all of the brilliant guests who have appeared over the years
on "Chicago Tonight," thank you for making me and all our viewers feel and think more deeply about the issues of our time. To all
of the WTTW field and floor crews—you are the very best in the
business. I owe much of my education about Chicago and national politics to Bruce DuMont, who for many years was the political
correspondent for WTTW and who was the program's very first
producer. Before she left to become a reporter for National Public
Radio in Washington, my former "Chicago Tonight" correspondent
colleague, Chitra Ragavan, took the time to read and critique the
first draft of many of these essays. She has my deepest gratitude, as
does Elizabeth Altick-McCarthy, the editor of WTTW's *Eleven* magazine. It was Elizabeth who first suggested that my columns in *Eleven*
magazine could be the centerpiece of a kind of "Callaway Sampler"
book. My thanks also to Jenny Epstein and Lisa Schoenfein, who
have edited my *Eleven* magazine columns in recent years.

My warmest thanks to my family at the William Benton Fellowships Program in Broadcast Journalism at the University of
Chicago where I have toiled part time for eight of the last eleven
years. My life would be a shambles without the tireless work of
Sharon Rosen, associate director of the Benton program. The staff
work of Lee Price and Alma Wood has been invaluable as has the
leadership of D. Gale Johnson, the chairman of the Benton Faculty Advisory Committee for the past several years. The earlier
work of Judith Mayotte and the pioneering work of the late Casey

Adams also made it possible for me to enjoy a productive intellectual and administrative life at the university. The friendship I have enjoyed with all of the Benton Fellows over the past eleven years has been one of the blessings of my life—thanks to each and every one of you for making Benton House a place of learning, friendship, and personal and professional growth. I am indebted to Hanna Gray, the former president of the university, to Barry D. Karl and to Jonathan Kleinbard for their unstinting efforts to make the Benton Fellowships Program a success. And I owe more than I can say to the numerous University of Chicago faculty members and Benton program guests who discussed and debated so many of the ideas expressed in this book. None of this wonderful intellectual experience would have been possible without the leadership and assistance over the years of Robert P. Gwinn, Peter Norton, and Fred Figge of Encyclopedia Britannica (which underwrites the Benton program), and all the members of the William Benton Foundation Board.

My thanks to David Halberstam and his wife, Jean Butler, for introducing me to my agent, Wendy Weil. My thanks to Wendy for her unflagging patience and support over the past twelve years. My thanks to Connie Goddard for introducing me to Jameson Campaigne, my publisher. Thank you, Jameson, for your faith. My thanks to Richard Altick, Dick Simpson and Martin Marty for special advice when the author was in doubt about how to proceed. Many thanks to David Wilson for all of his keyboarding and to Jean Franczyk for early research on the Problem Society essays.

To my beloved sister, Hamp, and her husband, Tom Karras, to my cousin, Charlie Dobbs, and his wife, Nan, to my late father's second wife, Carolyn, and her husband, Rick Wilson, to my first wife, Shirley, and our daughters, Ann Hampton and Liz, and her husband, Dan Foster, and to little Nicholas Callaway Foster—no man could be blessed with a better family. To Patrice, my heart breaks that we didn't make it to the finish line, but it was a hell of a run. Thanks always for the black balloons.

Introduction

My dad used to come to terms with things or offer miscellaneous thoughts by saying, "The thing of it is ...." And because Charles Ernest Callaway was a man unafraid of expressing his opinion on many things, "the thing of it is" became a familiar part of his rhetoric. As a small-town newspaper editor, he offered opinions in his columns and editorials. As an ardent anti-FDR Republican in a West Virginia Democratic stronghold, he knew the lonely feeling of holding to one's convictions in the midst of vocal, sometimes hateful, opposition. But for every opinion dad expressed, there were a dozen stories. He would sit back in his living room chair and begin with, "John, that reminds me of the time...." And these were stories that had beginnings, middles and endings. These, friends, often were not short stories. In order to love my dad, you had to listen and listen long and hard. My mom, God bless her soul, had an extraordinary ability to listen to these stories, even though she had heard them many times over the years. She also held opinions and could tell a good story, but Dorothy Garwood Callaway was at her best as a give-and-take conversationalist and kitchen debater.

Growing up in that household turned me into a researcher and a question-asker. I can remember coming to the dinner table at the age of six or seven and asking my parents something like, "Where's Corregidor?" I had heard the word "Corregidor" on the radio and the announcer or correspondent sounded worried. Neither my dad nor my mom was inclined to respond with something like, "Why, son, Corregidor is an island in Manila Bay in the Philippines and our boys have just been beaten badly there by the Japanese." Instead, either of them would say something like, "We have a globe right over there and we have plenty of newspapers and magazines in the living room. Why don't you find out for yourself." In my home, you were expected to be prepared when you came to the dinner table.

Dad's drinking started before dinner and would continue deep into the night (although to hear the clarity of his speech you would never know he had touched a drop). Mom would try, unsuccessfully, to keep up with him. Since my older sister, Hamp, would usually retreat to her bedroom to read, I found myself hanging around my parents, listening to and helping to "moderate" their kitchen discussions and debates. Since I did not know enough about the issues of the day to offer my opinions, I found myself gently intruding with questions or requested clarifications. It was a way of coping in my home. It was a way of being close to my parents without being too close. I learned to listen and to ask. It became a lifelong habit.

Another reason I may have developed into a question-asker instead of a commentator is that I didn't burst out of college thinking I knew everything (although my interracial, interreligious fraternity brothers had inculcated me with certain leftist dogma). In fact, as you will see shortly, I dropped out of Ohio Wesleyan University at the end of my third semester, just as I was developing a strong scholarly appetite.

Upon arriving in Chicago I soon began a journalism career that thrived on the asking of questions. As a nineteen-year-old police reporter at the City News Bureau, I learned not only to ask more specific questions but also to ask them quickly of homicide detectives and fire marshals, who had little patience with kid reporters.

The police reporting days were followed by general assignment reporting and wide-ranging question-asking for WBBM Radio and TV in Chicago. I learned at the feet of the master politicians. I would throw a hard ball question at Mayor Richard J. "Boss" Daley about police corruption and he would reply, slyly, "I don't know, John. What do you think?" The asking of questions dominated the rest of my career at CBS and my nineteen years in the PBS system. Whether it was eyeball to eyeball with a local politician, or on location with a nationally known figure for one of my PBS interviews (with the like of John Cheever, Leontyne Price or Dr. Jonas Salk), I asked the questions and listened patiently to the answers. You did not hear many "Thing of it is's" from me. Occasionally, someone would ask me why I took such great care to avoid expressing opinions in my work. Always, I would hide behind the argument of "fair" journalism. I did not, I would say, pretend to be "objective," because any halfway intellectually honest person knew that was journalistically impossible, but I did strive, I would always say, for "fairness."

That is why I can report that two of the most uncomfortable jobs I ever held were my assignments to come up with opinions. At WBBM Radio in the early 1960s, I was named editorial director and wrote the first editorials broadcast by the station's management. My editorials were among the worst ever broadcast on American radio. They were much too long (can you imagine a seven-minute editorial read by a general manager who didn't necessarily agree with the viewpoint he was reading?) and were so "on the one hand this, and on the other hand that," that they didn't get much said. I was so relieved to be relieved of that assignment after a couple of years. Later, in a part-time assignment for WLS-TV (ABC in Chicago), I was asked to comment on everything from books to movies to art in my role as "critic-at-large." I remember the general manager asking what was going on when the first segments I broadcast were short interviews. "We hired you to comment, not interview," he reminded me. Gradually, painfully, I began to form my own opinions about movies, but it wasn't easy.

As the years passed, I gradually began to come to terms with what it was to grow up in an alcoholic household and I came to understand the "dance" I danced conversationally with my parents—the "stay to the side of the grown-ups" dance and how it applied to my life and my career. It helped to receive some very patient and useful counseling along the way. And sometimes I got booted solidly in the seat of my intellectual pants. A good friend of mine, the church historian and prolific theological writer Martin Marty, of the University of Chicago Divinity School, asked me to be a speaker at a conference on medical ethics questions relating to the then fairly new phenomenon, AIDS. I begged off, saying that, while it was true that I had moderated some television programs on AIDS issues, it would be all I could do to come up with a few questions about AIDS, much less express any actual *opinions or insights* about the crisis. "Nonsense," retorted Marty. "We're all struggling for answers. Come struggle with us." He was saying to me that I didn't have to be an expert, but that I was a player in the field of communications about AIDS and I could, at the least, come testify as to what I did *not* understand about the issue and what it was like to have to deal on the air with that lack of understanding, if nothing else. It felt good to be scolded gently by my friend Martin and it felt even better to be a part of the conference and speak my piece about what I knew and didn't know.

At about that same time I was asked to host a series of radio tapings about the American judicial system. It was in researching the role of judicial fairness for one of those programs that I came further to understand how one can be independent, be fair and at the same time hold opinions. Good judges, the research said, were not empty vessels. They were expected to have experienced enough about life and the law to have solid opinions about things and at the same time not let those opinions unduly influence their opinions about specific cases. As one who truly wanted to be fair in his presentation of news analysis programs, I found that sensibility about the balance between opinion and open-mindedness to be helpful.

But most helpful of all was writing a monthly column for the WTTW monthly subscriber publication, *Eleven* magazine. The deadlines for that column were so far in advance that I didn't have to worry about taking sides in the scrimmages of daily news issues, but the short essays did give me a chance to get things off my chest and to follow my dad's footsteps in the telling of stories. Most of the shorter pieces in this book were published first in *Eleven*. Many of them are on the lighter side—just baby steps into the business of commentary. Many are seasonal because when you write for a monthly you think of the seasons as well as "issues."

The Problem Society essays are my attempt as a generalist to come to terms with the burdens of complexity in our lives. On my "Chicago Tonight" nightly news analysis programs I struggled for years to try to keep up with the specialists on a wide variety of issues. At the University of Chicago, where I have served as the director of the William Benton Fellowships Program in Broadcast Journalism, I sat in on hundreds of seminars led by specialists who really know their business. From the two perspectives of nightly news analysis and heavy duty special research at the University of Chicago, I developed a philosophy about how the development of complex specialization not only makes for almost impossible expectations placed on our generalist leaders but also, in the end, places a burden of cynicism upon ordinary citizens who feel disappointment with these leaders.

Forgive me my speeches. I have included a few speeches in this book because they are snapshots of my views of political developments over the years. Because I am constantly asked to speak, it turned out, ironically perhaps, that I came most solidly to my opinions through speaking, even before writing for publication.

And so, I hope you will enjoy the stories, examine my Problem Society thesis and perhaps even stop to think about some of the opinions offered here. You see, the thing of it is....

Personal, Please

1

Street of Dreams

The dean of men looked like Arthur Fiedler. He didn't hold a baton, but he had wonderful white hair and no-nonsense eyes. I suspect he had heard my story many times. I was washing dishes at the women's dormitory, but I wasn't making enough to pay the tuition, room, board and books. Mom and dad were broke. I had just finished my third semester at Ohio Wesleyan University at Delaware, Ohio, and, like the good West Virginia boy I was, decided to drop out for a while, make some "good money" and then return to school. I told the dean that I had decided to go to Chicago and get a job in the steel mills, but that I was nearly penniless and needed a small loan to get me on my way.

"Do you smoke?" he asked.

"No, sir," I replied, truthfully.

"Do you drink?"

"No, sir." Again, truthfully.

The dean then went on to explain that the university had a loan fund established by an alumna who wished to provide support for deserving, abstemious students. He promptly arranged for a $50 loan.

Back at the boarding house where I lived, I encountered my literary-minded roommates. One of them said something like, "John, this is a pivotal moment in your life. You'll want to write about this trip to Chicago in your memoirs or make a movie about

3

it. Fifty dollars is a not very romantic amount of money. It has very little aesthetic appeal." There ensued a "how many angels on the tip of a pin" type of conversation about what, for literary or cinematic purposes, was a memorable-sounding amount of money to take to Chicago: $27.40? $16.10? After debating for most of the afternoon, we finally decided that seventy-one cents had the ring of history to it. We spent the rest of the weekend eating hamburgers and fries, bowling, seeing movies and otherwise conscientiously spending the $49.29 right down to the last two two-cent Tootsie Rolls.

I hitchhiked a ride to central Indiana where I spent the night in a farm house and was generously fed. The next morning I hitched a ride to a place somewhere on the Indiana-Michigan border of the Chicago area. There I was picked up by a man who said he was a minister. I told him I was looking for a ride into downtown Chicago. He told me that would be a very dangerous and foolish thing to attempt and gave me the necessary $3.25 or whatever it was in those days to put me on a South Shore commuter train into the Loop. He wouldn't tell me his name or address so that I could send him the money. He simply told me to do the same for someone else once I got established.

I arrived downtown at the Randolph Street station early on the afternoon of February 6, 1956. I carried very little clothing and a copy of the New Testament and a paperback edition of David Reisman's *Individualism Reconsidered* in my tiny valise. The first thing I did was put that valise in a locker. That cost a nickel. Then I bought a *Chicago Tribune*. That cost another nickel. Then I walked up out of the station, right past the Chicago Public Library (which would become a second home soon thereafter), west on Randolph Street. I looked up at the marquees of the theaters and I felt an unexplainable rush of elation, an immediate sense of belonging, a deep, deep feeling that I had chosen the right city at the right time. And then I walked into a place on Randolph Street called Lucy's and bought a piece of pecan pie. I nearly fainted when I got the bill—thirty-five cents! Why in West Virginia you could buy a piece of pecan pie for a dime. I read the *Trib* want ads. They needed a dishwasher at Northwestern Memorial Hospital.

Garbed in blue jeans, work shirt, thin sweater and a very modest wool overcoat I got directions and trudged through the ice and snow the mile or so north to the hospital. The personnel office was closed for the day. I trudged back down Michigan Avenue to Randolph Street, past Lucy's as my mouth watered for another piece of pie and on to the Greyhound bus station where I immediately fell asleep on a hard waiting bench. The security guards chased me out a little after six o'clock.

Then I walked back east on Randolph Street to Wabash Avenue past the inviting, warm and expensive-looking windows of Marshall Field's. I walked all the way south under the clattering el on Wabash many blocks to the Harrison Hotel. There I discovered permissive security people and wonderful leather chairs in the lobby. I fell asleep again until the time that even those generous hotel cops had to escort me to the door. It was now nearly ten o'clock and I was starting to panic. I didn't know a soul in Chicago. My parents didn't even know that I had left college (I had a big fight with them and was thrown out of the house at Christmas). I walked back north on Wabash Avenue and happened onto a hotel called the Lorraine.

I still can't believe what I did next. I walked in and told the clerk the following story: my dad is a top reporter with a daily newspaper in Philadelphia (my dad was at home in Wheeling, West Virginia, where he was a reporter for a local newspaper). He was supposed to be here already, but he's late and I'd better get the room and wait for him. To my astonishment, then and now, the clerk said, "Fine" and gave me a key to a room. I later learned that perhaps the reason he was so accommodating was that he was an employee of an organization you didn't lie to in Chicago. I thought there were some rather tough-looking customers around that place!

The next morning I stole out of the hotel without paying the bill and headed for an employment agency on Jackson Boulevard that had been advertised in the *Trib*. There I explained my story to a man who looked very much like Robert Penn Warren, the poet and novelist. I told him I was nearly penniless and I had come to get work in the mills so I could someday return to college. He looked at me as if I were crazy.

"Do you know that there are thousands and thousands of grown men with families who can't get jobs in the mills?" he asked.

"No, sir, I didn't," I truthfully and shamefully replied.

"You didn't check anything out before you came, did you?" he asked.

"No, sir, I didn't."

I noticed that as we talked he kept looking at me and looking at a picture frame on his desk. Finally, he turned it around and there I was. "My son," he said. "Killed in World War II." And because I was a double for his son, he said, he was going to do something he never had done before. He, a normally hard-nosed employment recruiter, was going to lend me ten dollars of his own money, find me a place to stay and then find me employment. And he did all three. He sent me to the Traveler's Aide office in the Loop and it fixed me up with vouchers for the YMCA Hotel at 826 South Wabash Avenue. My tiny room there cost nine dollars a week. I bought my first Chicago steak at George Diamond's on Wabash Avenue. A few doors away, I bought my first Chicago blazer and trousers at Robert Hall's. Four months later, I lucked into a police reporter's job at the City News Bureau. Take home pay: thirty-four dollars, twenty cents a week. As I walked from the Y hotel up Wabash past the Harrison Hotel, the Lorraine Hotel, George Diamond's, Robert Hall's, Marshall Field's and west on Randolph past Lucy's, past Bensinger's where I watched the world's greatest pool hustlers, past the Greyhound bus station and then on over to 188 West Randolph where the City News Bureau was, I was almost always a few dollars in debt. But I was happy and very much at home in Chicago.

If someone wants to make a movie of my story of coming to Chicago, he will have to build his own set. They are tearing down my Chicago and, I suspect, your Chicago. I winced last December when I read that they had closed the Greyhound bus station on Randolph Street, boarded it up. And not only are Lucy's and Bensinger's long gone, but so is that entire wonderfully shabby block of Randolph on which they once stood. There are no lockers at the Randolph Street Metra station. On Wabash, Robert Hall is no more. The Lorraine Hotel is now a parking lot. The Harrison Hotel still stands, but there are no inviting leather chairs in the lobby. And the YMCA Hotel, heaven forbid, is now a luxury apartment building.

If only I had taken pictures of those treasured places. These were my personal landmarks of Chicago, my streets of dreams. At least they still live in my mind. And I hope, now that I have told you my story, that they will live for a while in yours.

2

*Back When Floods
Seemed Like Fun*

I am a son of floods, a possessor of deep, watery memories of growing up on the banks of the frequently overflowing Ohio River in my hometown of New Martinsville, West Virginia (40 miles south of Wheeling and 100 miles south of Pittsburgh).

For us kids, floods were fun. Just about the time we couldn't abide another spelling or math test in the schoolroom doldrums of March, the waters would rise and we would be sent home. We loved putting on hip boots, searching for spare rowboats and sharing in the excitement of preparing for the approaching waters. And floods were a tremendous builder of self-esteem. We felt so darned important helping our parents move all of the canned goods (everyone canned fruits and vegetables and kept them stored in basements during those World War II days), dishware, and other household possessions up to the second-floor bedrooms. I was particularly proud of helping my mother, whose heart condition prevented her from going up and down the stairs much. I wish I could have been more help to dad, who strained his gut moving the piano out of harm's way.

Another reason the Ohio River floods were fun is that they were dangerous. These weren't the tragic flash floods that you see so often, but they did come upon us much more quickly than we expected. I can remember walking out into the fields around our home and feeling queasy as I saw the waters creeping up on us. We were never sure if we would get all of our possessions upstairs before the muddy waters surged into the living room on the first floor.

And even when we succeeded in moving everything upstairs, we then had to sweat out whether or not the waters would seep through the first-floor ceiling into our jam-packed bedrooms. During one of those 1940s floods, the water came within an inch or two of the second floor.

We thought our parents were having fun, but they were not. My dad's weekly newspaper was located very near the banks of the Ohio and so it took the first big hit of the flood. Moving all that type and press equipment out of the way was about as much fun as a spinal tap, not to mention the financial loss of being flooded out of business for a week or two.

During the flood, my sister and I would huddle in a furniture-filled bedroom and play Monopoly or try to read by candlelight. Eating cold sandwiches for lunch and dinner was no hardship at all for us, but our sensible parents probably yearned for a good, hot meal.

I remember we could step out the window of our bedroom onto the roof and climb directly into rowboats which were sitting there at second-story level. Mom hated to see my sister and me go out with dad in those rowboats—she feared that somehow we would be caught in some furious tide and swept out into the Ohio River never to be seen again.

After the waters receded, reality set it. For those of us who now enjoy the comfort of hardwood floors and plaster walls, it is almost unimaginable to think about what our old, rickety, wood-frame, wallpapered house looked like after a flood. You hose and hose and still you can't get rid of the mud and dust. The wallpaper peels. Tiny fish get stuck in the woodwork. The gas stoves don't light correctly. The woodwork bulges with water damage.

Just when you think you're starting to get the interior of the house clean, someone walks in from the front yard, which is inches high in caked mud. That someone leaves mud tracks all over the house. Sometimes that someone got his bottom paddled because he didn't wipe his feet correctly.

But then summer would come and the once mud-caked yard would burst alive with wonderfully rich, green sod, nurtured by all of the flood's nutrients. The place would be alive with flowers and tree blossoms and worms and little field mice that would run all over the house.

There were no investigations. No news conferences. No blame. Floods of my Ohio River Valley boyhood were just a natural way of growing up, in more ways than one.

3

❧

Days of Our Lives

When my parents were living, I viewed Mother's Day and Father's Day as something of a pain in the rear. "I'll let my parents know I love them and think about them when I want to do so, and not when the nation's florists and retail gift sellers want me to" was my caustic thought. I found something obligatory and obnoxiously commercial about these "days" not only for moms and dads, but also for secretaries, spouses, and all of the rest of the various beneficiaries of special days. I wasn't even thrilled to be on the receiving end of any of those days.

But now that my parents are dead, I don't quite feel the same way. It now would give me great pleasure to be able to celebrate Mother's Day with Dorothy Garwood Callaway in May and Father's Day with Charles Callaway in June. Those so-called "commercial days" would simply give me one more opportunity during the year to talk with my parents or be with them and in some small way, love them. This is written, of course, under the general heading of "Things You Now Know That You Previously Took for Granted."

In our culture, I think it is regarded almost as unmanly to permit yourself to feel, much less state publicly, how much you miss your deceased parents. I remember a noted journalist once remarking during a speech about how much grace under pressure President Ronald Reagan exhibited after he was felled by a bullet from a would-be assassin. Reagan was able to quip to the surgeons just

11

before they operated to remove the bullet, "I hope you're all Republicans."

The famous journalist said that if it were he who was about to undergo surgery he probably would have said something like, "I want my mommy." His admission was greeted by a huge outburst of laughter from the audience. All too often, in our culture, it is regarded as laughable to think that an adult male might want his mother in a moment of crisis.

Perhaps that is why I was so genuinely shocked at something that the late, very tough, West Side Chicago Alderman Vito Marzullo said some years ago. Marzullo was being interviewed for a documentary being produced by my friend Tom Weinberg. Tom was performing one of those video miracles of his whereby he gains the confidence of someone who normally isn't very open with reporters.

So there is Marzullo, as tough and crusty as they come, looking into the camera and saying something about the fact that he had made good in this country and that he had done so for fifty years without his parents, who remained behind in Italy. And you could see the pain in his face. You could see in that priceless moment of television how much Vito Marzullo loved and missed his parents. Now that may not seem like a very remarkable thing for a man to say, but it was a shocking thing for me to hear. I just took it for granted that Alderman Marzullo and thousands of others, including yours truly, had done nicely in this city pretty much without having our parents around every day to help us. We had left home and we had made good. As Ross Perot would say, "It's that simple."

Well, as is the case with most things Ross Perot says, it is not that simple. Yes, we know that it is natural when you are growing up to want to distance yourself from your parents. And yes, we know that if you experience that distancing in a natural way, you will grow closer to your parents later, enabling you to join so many who learn to say, "The older I got, the smarter I realized my parents were."

But for those of us whose parents have been deceased for many years, I think there is a special problem. As the years pass, it is more and more difficult for some of us to acknowledge how much we miss our parents, however self-sufficient we think we've grown. And so as we prepare to celebrate Mother's Day and Father's Day in the next two months, I want publicly to acknowledge how much I miss my mom and dad.

I miss listening to mom joyously playing the piano. I miss her incisive questions and commentary about world events. I miss her home-baked pies and cakes. I miss her listening to me with her laser-like intensity. I miss her genuine interest in sports.

And I miss my dad. I miss coming home to West Virginia and waking up to the aroma of the bacon and eggs he would be cooking in the early morning. I miss his interminable stories about Bert the Mule who worked in my grandfather's coal mines. I miss his easy company on a golf course. I miss seeing him pat my mom on the fanny when he thought no one was looking.

I miss the parties the two of them used to host in the early 1940s when parties were parties and people told stories and debated politics and drank whiskey and smoked cigarettes and wouldn't go home till dawn. I miss sitting all night in the summer heat and playing bridge with them and my sister. I miss standing in the kitchen and eating sardines and crackers with them while arguing politics. Damn, I miss them.

4

❧

My Summer Job at the White House

I don't usually brag about this, but I once worked at the White House. No, I didn't write speeches or advise the president. I washed dishes, waited tables, cooked short-order, hauled garbage, and tended the gas pumps. My White House was not the one at 1600 Pennsylvania Avenue. It was the White House restaurant on Route 2, just north of New Martinsville, West Virginia.

Dave Sulsberger's White House restaurant is where I, at the age of sixteen, worked during the summer of 1953. Now, I have not served in the United States Marines. And I did not have the honor of playing professional football for either Vince Lombardi or Mike Ditka. But I am here to tell you that working seventy hours a week for $35 for Dave Sulsberger in the summer of 1953 ought to count for something in the Blood, Sweat and Tears Department of life.

Mr. Sulsberger, who worked at least 100 hours a week himself in that fried-chicken and hot-turkey-sandwich-with-mashed-pota- toes-and-gravy-joint, smiled ironically when he gave me my first assignment at the White House. I was to remove all of the grease that had caked on the huge outside vent of the short-order frying stoves—grease that must have been accumulating since West Vir- ginia became a state in 1863. He gave me some kind of anemic household cleanser and scraper and told me that after I had finished with the vent I was to unpack all of the boxes of canned vegetables and sauces and then I was to wash all of the dishes that had accumulated during the day. And, oh, would I also take care of the gas pumps for the rest of the evening? Dave said he had to go somewhere and would be back by 4 A.M. to drive me home. And you thought the Clinton White House kept long hours.

I learned many things during my summer at the White House. I learned that no amount of cleanser and scrubbing can remove years of grease from a fried food vent. I learned that if, at 2 A.M., you mistakenly fill a chicken farmer's truck with diesel fuel and that chicken farmer's truck uses regular gas, that the chicken farmer's truck will inevitably come to a smoky halt several miles down the road. I learned that you will hear invective from the chicken farmer that would make the Lombardis and Ditkas of the world blush.

I learned that after you work all night and want to see your girlfriend for a few hours before you start your next 4 p.m. to 4 a.m. shift, you will learn the meaning of sleep deprivation and will always feel the deepest respect for people like big-city cab drivers who must work at least fourteen to sixteen hours a day to make a living.

The next summer—the summer of '54—was even more fun. I lucked into a job on what was known as the "shit crew" at the local chemical plant. The good news is that the hours were about half of what I worked at the White House and the pay was about double. The bad news was that those few of us who were summertime help were given the lowliest, most dangerous once-a-year assignments at the plant. We were soon-to-be college boys. In other words, we were expendable.

We laid a railroad track siding through the plant property that summer. A picture of me trying to pound a railroad spike straight down in ninety-degree weather will not land in the Hand-Eye Coordination Hall of Fame. We hauled 100-pound bags of chemicals out of box cars. One day we were ordered to hose out the sludge from the bottom of a huge container that had once held hundreds of thousands of gallons of chemicals. My buddy and I were told to hold onto the powerful hoses tight because if we let go of them the power of the water in the hoses could whip us into a bloody pulp.

My last job that summer could have killed me. I was assigned to take dozens of rags and dry the very damp, inside walls of a benzene rail car. It was like being asked to take those rags and dry the Atlantic Ocean. I was squeezed into an airtight rubber suit and fitted with a gas mask. I was warned that if I started to feel a kind of cool sweat (as opposed to a hot sweat that already had drenched my body) I was to exit the tank immediately—that would be the sign that the benzene fumes had penetrated the rubber suit. And I was told that the benzene would turn me blue and that, in the absence of fast medical attention, I would die. Oh, to be back at the White House scraping grease off the vent. After what seemed like half a day of getting the damned rubber suit on I finally climbed atop the tank car and shinnied my way down into its cool, dark interior, armed with dozens of dry rags. I had been drying the walls with those rags for only ten minutes when I began to feel a very pleasant, comforting, cool sweat. Pleasant? Comforting? God, get me out of here! So up and out I climbed and off came the rubber suit and gas mask. They took me to the nurse's office where I was bathed down with alcohol. Then I did it all over again. Same result. In the tank for ten minutes and a nice, cool sweat.

I never did find out if they got that benzene tank dried. But I went off to college with a renewed respect for people who labor for a living. So when I hear about a politician who won't fund summer jobs for kids because those jobs are "pork" or "don't lead to anything," I'd like to hand him some cleanser and order him to finish scraping the grease off that vent at the White House.

5

~

The Summer Jobs Debate Continues

Sometimes a throwaway line can be most counter-productive. Some of you wrote and called with supportive comments about my summer jobs column. Apparently you were pleased to know that the overweight guy who now sits behind a desk moderating a news analysis program did some honest, sweaty work in his youth. But several of you wrote or called to say that while you were moved by my accounts of washing dishes, scrubbing grease from a short-order fry vent, waiting tables, filling gas tanks and working in a chemical plant, you were severely disappointed with the column's conclusion in which I wrote:

"So when I hear about a politician who won't fund jobs for kids because those jobs are 'pork' or 'don't lead to anything,' I'd like to hand him some cleanser and order him to finish scraping the grease off that vent at the White House (restaurant where I worked)."

These readers felt that my all-too-apparent support for government-funded summer jobs revealed, at best, a sad ignorance on my part of what a fraud government-funded summer jobs are and, at worst, the kind of gooey, liberal economic views held, they feel, by all too many folks in the news media.

Well, it's a bit out of season to engage in a summer jobs debate, but let me try to respond to my critics in a way that will serve the larger purpose of discussing with you this business of those who, like former President Reagan, say that government is the problem and those who, like President Clinton, feel that government can play a major, constructive role in our lives. First of all, the friend who wrote me to describe the ending of my column as a non sequitur is, I believe, correct. If I were going to end a column with a meaningful plea for government-funded summer jobs, I should have started the column with something that would have premised my conclusion. Second, while I am prepared to defend some government-funded summer jobs, I utterly failed to make it clear that I would hope that most summer jobs or most jobs of any kind would be in what economists call "the private sector" (don't you love terms like that?). I am in the camp that believes that the best social program is a private job. Jobs that create meaningful work and income enable people to provide for themselves the basic necessities of life and maybe even a beer and a ballgame or two. Give a person a chance to earn enough income and material comfort and you may find a person with enough dignity and self-esteem to involve him or herself in the larger pursuits of life. Deny that and you may encounter drugs, crime and despair. So three cheers for private jobs.

But what really pains me about those who were so quick to jump on the notion of a government-funded summer job is that many of them think nothing of silently and perhaps even enthusiastically supporting other government-funded jobs. Many of these anti-government patriots don't whisper a word about billions in waste in defense spending. They will tell you the government should keep its nose out of private enterprise, but they will cheerfully accept mortgage deductions, real estate tax deductions, agricultural subsidies and the rest. You will not find them complaining about the fact that even though the Cold War is over, the U.S. is prepared to spend $28 billion on intelligence services and activities this fiscal year. Twenty-eight billion dollars! These people who tell you government can do no good often are people who graduated from land-grant state universities. They say they are against a federally directed industrial policy (and in my view they are correct on this), but they don't have the grace to acknowledge that a tax code which gives them every-which-way tax breaks adds up to nothing more than a federally directed industrial policy. But risk wasting a few million on some summer jobs for mostly non-white inner-city kids and they scream like a scalded rooster.

Look, I wasn't born yesterday. I know there is waste in government-funded summer jobs as I know there is waste in big private corporations. I'm not all that big on government-funded jobs, but the fact is that many of the people who work for the government, full or part time, earn their pay and then some. As a matter of fact, what I didn't tell you in that earlier column was that one of my first summer jobs was on a government payroll—the park system of my little hometown in West Virginia. I worked my butt off that summer cleaning up around that park. So don't tell me that a government-funded summer job can't be honest work. I argue that if we were prepared to invest a third as much in programs for inner-city kids as we were to defeat the Communists that, waste and all, we would begin the work necessary to rid this country of its greatest enemy—an angry, uneducated, unemployed generation of inner-city kids. If you want it to be a totally private initiative, that's okay with me. If you want it to be a mix of the two, fine. But understand that if it is a great undertaking, there will be, just as there was in World War II and in the Cold War, great waste. And it will be worth it.

6

❧

Sugar Baby

All right, I'll confess. I'm an addict. A recovering addict. A sugar baby. What's a sugar baby? A person who has consumed large doses of refined sugar since early childhood and is hooked on it. We tend to mask this addiction with one of the most cloyingly cute phrases of avoidance and denial ever created: "Oh, he's got a sweet tooth."

My first recollections of sugar take me back to my childhood in West Virginia during World War II. I can remember my mother—a hard-working newspaperwoman during the week working even harder on weekends—baking angel food cake, chocolate cake with deep chocolate icing, cupcakes, chocolate chip cookies, fudge, and pies: apple, cherry, pumpkin, or my favorite then and forever, lemon chiffon with graham-cracker crust. My sister and I would assist in the confectionery constructions by cleaning the icing bowls with our fingers.

Not all of mom's baking was for us. Some of these items were given away to Cub Scout bake sales and similar good causes. In West Virginia, if anyone died you took baked goods to the house. Sugar was the currency of shared grief. But there were always pastries around our house. And I remember one summer when my parents really got into making, or should I say churning out, wonderful, luscious, creamy homemade ice cream.

And then there are my memories of individual sugar episodes. My mother had to cover a local social event one evening and left my dad with the responsibility of making dinner. At my sister's insistence, his first course of the evening was white bread covered with sugar!

Another time, I remember eating in one sitting an entire box of chocolate-covered cherries that had been sent to the family for Christmas. And I should add that much of this sugar was washed down with sugar-filled soft drinks, which were usually available in our home.

As a child, my day usually would begin with sugarcoated cereal upon which I placed a teaspoon or two of sugar. On the way home for lunch, I would carefully avoid being seen by me sister and sneak into the bakery, which was strategically located directly across from our elementary school. There I would buy at least two raised doughnuts (pure concentrations of yeast and sugar) and wolf them down on my way home. They cost two for a nickel. After school, I would rush to another big sugar fix with a chocolate milkshake at the ice cream shop, which also was located very near the school.

I began selling newspapers on the streets at age seven. One of the main things I did with my earnings was buy ice cream sodas and soft drinks and black-market bubble gum (hard to get during World War II). These and other sweets served to give me a sense of reward for my early childhood labors and also provided me with sugar highs of sorts.

Was I a fat baby? Surprisingly, no. From grade school on I played sports for hours on end when I wasn't delivering or selling newspapers. Maybe that helps account for the fact that I was able to remain slim. I did have plenty of tooth decay, however, and retain painful memories of dental visits.

By the time I came to Chicago in the mid-fifties I still was a slim, 170-pound lad of just under six feet. That quickly changed. In the early days you could find me sneaking milkshakes at various soda fountains around City Hall after covering Mayor Daley.

At night, I began drinking alcohol. Not scotch and water. Not martinis. No, I drank sugar. Bourbon and seven, and vodka and tonic. Might as well drink chocolate milkshakes. Except those mixed drinks led to a habit even more deadly than sugar. Salt. I found myself eating bags of potato chips and slice after slice of rich, cheddar cheese so that the sugary booze wouldn't intoxicate me too quickly. As a matter of fact, I was not drinking so much for intoxication as for a sugar hit, which would enable me to stay up late and begin an adult lifetime of late-night reading.

Was I still slim? Ho! This kid shot up from about 170 pounds at age twenty-two to more than 200 in about three years. And then with each passing year after that I added a pound or two. And then I would go on diets and lose some. And then put the weight back on. The miracle is that I never experienced serious illness or heart problems.

Nearly three years ago I decided to do something about this pattern. I decided to stop drinking. I thought, if I can stop this vodka and tonic nonsense at midnight I can then stop the potato chips and cheese nonsense before my arteries get so clogged I'll need Drano. So I stopped. It was amazingly easy. No more bourbon and seven and no more vodka and tonic. Good for me!

Ho! Guess what the kid started doing at midnight? Ladies and gentlemen, the John Callaway Midnight Research Replenishment Hour is now brought to you by the makers of Häagen Dazs ice cream and Ann Sather cinnamon rolls! Yes, friends, John Boy here went back to his childhood of pure sweets. It was pitiful. And so this continued until last November when I had a little talk with myself and suggested to myself that ice cream every night might finish me off more quickly than booze, chips, and cheese. And so I stopped eating refined sugar. No ice cream, no cake, no cookies, no nothing.

Was it easy? It was awful. I thought I was going crazy. The first month was a nightmare.

But then it got better. I started eating a lot of fruit as a substitute for baked goods and ice cream. It worked. And then some other, huge, life-changing events began to happen as a result of saying so long to sugar.

7

❧

Sweet Success

When I left you last month, I had confessed to my sugar addiction, hooked on everything from mom's lemon chiffon pie during World War II to Ann Sather cinnamon rolls in the go-go 1980s. I had established that even my drinking habits were sugar-pops—vodka and sugar-filled tonic and bourbon and sugar-filled Seven-Up. I proudly reported to you that I called a halt to the liquor and soft drink madness some time ago and, even more miraculously, had ceased eating refined sugar, desserts, ice cream and all that good stuff since November 1, 1989. And, I concluded, saying goodbye to sugar had resulted in "other huge, life-changing events." As I look at those words, it is clear that saying goodbye to sugar did not result in any reduction of my lifetime addiction to hyperbole. I'll report the changes. You decide if they are "huge" or "life-changing".

Before I report any change, however, let me confess one of the by-products of my lifelong sugar habit. I was a night person. Except for being born at high noon on a very hot day in August 1936, I had been a night baby, a night boy, a night man for just about all of my fifty-three-and-a-half years. Back in World War II, when I was sneaking raised doughnuts on the way home from school for lunch and sneaking chocolate milkshakes after school before delivering newspapers, I also was sneaking wide-awake pleasures in or out of bed after supposedly being put to bed. At age seven, aside from playing imaginary football with my teddy bear, I can remember slipping into the hallway after midnight and overhearing my parents talk in their bedroom. It was not ordinary talk.

My mother and father ran a small-town weekly newspaper in West Virginia (the *Wetzel Republican,* for those of you keeping notes). I could hear my dad say, "Lemon, Mr. and Mrs. William." And my mother would reply "Lemon, L-E-M-O-N, Mr. and Mrs. William." Name after name into the night they would chant, proofreading the endless lists of guests at a wedding or families who had made news by driving all the way from our hometown of New Martinsville to go shopping in the big city of Wheeling, some forty miles north along the Ohio River. (That I grew up hearing them take such painstaking care about how they spelled the names of people who graced the pages of their newspaper may account for why I still go crazy when the Chicago newspapers spell my name "Calloway".) And if I didn't overhear them proofreading the columns of their paper, I overheard them arguing Franklin Roosevelt's war policies or wondering out loud why their son, John, wasn't doing better in school.

And when I was sick (and it seemed I was sick for a good bit of every winter of my early childhood), I would quietly tune the portable radio by my bedside to after-midnight, clear-channel radio shows from WHAS Louisville or WWL in New Orleans. I was not only a sugar baby, I was a night baby.

Later on, in high school, I set pins in a bowling alley five or six nights a week until midnight. Exhausted, we pin boys would trudge to the all-night truck stop across the highway and gulp down hot turkey sandwiches, mashed potatoes with gravy, and chocolate milk. Fully resugared and fortified, I did my homework until two or three in the morning. My teachers were less than thrilled with the zombie-like appearance I made in their morning classes.

In college, I found every excuse imaginable to postpone homework until midnight when I would eat french fries and drink milkshakes and then knock off three or four hours of reading.

And as a journalist in Chicago, I regularly did my reading and writing homework until three or four in the morning. All of this after having knocked back a couple of vodka and tonics and scarfed down a plate of cheese and chips or crackers just after midnight. Sugar man.

All of this meant, of course, that I was getting to work in a state of fatigue, irritable with any early-morning meetings I might be required to attend or exhausted if a breaking news story required my presence anytime before ten. No power breakfasts for this kid. No prayer breakfasts. No breakfasts of any kind unless it was a sweet roll at work.

Finally, I got some help. A friend helped me figure out that I was addicted to sugar. Sugar, we concluded, was my work drug the way cocaine is someone else's work drug. Go at it from ten in the morning until midnight, take a sugar hit and go at it until three or four in the morning when the sugar drop would kick in, and I could finally sleep.

So what happened when I went off sugar last November? At first, not much of anything. And then in December I experienced the most fluctuating waves of insomnia I've ever endured in my life. Up till seven in the morning one day, sleep till noon another day, back and forth for a month. All the while going crazy without sugar (try that at Christmastime, friends).

Then came January. The New Year. A new beginning for sugar-head Callaway. I became ... A MORNING MAN! Born again! Up with the sun!

At first, I behaved like one of those super-puritan CEO types who get up at four-thirty or five and read three newspapers, five reports, write twenty letters, make fifteen calls and plan a day's activities by the time their employees show up for work at nine. Then, gradually, I evolved into something resembling normalcy— getting to bed a little past midnight most nights and getting up around eight. Sometimes I slip and read till one or one-thirty, but usually only on weekends.

How does it feel to be a morning man? Great. I eat a good, healthful breakfast at home. I read the newspapers. I'm better organized at work. Without dieting (except for cutting out sugar) I lost ten pounds in the first three months of the new regimen. I'm also feeling good enough to work out in walk/run three-mile stints three or four times a week.

So, root for me to keep off sugar and to get to bed early. But, please, don't invite me to any power or prayer breakfasts.

8

⮾

Baby, It's You

It's June. Month of romance and weddings. You want a love story? I'll tell you a love story.

The year was 1983. She was a twenty-two-year-old New Trier High graduate appearing in her first starring role in the new Broadway musical *Baby*.

He was a twenty-six-year-old graduate of Providence College who had landed a small part in the television soap opera "All My Children". He had a hot date to see the very first preview of *Baby*. When our heroine took her curtain call that night, he was struck by her "graceful bow" and the "refreshing way she interacted with her fellow cast members—no ego trip." He was in love. Forget the hot date.

Within a week, he returned to see *Baby* but he was too shy to wait backstage and introduce himself to the object of his growing affections. When he wasn't taping "All My Children" performances he waited tables at Joe Allen, the popular theater district restaurant where cast members of *Baby* often met after the show. Relentlessly he circulated word of his interest in the young woman. Word got back to her that an attractive young man was making inquiries about her, but she wasn't interested. She had experienced one date based on someone who had written to her after seeing her on the stage and it was a disaster. No more "stage door Johnny" dates. Besides, she was very focused on her career.

Finally, after seeing *Baby* seven times in four months, our hero screwed up his courage and waited outside the stage door to meet his lady love for the first time. She shook his hand and walked away without uttering a word. "I was devastated," he later said.

But not defeated. He had learned from the other cast members that in Central Park on Thursday afternoons the cast of *Baby* played softball with cast members of other Broadway productions. And so, on several Thursday afternoons thereafter, he would show up, standing quietly behind the bleachers, to watch his lady love running out ground balls to first base. The other cast members knew he was there. She didn't.

One Thursday he finally came out from behind the bleachers to watch her play. The other cast members cajoled her into speaking to him. The ice was broken. She invited him to join her at a Memorial Day Mets baseball game the following weekend. She would be singing the National Anthem at Shea Stadium—the pinnacle of success for her, a lifelong Mets fan. What she didn't tell him was that she was determined not to lead him on and that she had purchased tickets for fifty-nine other persons to attend the game with them, including relatives! It would be Chaperon City.

It was a miserable first date for the young man. She intentionally seated him far away from her. It rained. She hardly spoke to him. Finally, he took the subway home, alone.

But still he didn't give up. Every day he would call and leave a message on her phone. And every day she would *not* return his call. He was about to throw in the towel. As he recalled later, "One night I was out with some friends, got really loaded and left a message: 'Okay, I think I'll just leave you alone from now on.'"

She returned *that* call and a few days later they met for dinner at a Mexican restaurant in New York. They talked until 6:30 the next morning and began seeing each other regularly.

One evening the following June she had just returned from a production in Milan and was expecting him to pick her up in a cab and take her to dinner. Instead, there was a limo waiting and they drank champagne and watched the Mets as they tooled uptown. The limo left them off in Central Park, and the young man took her to the bleachers where he used to spy on her playing softball. She had always told him that if he ever proposed to her, he must get down on one knee to do it. Thus, he lowered himself to one knee and asked her to marry him. She accepted, sobbing with emotion both at the prospect of getting married and at the fear of getting mugged in Central Park.

But that is not the end of this love story.

At their wedding reception, the young man sang a song from *Baby* to his bride, "I Chose Right." It just so happened that attending the wedding reception that evening was Richard Maltby, Jr. who wrote the lyrics to that song. And it turned out to be the reason why the young husband was cast as the leading man with his wife when the production of *Baby* was brought to Marriott's Lincolnshire Theatre two years later. So here were a husband and wife singing to each other in the musical which brought them together. How much more romantic can you get than that? Well, just a little bit more.

On February 17, 1991, they finally stopped singing *Baby* and gave birth to one. The relieved mother is Liz Callaway, now appearing in *Miss Saigon* on Broadway. The proud papa is Dan Foster, who has left "All My Children" to seek fame and fortune in New York's theater world. The *Baby* is Nicholas Callaway Foster.

It's June. Month of romance and weddings. That's my love story for you.

Career Confessions

9

ᑐ

This Had Better Be Perfect

It was late spring of 1956. I had hitchhiked to Chicago a few months earlier and ended up living at the old YMCA Hotel on South Wabash. I was a $50-a-week billing clerk during the day and a lonely aspiring actor and playwright at night, dreaming on a tiny pulldown wall-bed in a minuscule $9-a-week room at the Y. I was always hungry and at week's end could always be seen bumming $5 off one of my buddies to get me through to the next paycheck. If only someone would discover my great acting and writing talents. If only someone would give a nineteen-year-old college dropout his first big break.

One night the director I was working with at the Y's theater group took me aside and said, "John, I like you very much, but you are just about the worst actor I have ever had to try to work with and I fear that as a playwright (I was trying to compose a twentieth-century update of *Everyman*) you aren't much better." As I forced back the tears of rejection, he went on. "You may not realize it, but you are always talking about your parents and the newspaper business back in West Virginia. Clearly you have a deep love of journalism."

"Well, I suppose that's true," I gulped.

Then he said something which changed my life forever.

"There's a place here in town I've heard about called the City News Bureau of Chicago. They hire young reporters and sometimes those reporters get free meals at political banquets." That was enough for me. Any job that included the prospect of a free meal now and then sounded ideal. I quickly submitted my application to the City News Bureau and to my astonishment, two weeks later I was hired.

The bad news, as it turned out, was that there were no free meals. City News reporters covered police beats in those days, not political banquets. And my new pay was only $34.20 a week, take-home. The good news was that I had lucked into a job with an organization that was once dubbed "The West Point of American Journalism." As my father told me when he learned I had been hired at City News, "Son, if you can make it there, you can make it anywhere."

He was referring to the fact that dozens of graduates of the City News Bureau went on to hold top reporting and editing jobs at newspapers all over the nation. He also was referring to the fact that the regimen at City News was so tough that many young recruits simply quit. They couldn't take what you had to endure at this journalistic Quantico.

After serving two weeks as a copy boy, I was sent out on the police beats. A veteran reporter (someone who had been with City News, say, two months) was assigned to show me the ropes the first day. He had to show me how to use a pay telephone! Honest to God, I didn't know how! Back in West Virginia, we just picked up the phone and asked the operator to get us, say, 246.

One of my first days out on the Englewood police beat I was sent to cover the murder of an old woman who had been stabbed seventy-one times and left to die in a Jackson Park washroom. A few days later my editor dispatched me to an alley near 55th and Halsted where a nude young woman had been left to die, half her head chopped off by her assailant. Not long after that I found myself reporting the case of a man who shot his wife between the eyes and then turned the shotgun on himself. I learned a lot about life and death in Chicago but I did not sleep well at night.

The editors were an unforgettable cast of foul-mouthed, journalistically meticulous, personally idiosyncratic tyrants. There was Walter Ryberg, who in the midst of a huge breaking news story would pace the city room and say, "Oh, to be in Düsseldorf." There was Larry Mulay, who could dispatch six different reporters to six different stories and at the same time never stop cleaning the top of his desk with his bar towel. And then there was the legendary A. A. "Dornie" Dornfeld, the night city editor whose command of invective would have intimidated Mike Ditka.

All of these editors, particularly Dornie, were sticklers for detail. Hence the City News motto, "If your mother says she loves you, check it out."

A colleague of mine publicly boasted that he would be the first reporter in City News memory to phone in a story to Dornie and not have Dornie call him back with a follow-up question to be answered. One night my pal thought he had achieved his great goal. He telephoned Dornie with an incredibly detailed account of a multi-car accident that occurred on South Lake Shore Drive. The colliding cars finally had come to rest on some weeds near the beach. There were several injuries. My colleague had it all: names, addresses and occupations of the victims, time of accident, circumstances of accident, hospitals where the victims were taken, updated condition of the victims, etc., etc., etc. No detail was left unreported. A short novel, as police reports go. Nope. It wasn't to be. Dornie called the reporter in a few minutes with one follow-up question: "Chum," he blared (he always called you "Chum"), "what *kind* of weeds?"

Those are the kinds of stories that will fill the air early next month as reporters and editors from all over the nation meet in a Chicago hotel ballroom to recollect their early police beat days and to help celebrate the hundredth anniversary of the City News Bureau of Chicago. I'll be there and I hope my pal has by now checked out what kind of weeds those were and is there to tell Dornie in person.

10

❧

Rules That Were Made to Be Broken

Are you a stickler for rules? Do you follow not only the substance of the law but the letter of the law? If so, have you ever experienced a gut-wrenching situation in which it just killed you to have to be true to your insistence on being a straight arrow? I was almost in such a situation about twenty years ago. Thank goodness I found an escape hatch.

It happened when I was with CBS Radio in New York. I was thrilled to learn that I would be able to meet and interview David Niven. He was my idea of a truly sophisticated, urbane, world-class movie star. Please pardon the pun, but he had so much savoir, it wasn't fair.

Mr. Niven was in Manhattan to promote his newly published *The Moon's a Balloon,* a delightful autobiography which became an instant best-seller. He was still in his dressing gown when he graciously greeted me and my radio engineer in a suite at the Hotel Pierre on Fifth Avenue. He apologized for being in his robe and said that he had been up quite late the night before attending parties in his honor.

Before the interview commenced, David Niven said to me, "Mr. Callaway, before we record anything, I must ask you a favor."

Instantly I replied, "Mr. Niven, I would be pleased to grant you a favor."

He said, "I know this might sound strange to you, but I have a question that I want you to ask me during the course of the interview."

My heart dropped. If David Niven had asked me for the shirt off my back it was his. If he had asked me for the last one hundred dollars in my bank account (that was about how much it was in those days), it was his. But, horror of horrors, he had asked me for a favor that I could not conceivably grant. I said to him, "Mr. Niven, you'll never know how much it pains me to say this, but I can't let you do that. The rules at CBS prohibit a guest telling an interviewer what to say or what to ask. The rules are very rigorous and very specific about the interviews having to be spontaneous and unrehearsed. I'm just terribly sorry that I can't accommodate you."

A look of utter dejection crossed Mr. Niven's face.

"But, Mr. Callaway, this is urgently important. I implore you to let me tell you a question to ask me during the course of the interview."

I was in a state of deep despair. He was a good and gracious man, a man I had taken an instant personal liking to upon meeting, and I couldn't provide him with the one simple thing he needed. I felt like a total jerk. But suddenly I remembered something. "Mr. Niven," I exclaimed, "I think I can help you! If I'm not mistaken, one can circumvent or bend the CBS rules if one simply takes care during the course of the broadcast to tell the listeners or viewers that the rules were circumvented. If I'm not mistaken, this has been done in those rare instances where interviews have been paid."

"That's wonderful, Mr. Callaway," Mr. Niven shouted. "Let me now tell you what questions I want you to ask me."

"Go right ahead, Mr. Niven."

"At some point during the course of the interview, I want you to ask me what I did yesterday for lunch."

I truly was perplexed. All of this pain and distress had been over a question as innocuous as what my guest had done yesterday for lunch? The only thing difficult about a question like that was that it was the kind of chatty, gossipy question that, frankly, I prided myself on not asking. I was about much more substantive business in my interviews, I pompously thought. But what the heck, if my new pal David Niven wanted me to ask him what he did yesterday for lunch, who was I not to go along? All I would have to do is tell the listeners sometime during the interview that Mr. Niven had told me to ask him that question.

And so we rolled tape and I asked questions about David Niven's remarkable life and career and received warm, entertaining and sometimes very moving answers.

And about three-fourths of the way through the interview I said to myself, "I'd better get this what-did-you-do-for-lunch-yesterday business taken care of if I ever want to see this wonderful man again." And so I said something like, "Well, David Niven, here you are, back in Manhattan where you certainly enjoyed some of the more spectacular days of your youth. I wonder what it's like coming back here now. I mean, for example, what did you do yesterday for lunch?" Awkward as could be, I got the infernal question asked.

David Niven's eyes lit up. His posture straightened. He said, "Mr. Callaway, you'll never know how much it pleases me that you asked me that question. All of my life I have wanted to say the words which will answer the question. Forget about all my starring roles. Forget about all the beautiful women I have been privileged to perform with in Hollywood. Forget about all the film awards and honors. Mr. Callaway, all of my life I have wanted to say what I'm about to say in answering your question, 'What did you do yesterday for lunch?' [Long, dramatic pause.] *Mr. Callaway, yesterday I had lunch with my publisher.*"

Well, I don't know if that answer means anything to you or not, but it meant something to me. I have told that story to some groups and there is very little response. But if I tell it to a group of writers or book lovers there almost always is a roar of laughter of appreciation.

What David Niven was telling us was that all of his adult life he not only wanted to write, but also wanted *to be known as a writer.* By comparison, his acting was, for him, a sidelight. Now, with the publication of his autobiography, this great film star finally had come into his own, and the very essence of being a writer in New York, of course, is being able to say, "Yesterday, I had lunch with my publisher." Now, all of you straight and narrows out there, aren't you glad I found a way to bend the rules?

11

~

To Lie or Not to Lie

It was the winter of 1967 and I was host of the Sunday evening "Nightline" (take note, Ted Koppel) program on WBBM Radio. The documentary/interview/call-in show lasted three or four hours and I was so energized at the end of it I could never get to sleep unless I cooled off over a few at my favorite Near North Side watering holes. I was lucky if I got home by 3 A.M. and could fall asleep by 5 A.M.

My boss at WBBM, the late, great E.H. "Ernie" Shomo, stopped me in the hall on Friday afternoon and said, "Kid, I know you like to sleep in on Monday mornings after being up all night, but we've got an important meeting I want you to attend Monday morning at 10." I said I would be happy to be there, but that Sunday evening I did my usual all-nighter after the program.

After about four hours of sleep, I woke up feeling really groggy; some might say hung over. My wife and two daughters had already left for work and school and I noticed the telephone was off the hook, replaced it and then shaved, bathed and headed for work. As WBBM news director, I always listened to the news as I drove to work, but on this particular Monday morning I couldn't bear the thought of listening to anything, so I drove to work in silence.

When I walked into my office, I had barely removed my coat when Jeff Kamen, one of our star reporters, rushed in, grabbed me by both shoulders, looked me in the eye and said, "You don't know, do you?"

40

"I don't know what?" I replied as I noted that he was wearing a rain slicker that was covered with soot.

"You don't know, do you?" he hissed again, looking at me incredulously.

"I don't know what?" I replied, more impatiently.

"McCormick Place burned down last night!" He shouted.

"What?"

"McCormick Place burned down last night!" He paused, looking into my dumbstruck eyes.

I was dumbstruck because I couldn't conceive of how the relatively new convention and trade show hall on the lakefront could have possibly burned to the ground. "Your phone was off the hook last night, wasn't it?"

"Yes, I guess it was," I said, remembering that I had put it back on the hook when I awoke.

Then Jeff assured me. "Ernie doesn't know that you didn't know. We've done a good job covering the fire. Everyone in the newsroom will protect you. I've got to get back out there."

With that, Jeff left. Before I could regain my senses and in a scene perfectly suited for farce on the stage, my boss, Ernie Shomo, promptly walked into my office, seemingly bursting with pride. "Great job, kid! Sensational coverage! Do you think we ought to keep doing what we're doing?"

The problem was that I, the station's news director, did not have a clue as to "what we were doing." What should I do? Should I lie? Or should I tell the truth?

I lied. "Yes, Ernie, I think we should keep doing what we're doing."

"Swell, kid, so do I." And with that, my impeccably dressed boss swept out of my office.

Panic-stricken, I raced into the newsroom to find out "what we were doing." I was delighted to learn that WBBM had thrown out its regular talk format and was using its valuable airtime as a clearinghouse for the hundreds of persons who had been affected by the fire—trade show people who needed help, etc. If I had known that's what we were doing, I assure you I would have said what I said anyway to Ernie Shomo. As far as I know, Ernie went to his grave years later not knowing that I didn't know a thing about the McCormick Place fire.

Ernie was also a peripheral part of another and related memorable moment for me at WBBM. There was a change in management at CBS Radio in New York later that year and the new executive vice president who would oversee the operation of the owned stations was in town to meet Shomo and the other WBBM executives, including yours truly. We all were sure we were going to be fired in a wholesale shake-up of the station.

So I was nervous when the new bossman from New York, Sam Digges, walked into my office and introduced himself. He said he looked forward to talking with me at a luncheon with my colleagues at the Tavern Club, just a few blocks from WBBM. Wanting to make a good impression, I made sure I checked all the news wires very carefully so that I would be up on all the latest news at lunch. Never hurts to impress the new brass, especially if you're an endangered executive.

And so, you might imagine how chagrined I was when I walked into the Tavern Club and Sam Digges took me aside and said gravely, "It's too bad what happened at O'Hare this morning, isn't it?"

My heart sank. Here I am, news director of the CBS-owned station in Chicago, and I don't know about a tragedy that just happened at O'Hare and this new boss from New York *does* know about it. Do I lie? Or do I tell the truth?

I told the truth. "Mr. Digges," I confessed, "I'm sorry, but I don't know a thing about what happened at O'Hare."

He looked at me with a twinkle in his eye and a slight smile on his face and said, "That's good, John, because nothing happened at O'Hare." Digges was just trying to get a quick read on whether or not he could trust one of his new employees.

Years later, when I worked with Sam as his right-hand man in developing the all-news stations for CBS Radio, I told him not to think of me as someone incapable of telling a lie. I told him the story of my performance with Ernie Shomo after the McCormick Place fire.

12

~

What Did He Say?

It was my first week on the job for WBBM Radio and WBBM TV in Chicago, back in the early spring of 1957. I was fresh out of that journalistic boot camp, the City News Bureau of Chicago. I was twenty years old and had just been placed on the CBS payroll for $90 a week—an incredible salary increase over City News. I had arrived.

One of my first assignments was to interview the attorney general of the United States, William P. Rogers (who later would become Richard Nixon's secretary of state). Mr. Rogers and his Justice Department were coming down hard on the teamsters union that year (aren't they always coming down hard on the teamsters union?) and I was instructed to try to stop the attorney general as he stepped off his plane at Midway Airport and quiz him about the teamsters inquiry.

As I awaited the deplaning of the attorney general I felt so proud standing there on the tarmac in my new suit, new shirt and tie, and new shoes, while holding a microphone as a camera crew stood poised for action behind me. If only those editors at the City News Bureau who had yelled at me over the tiniest mistakes could see me now. If only my dad, who labored for decades as a respected but low-paid newspaperman in West Virginia, could see me now.

The next thing I knew the attorney general of the United States was striding toward me and shaking my hand. To my amazement, he actually agreed to be interviewed. The assignment desk had written the questions for me, so all I had to do was ask them.

Within three minutes, the interview was over. I thanked the attorney general and the camera crew handed the film (there was no videotape in those days) to a courier who rushed it back to the processing lab near CBS. With a little luck, the interview would make the six o'clock news.

Before I journeyed on to the next assignment with the camera crew, I went to a pay telephone to let the radio news bureau desk know about the interview with William Rogers. I was not an on-air reporter at the time (only Mr. Rogers' words would be excerpted for the television interview) and so my instructions were to tell the radio desk what the story was so that it could write it for possible use by our staff news announcers at WBBM Radio.

The legendary Chicago newsman Mike Neigoff was on the desk.

"I got the attorney general to stop for the interview," I screamed ecstatically.

"Great, John. What did he say?" responded Neigoff.

"Well ... uh, uh, uh." (Jack Benny might have said, "I'm thinking. I'm thinking.") "Well, I can't remember a single thing the attorney general said."

I trembled with fear that I would be fired on the spot.

"Well, kid," Neigoff replied, "maybe that will teach you to listen."

I had done everything on that assignment but the one thing than mattered. I had not listened. And so when people ask me today what is the essential element of interviewing I often tell them that story as a way of saying that listening is the essential element not only of interviewing but very frequently of living.

From time to time, I read articles about the *technique* of listening. I am sure that there are techniques which will help us become better listeners, but to me listening is much more than technique. The reason I didn't hear what the attorney general said was that I wasn't *prepared* to listen to him. Not only was I so taken by my own sense of self-importance that I blocked out everything else around me, but I also brought absolutely nothing to the interview. I hadn't begun to prepare. I didn't know a thing about the man I was interviewing and I knew nothing of the details of the teamsters union investigation. Furthermore, I knew next to nothing about what was going on in this world when I was twenty years old. It takes experience to be a good listener.

But experience is not enough. You must also care. One of the most painful, rejecting experiences in life is to be patronized instead of listened to. We all do it. Our mind is somewhere else and we look at the speaker eyeball to eyeball but we aren't taking in a thing and he or she knows it. There is a certain woman I know who drives me absolutely bonkers this way. I'll start to say something like, "The idea under ..." and before I can say the word "discussion" or even begin to state my thought she will intrude with a seemingly earnest but patently phony "uh huh." They keep coming, these badly placed and insincerely uttered "uh huhs," and it is all I can do to speak another sentence. I would rather she say directly to me, "I'm busy and I don't have the time to listen to you and if I did I wouldn't listen anyway."

Maybe I was spoiled by my mother. When Dorothy Garwood Callaway listened to you, she peered deeply at you and drank in everything you had to say. You felt as though you were the only person in the room. I didn't realize it until recently, but she was bringing everything she knew, everything she felt, everything she was as a human being to that moment of listening. You could *feel* her listening. It is a wonderful thing to be listened to that way. That's why to me, listening is loving.

13

∾

Her Heart Belonged to Daddy

People sometimes ask me, "Of all the interviews you've ever done over the years, which one is your favorite?" I hem and haw and evade. Of the many satisfying interviews over the years, no one person stands out way beyond the others. But when I am asked, "What has been your most difficult interview?" I respond immediately. No ifs or buts. Margaret Truman.

Now it is not my custom to criticize my guests because (1) as host of the program I think it is impolite to criticize—at least in public—your guests and (2) who knows, I might have to interview that person again some day. But because my difficult experience with Margaret Truman has a happy ending, I'm sure she would not object to my telling this story.

It was back in 1976. Margaret Truman was on a media tour with the publication of her book *Women of Courage.* This was the pre-mystery writer Margaret Truman. The book was about well-known and little-known women in American history who had achieved great things long before the modern women's movement. In preparing for the interview, I had read the book twice and enjoyed it very much. I was delighted to have an opportunity to meet Margaret Truman for the first time and to give her an opportunity to tell the then current generation of women's liberationists about their courageous grandmothers and great-grandmothers.

In reading a slew of magazine profiles of Margaret Truman, I became very aware that most writers and interviewers focused on her relationship with her father, Harry S Truman. As I read these interviews and profiles, I thought to myself, "How very tired she must be of talking about her father, about being perceived only as the daughter of a former president of the United States." I thought it would be particularly appropriate to interview her on her own merits—not her father's—as a part of a book interview devoted to the celebration and acknowledgment of American women in history who had achieved great things on their own.

As is my custom in preparing for one-on-one author interviews, I wrote a full page crammed with questions and notes so that I could absorb the book and my thoughts in such a way that I could talk with Ms. Truman eyeball to eyeball without consulting those written questions. This was my way of trying to establish a warm, intimate connection with a writer and it usually worked. When most authors discovered early in an interview that I had read their book or books and cared deeply about them and their work, they opened up like lovely flowers.

But that didn't work with Margaret Truman. I would ask a question and she would respond in a rather matter-of-fact, very brief, almost terse manner. Well, I thought, maybe her mind is elsewhere. Maybe she is at work on another project and has left this one behind mentally.

But there was something about Ms. Truman's voice and manner which suggested something more at work than boredom. She seemed almost stubborn in her clipped responses. I was close to panic. I had ripped right through the main theme questions for her in about ten minutes. How in heaven's name were we going to fill the rest of the half hour? In desperation, I blurted out, "You know, you remind me of your father!"

"Oh, how so?" she replied.

I then proceeded to tell her the story of my first encounter with Harry S Truman. It was in 1958 and Mr. Truman, who had been out of office for six years, was on one of his periodic visits to Chicago. As was his custom, he would take one of his famous early-morning walks up Michigan Avenue, meet informally with Mayor Richard J. Daley at City Hall, have lunch and then meet with the local press for a news conference. I was thrilled to be among those questioning the former president. I was at the Blackstone Hotel with a camera crew from WBBM-TV. I was twenty-one years old.

It so happens that, at the time of Mr. Truman's news conference, the U.S. government was undergoing a foreign affairs crisis. Lebanese President Camille Chamoun was trying to amend the Lebanese constitution and serve a second term as president. There was rioting in Lebanon. The Eisenhower administration feared both Communist mischief (in those days almost anything bad that happened was attributed to communism) and pan-Arab nationalist ferment. Ike and his secretary of state, John Foster Dulles, were giving serious consideration to sending the U.S. Marines into Lebanon (sounds familiar, doesn't it?).

As our cameras rolled, I asked the former president, "What do you think President Eisenhower should do about the situation in Lebanon?"

"Son, politics stops at the water's edge," replied Mr. Truman.

"But, Mr. President, as leader of the loyal opposition in this country, don't you have an informed opinion on this critical foreign affairs issue?'

"Son, politics stops at the water's edge."

I followed up once more. "But, Mr. President [you always call former presidents 'Mr. President'], as the former president of the United States you are kept up to date with intelligence briefings. You are the *one* person outside the administration who is qualified to comment on this crisis."

Harry S Truman sat back, smiled wryly and said to me, "I've already been over to City Hall to pay my respects to Mayor Daley.

Bess [his wife] is shopping at Marshall Field's. If you have the time and enough film in that camera I'll be happy to sit here for the rest of the afternoon and tell you what I've already told you, 'Son, politics stops at the water's edge.'"

Well, that broke the ice with Margaret Truman completely. She said that sounded just like her stubborn, principled father. The minute she started talking about her dad she became warm, animated and engaged. Her heart belonged to daddy.

I will never forget how pleased I was the following week when her office called and asked for a tape of the interview. What was at first my most difficult interview experience became one of my favorites.

14

❦

So You Want to Cover the Academy Awards, Huh?

It's that time of year again when our favorite movie stars are hyped for Oscars. You may not realize this, but I'm something of an expert on the Academy Awards, the way someone who has been rear-ended in a car accident is an expert on highway safety.

About ten years ago, when I caught the management of Channel 11 in a generous moment, I was permitted to moonlight as "critic-at-large" for WLS-TV, Channel 7.

I thought covering the pillow-soft movie beat would be a breeze after having reported on race riots and murders. Little did I know that Michael and Jeffrey and Gene and Roger deserve combat pay.

One Friday I dodged rats running all over the floor of a cavernous State Street theater while trying to appreciate the finer points of a Kung Fu movie. I'll not soon forget the time I was sitting in a suburban movie house and a Refrigerator Perry-like teenager suddenly lurched back in his deep swivel chair and cracked my knee full square, causing me to limp for a month.

Channel 7 forgot to provide me with protective gear to wear while covering the cinema. Squandering some of the proceeds of my newfound part time work, I popped, for the first time in my life, for a very expensive silk summer suit. Foolishly, I wore it to a screening. As I sat down, the right pocket of the trousers slid over the movie chair arm and the sound of shredding silk cloth could be heard well over the soundtrack.

They never were able to repair those trousers. A few weeks later, having not learned anything from that experience, I splurged for a pair of Bally loafers at a cost that was totally responsible for the 1982 U.S. balance of payments deficit. Immediately in front of me, a child turned around in his seat, stared innocently at me and accidentally dropped one of those ten-dollar twenty-five-gallon movie drinks— all over my beloved Ballys. They were not able to remove the grape stain from those shoes. Clearly, God meant me to wear cords and Hush Puppies.

The movie beat did have its compensations. One day, my brilliant producer, Marsha Jordan, and I were told that we were being assigned to cover the 1982 Academy Awards. In addition, we were to come up with a series of reports about Chicagoans who had made good in Tinseltown.

It was during the field interviews with the ex-Chicagoans in Hollywood that I came to know and hit it off big with the very capable and charming camera crew loaned to us by our ABC sister station in Los Angeles. I was delighted to know that this crew had been assigned to me for the interviews I would do the following Monday with Jane Fonda, Bob Hope, Cary Grant and other stars who would stop and talk with me on the red carpet leading to the Oscar ceremonies inside the Dorothy Chandler Pavilion in downtown Los Angeles.

Memo to anyone who has to cover the Academy Awards. Get there early. The line of limos was backed up so far that rainy Monday that I had to run for more than a mile to get to the red carpet area. But I would be okay—I saw my on-loan camera crew in the drenched sea of other camera crews standing by to interview the stars. But when I met them the cameraman looked at me as if he had to report a death in the family.

"John, pal," he said. "I don't know how to tell you this, but the rain has short-circuited our camera and we're totally out of commission and there won't be another one available out here."

Why me, God? But I had survived rats on State Street, and I would survive this. I caught up with Marsha and told her my strategy. I would take very careful, timed notes on the actual telecast (which would play on Channel 7 in Chicago because it was a network broadcast) and would build my script around segments from that, intercut with segments of interviews with Oscar winners who were always interviewed by pool reporters inside the Pavilion following their awards. We did have a camera crew inside for that assignment. Brilliant recovery plan, we agreed. I immediately called my tape editor, Linda Gerber, back in Chicago and told her to screen the telecast with me so she could be familiar enough with it to edit the tape cuts we needed based on my notes.

The rest of the night was easy. I took notes on the Oscars telecast and asked questions of Warren Beatty and other stars who won the prizes and then Marsha and I hightailed it out of there and caught an early morning flight back to Chicago. En route, I wrote my script, carefully leading into sound bites I knew we could lift from the Monday night Oscars telecast. I had talked with Linda back in Chicago and she had isolated the sound bites we needed. Nothing could stop us now, not even the fifty-mile-an-hour-plus winds that greeted our plane as it bounced its way down the runway at O'Hare at shortly before one that afternoon. God meant us to make the 4:30 news.

Really? When we arrived back at the ABC building we were met at the newsroom door by our bosses. They had the same expression on their faces that the cameraman had on his face in Los Angeles. Something has gone horribly wrong.

They proceeded to inform us that during the time we were in the air, they had discovered that the production company which produced the Oscars telecast owned the exclusive rights to the telecast and that even though it was broadcast on ABC-TV, the parent company, we couldn't broadcast a second of the Oscars telecast! No Oscars telecast, no red carpet interviews. Just some backstage stuff. May I go back to covering City Hall?

In the end we did what you should always do. We played it straight. I went on the air, told our viewers about our camera short-circuit, told them we couldn't show them Oscar highlights and that we would show them the clips from movies that won the Oscars and segments of the backstage interviews with Oscar winners. Baling wire, I think you call it. So give me war, give me pestilence, give me floods, but, please, never assign me again to our beloved Academy Awards.

15

∽

The Archival News

The producing team has obtained guests who are among the best experts in the business. The introductory video report is beautifully photographed and edited and astutely written and delivered by the correspondent. The director calls the shots that show the conversation in a most engaging way. The technical and engineering crew handle their live on-air assignments with efficiency and grace. The host of the program has been given in-depth research resources and the time to prepare for the interviews. The underwriters who help support the program financially are the cream of the business crop. Audience size is large enough and demographically on target to merit the advertising investment. Top management goes against conventional public television thinking and places the program in prime time where it can succeed and then gives it the freedom to grow and the resources to prosper editorially.

That's the way it is more often than not around WTTW during these days of our thirty-fifth year. It's that way because WTTW President Bill McCarter and his staff place local programming at the heart of the station's mission. It's that way because the long-range investment in local programming is now paying off in large audiences and in excellence of programming content.

It wasn't always as easy as it now looks. We had to stumble around a bit before we could fly right, particularly in the nightly news and public affairs area. I'm proud of our fledgling nightly public affairs offering, "The Public News-Center" (1975–1978), but I'll never forget the letter an irate viewer wrote complaining that she had read all of the favorable publicity prior to the inauguration of the program, had watched it carefully for two months and found that it was "not a whit better than the 'CBS Evening News' with Walter Cronkite." There was a grim lesson in her letter: Viewers don't care if you have only a few thousand dollars to invest in your start-up local programming against tens of millions spent on the well-established network competition—you'd better be good if you want them to switch the channel to you.

Among my fondest "growing pains" memories of the early WTTW years:

August 9, 1974 Remember what happened? Richard M. Nixon became the first president of the United States to resign. We mounted what became my very first live public affairs special at WTTW, a three-hour extravaganza in which I interviewed eighteen guests. The studio air-conditioning also resigned that night. The temperature in the studio hovered near 100 degrees. Result: your overweight host lost five pounds in one broadcast!

October, 1974 Joel Weisman and I were hosting a three-hour "politithon" in which we conducted quickie interviews with every congressional candidate in the metropolitan area. Joel and I had never hosted a program with this many guests and this much complexity, but about two hours into it we were chugging along without a major fluff and feeling pretty good about ourselves. We sat in chairs in front of a beautiful twelve-foot-high flag-like red, white and blue backdrop that extended for nearly the entire length of one side of the studio. Here we were in the midst of interviewing the long-shot socialist candidate who was telling us how running his dry-cleaning business would make him a better congressman when IT happened. IT began as a slow groaning sound that escalated into a screeching, shiny, industrial-strength sound neither Joel nor I will ever forget. The entire red, white and blue flat behind us had collapsed, barely missing us and our would-be congress-man! Joel started grinning and laughing in such a contagious way that I nearly lost control. I just barely managed to keep a straight face, but by that time our socialist dry-cleaner candidate was up in arms because he thought we were laughing at him. If you are reading this, sir, our deepest apologies.

March 30, 1981   I was on the Near North Side for one of my very rare downtown lunch appointments. It was a leisurely visit with a former colleague who was making me an offer to join him at a network-owned station. Near the end of the lunch his pager started beeping. When he returned from calling his newsroom he told me that an assassination attempt had been made on the pres-ident but that Reagan had not actually been shot. I raced to my car and limped through heavy traffic back to WTTW. By the time I got to the station more than half an hour had elapsed—a life-time in the business of reporting a crisis of this magnitude. We had not told our viewers (mostly children at that hour of the day) a thing about the events in Washington. As our principal public affairs on-air presenter, I thought that I had failed WTTW. But it turned out that by the time I read our first bulletin on the air, I had the story correct, tragically enough. The president had, indeed, been shot. We had it right. Later, in memorializing how lucky I was, I coined a new slogan for our public affairs efforts: "Chan-nel 11 Archival News. We get it straight, 'cause we get it late."

16

~

Cover Story

For once I was seated next to a beautiful young woman. Not a screaming child. Not a snoring salesman, but a beautiful young woman, who, it turned out, was also very smart. Soon after our flight to New York departed from O'Hare, we began a wide-ranging conversation, which was so pleasant that it seemed over before it began. It was the kind of flight I had fantasized but seldom experienced.

As the jetliner descended toward LaGuardia and the pilot issued his final seat-buckle instructions, the young woman turned to me and said, "Do you mind if I hold your hand?" I (who was between marriages at the time) assured my lovely companion that I surely would have no objection if she held my hand.

What was it? I wondered. Was it my post-divorce charm? Was it my slimming back from pretty darned fat to just reasonably overweight? What was it that this woman saw in me?

Well, it turned out that it wasn't my charm or my reduced weight. I just happened to be another human being she could hang on to at a critical moment in her life. She quickly explained, with some embarrassment, that she had just finished taking her bar exam and was sure that she was going to die before she learned the results. She said that everyone she knew in her law school class was experiencing the same kind of trauma—the "I'll get hit by a truck crossing the street and will never know if I passed the bar" kind of nightmare. She was afraid the plane would crash.

And so she hung on tightly to me as we glided safely into LaGuardia. We shook hands at the gate and I never saw her again. That young woman's fear reminds me of my own recurring nightmare. And when I say recurring, I mean recurring—I have this fear dream at least twice a year and have had it for at least fifteen years. Before I get to the specifics of it, let me confess that my dreams are not the wildly exotic, colorful, complex impossible-to-interpret dreams which so many of my family and friends like to share. Their dreams will keep psychiatrists busy for years. My dreams are so obvious that even I can understand them. For example, if I have been criticized in the press, I'll dream that I'm walking down the street and people are shooting at me from rooftops. Subtle, huh?

My recurring work dream is that it is just a minute or so before seven o'clock in the evening and I am late for my on-air assignment. As I walk into a huge auditorium-based remote broadcast site, I see that everyone is waiting for me. There are at least six panelists. There are hundreds of persons in the audience. The only problem is that I don't know who the guests are or what the topic of the program is. I am supposed to sit down and immediately interview the guests on the stage. I always wake up about the time I have to reveal to the audience that I don't know what's going on. (I know, many of you who have watched my broadcasts over the years will say that it is entirely true that I don't know what's going on and that the dream simply reflects, once again, a not-so-subtle reality.)

My real broadcast nightmare is no dream. It is a reality that I have sweated through (literally) for years. If you said to me at six o'clock in the evening, an hour before my broadcast, "John, the president of the United States is dropping by and you have to interview him live for two hours without any special preparation," I would grumble but then I would say, "Okay, let's do it." Or if you said to me, "John, we need you to be here in an hour and make a sixty-minute speech without preparation or notes," I might make a discreet inquiry about the honorarium, but I would be there and I would deliver.

But if you are a broadcast executive who asks me to moderate the next mayoral debate and to introduce the debate by reading several formal paragraphs of boilerplate copy describing the rules of the debate, who the candidates are, and who the journalists-questioners are, I go into shock.

I have moderated many debates and introduced dozens of special forums in my thirty-six years of broadcasting. Never once have I read the opening copy without almost choking on the air. My throat goes dry. My heart pounds. I gasp for breath. I see my career going down the tube.

One steamy night in Carbondale, Illinois, I had the awful responsibility of moderating a live gubernatorial debate. The temperature in the studio was about 110 degrees. I was on antibiotics for a sinus infection. All of that combined with my debate-intro phobia caused me to come within inches of fainting—live, on air.

How have I dealt with this? At first, I tried to fake my way through. When a producer would ask why I gasped in the middle of the copy, I would mumble something about heartburn or the teleprompter moving too fast. Finally, I started confessing my problem to my colleagues, much as I'm telling you here. They were just wonderful about it. They would work with me to devise points in the introductory copy where I could go directly to the candidates if I couldn't find the breath to finish all the boilerplate copy. Even before my live introductory news report or essay on "Chicago Tonight," my producer will whisper over the intercom into my earpiece a reassuring, "Good luck, John." That really helps.

I think, after years of sweating and reflection, that my aversion to the reading of formal introductory material is a deep resistance to being used in an announcer's function. I'm particularly uncomfortable reading copy that I haven't written. And if I think the sponsors of a debate and the candidates are all staring at me watching for a slip, I feel like the kid at a high school speech contest who fears making a fool of himself.

And so, if you see me freeze some night while I'm reading copy to introduce a program or debate, forgive me.

And to the young woman I flew into LaGuardia with that night many years ago, I do hope you passed the bar. And, by the way, if you're in town the next time I have to moderate a debate, would you come over and hold my hand?

Christmas Isn't Easy

17

~

Blue Christmas

Christmas isn't easy. A few years ago, WTTW hooked up with the Church Federation to offer a Yuletide hot line. The volunteers were swamped with calls relating to everything from pleas for food to suicide threats.

When Channel 11 established the hot line, I joked with colleagues that the station already was generous with staff benefits. They didn't have to go to all the trouble to set up a special Christmas telephone emergency service for me. I never did call the hot line, but I could have. It's no joke, Christmas makes me sing the blues.

When I was a sophomore in college, I came home for Christmas and ended up in a great big fight with my mother over the most bizarre incident. One night during the holidays my dad lent me his DeSoto to drive twenty-six miles down the Ohio River and see an old girlfriend from high school. As always, the deal was that I was to replenish the gas tank with at least the same amount of gas I used. No problem. After the date, I dutifully headed for the restaurant–gas station where I had worked the previous summer. Knowing the boss very well, I simply pulled up in front of a pump, helped myself and then went in and paid the $2 or whatever it was.

I drove home without incident. Little did I know that I was lucky to have got home at all. I spent the next day with chums and arrived home late to be greeted by Dorothy Garwood Callaway, *my very, very angry mother.* Dad had gone to bed, so it was mom who informed me at the top of her lungs that because of me the DeSoto had spewed dark fumes as dad drove it to work and then conked out on a very icy, precarious stretch of narrow road, thus endangering dad's life and causing him to lose a day's work.

Why hadn't I confessed to them the night before that I had filled the car with *diesel fuel?* my steamed, esteemed mother wished to know. I told her truthfully that I didn't realize I had done any such thing. She didn't believe me, and there was a reason for her mistrust.

I was known as the "diesel fuel kid" in those parts, following an incident the previous summer at the same restaurant–gas station when I had accidentally filled a chicken farmer's non-diesel truck with diesel fuel. That poor fellow hadn't driven more than three miles down the road when his chicken truck died in a cloud of diesel fuel smoke. So my mother was sure that I couldn't have driven dad's car without knowing it was smoking diesel fuel. But the truth is—and she didn't believe me that night—I drove the old DeSoto home without a hitch. But dear mother, inspired by a few post-Christmas highballs and sure that I was lying, pronounced me a prevaricating coward and threw me out of the house! There I was, hitchhiking my way back to college in the cold, *not* humming "Have Yourself a Merry Little Christmas."

But that actually was a lot less traumatic than the Christmas of 1941. I was five years old and thrilled to be the recipient that Christmas morning of a brand new Lionel electric train set. Dad took great pains to explain to me that it would be necessary for me to take very good care of the train, the track, and other shiny new equipment because there wouldn't be any replacement parts for maybe years to come. He reminded me that the Japanese had bombed Pearl Harbor eighteen days earlier and that we were at war.

Included in my Christmas extravagance that year were some black balloons. They were wonderful, big blow-up balloons. They made an awful pop sound that scared everyone silly when I would fill one up and then place it on top of a red-hot room heater we had in those days. Just before bedtime I took the last of my black balloons and placed it on top of the heater. Once again it exploded but this time no one jumped and yelled. Only my dad came into the room. He looked matter of factly at me and said, "Son, that was your last balloon. Because of the war there probably won't be any more made for years and years."

There was a quiet finality in his voice that cut through me like death. In a flash I experienced a kind of deep understanding that the party was over. The war would mean sacrifice of many kinds for years and I might not possess one of my beloved balloons for many, many years. I wept that evening the tears of one whose best friend has died.

You can imagine how touched I was, then, on a recent Christmas when my wife, Patrice, presented me with one last special gift. Two black balloons.

If you visit our home you'll find those balloons in my library, and in our kitchen you'll also find other reminders of my Christmas memories. You'll find four plain glass soup bowls that retail for about a dollar or less each at factory outlets. We've had them for years, and they are a reminder of the four plain glass soup bowls I paid five cents each for and gave to my mother one Christmas when dad was out of work; we were broke and there wasn't much on the table.

My mother would say for years after that those bowls were the nicest Christmas gifts she had ever received. They were still on the shelf in their home in West Virginia when I arrived for her funeral on the day before Christmas twenty years ago. Christmas isn't easy.

18

⌒

Oh Christmas Tree, Oh Christmas Tree

Christmas isn't easy. I'm not talking about experiencing the kind of holiday blues that moved me to begin this column last December with the sentence "Christmas isn't easy." No, I'm talking about a problem of even greater complexity and psychological turmoil than one's childhood Christmas traumas. I'm talking about the problem of purchasing a Christmas tree.

Tell me I have to have root canal work. No problem. Tell me our plane has to make an emergency landing in Cleveland. No problem.

Tell me that Mike Wallace of "60 Minutes" is calling and wants to interview me about my income tax returns. No problem.

Tell me it's time to buy the Christmas tree.

We've got a problem.

My Christmas-tree phobia goes back to the days when my daughters were very young and I was very broke. Being very broke meant that I usually waited until the last paycheck prior to Christmas before I went tree hunting, not to mention gift shopping. That meant that I found myself Christmas tree shopping just a day or two or three before Christmas when two overwhelmingly obvious circumstances would manifest themselves: (1) there were no decent Christmas trees left, and, (2) it was usually colder than a bill collector's heart.

Those ungratifying circumstances were usually exacerbated by the fact that in those days I invariably went Christmas tree hunting after putting in a ten-hour day reporting on everything from murders to fires, followed by some kind of holiday drinking contest with colleagues at a nearby establishment of good cheer.

So there I would stand, huddled in my wafer-thin overcoat (they didn't have down jackets in those days), shivering in the falling snow at some wind-swept lot on Chicago's North Side, trying to peer through my fogged-up glasses with my alcohol-fogged-up eyes, trying to discern which of the poor orphan trees remaining I should rescue and take home.

Invariably I would choose the wrong tree. I would be instructed to get balsam. I would forget and choose a Scotch pine.

Invariably, because the trees were frozen stiffer than a corpse at the Cook County morgue, I would return home with a horribly disfigured tree—discovered only upon the post-thaw examination. Invariably the tree I bought was too short or too tall. Invariably, the tree would not fit into the holder and I would be dispatched into the cold to try to find a larger or smaller holder. I simply couldn't get it right.

Now my children are grown up and now I have enough money to buy any tree I please but it's still traumatic for me to hear the words, "It's time to get the Christmas tree." My self-confidence evaporates. My knees shake. My heart pounds. Will I know what I'm doing?

I would have known what I was doing with Christmas trees and anything else having to do with Christmas if I had only had access years ago to the wit and wisdom contained in Michelle McKenzie-Voigt's "Christmas Party Notebook." (Michelle is a long-time colleague on my "Chicago Tonight" program.)

In a cover memo Michelle attached to her precious Christmas party notebook she wrote,

"We've had a Christmas party every other year since 1979. That's a lot of parties! I simply don't see much sense in making the same mistakes over and over just because I failed to note what worked and what didn't. I'd be pretty foolish NOT to make notes, because after 730 days have rolled around again, I can scarcely remember where I live, let alone what foods people have enjoyed. And I've learned a lot, too. I've learned that people don't drink green punch. I've learned not to put candles down low where the dog can knock them over with its tail. I've learned not to serve grapes with seeds. Or ANY kind of Jell-O mold. Or shrimp with the shells on. We're talking priceless information here, acquired at great cost and the agony that only personal experience can possibly provide."

You can imagine, then, my joy when I opened Michelle's Christmas party notebook and found, on the first page beyond the index, a page entitled "Tree Notes." Here, in part, is what it says:

"We get balsam.

"It is eight feet, three inches from the inside of the assembled tree stand to the living room ceiling, so we can get an eight-foot tree.

"Remember to take the measuring tape with us when we get the tree.

"BUT DO NO CUTTING UNTIL THE TREE IS UP! In 1990, we took off way more than we needed to, even though we measured.

"In 1990, it took 1½ hours (once we got home) to put the tree up and put the lights on. This assumes, of course, that everything has been readied: the furniture moved, the stand assembled, etc.

"It takes me five hours to put on the ornaments once the lights are on and assuming I'm alone.

"Consider unpacking all the ornaments and decorating the *house only* on Thanksgiving weekend. It takes a day and a half to buy and do the tree, so do this the first weekend of December."

And so this incredible notebook goes; with sections on party ideas (let's add broccoli cheese soufflé to the menu); schedules (book party help no later than June); menus from every year since

1981 (they had Cranberry/Cherry Jell-O Mold back then); guest lists complete with who RSVP'd and who didn't (the CIA would envy her thoroughness); gifts received and who gave them; inventory lists of party supplies (200 forks, 200 knives, 100 spoons, three fire logs, etc.); on down to an accountant's dream of an expenses section.

I won't tell you more. If there is a publisher out there looking for a great new Christmas book, call Michelle McKenzie-Voigt.

As for me, I'm going out there now and see if I can't find a good eight-foot balsam. Or was that a Scotch pine?

19

∾

Home for Christmas!

Christmas isn't easy. No, I'm not talking about trying to find a full-bodied, attractive Christmas tree on Christmas Eve. And I'm not talking about trying to assemble an-impossible-to-assemble toy for your child after midnight on Christmas morning. No, this time my "Christmas isn't easy" lament is about kids who arrive home for Christmas from their first semester at college. They departed for college as your beloved, darling, clean-cut, high-achieving, God-fearing and -believing adorable children. And now they have returned, evil little atheists who have been transformed into perhaps the only true Communists left on the globe. And you, their dear parents, are filled with sentimental mush about Christmas when these "I have seen the light and I know everything" monsters come dragging in from the Halls of Ivy to ruin your egg nog-inspired dream of a 1950s Christmas homecoming.

I know whereof I write, because I was one of the little monsters. Permit me a story.

On the lovely late summer evening prior to my leaving for college at Ohio Wesleyan University, my dad took me aside for a little chat. "I notice you've received a lot of mail this summer from the fraternities at Ohio Wesleyan," he said. "Yes," I said, puffing up like an adder. "All of them want me to join." "Well, that's very nice. But I just wanted you to know that if you join a fraternity you don't have to worry about coming home ever again. And don't worry about having anything to do with me."

Utterly shocked, I asked my father whatever in the world was he talking about. He explained that when he was in college he joined a social fraternity and thought it was a wonderful experience until he learned that social fraternities did not accept Negroes (the term used in those days) or Jews. He told me that he never had been more ashamed of anything in his life than his belonging to a fraternity that discriminated on the basis of race or religion. And he said he simply would not stand for his son to indulge in the same behavior.

Now in this day and age you might be tempted to say, "So what's the big deal? You simply were blessed with a fair-minded, sensitive father. Thank your stars." But you have to understand who my father was to appreciate the shock I experienced. To say that Charles Callaway was to the right of Attila the Hun is to practice rhetorical restraint. He hated FDR. He hated anything smacking of government interference in business or private life. Aside from the time he had complained that a Lebanese family was being discriminated against in our town, he had said little around the house that struck me as racially progressive. That was understandable since we lived in a West Virginia town that was lily white and mostly Protestant. Racial and religious tolerance were, up to that shocking moment, non-issues in our home.

And so, I had my marching orders as I showed up at Ohio Wesleyan the next day. Dutifully, I accepted the invitation to each fraternity on campus to be "rushed," that is, to listen to the exhortations of each fraternity leader on why I should join. I would listen politely, and then ask the key question: "By the way, do you accept Negroes and Jews into your fraternity?" There would be much coughing and sniffing and each spokesman would mutter something about how he would dearly love to accommodate all races and religions, but provisions in the national organization's charter forbade him from doing so. I politely would shake his hand and leave without comment. I was so proud of myself. Meet John Callaway, conservative son of conservative West Virginia newspaper editor, newfound *liberal*.

But the glow of being a progressive faded. After having turned down what I thought was the last fraternity on campus and having contemplated what it would be like to be an "independent" on a campus where 95 percent of the men and women belonged to fraternities and sororities, I was feeling depressed and lonely.

It was about then that I found myself walking down a street and hearing a wonderful trumpet sound emanate from a house. I checked it out and discovered that it was a fraternity I hadn't visited. It turned out to be Beta Sigma Tau, the only inter-racial, inter-religious, inter-national social fraternity in the country at that time (to the best of my knowledge). The place was hopping with kids from all over the world, of many races and religions. I joined at once.

Later that night I called my dad. "Guess what, Dad. I've joined a fraternity." Long silence on the other end of the phone. Really long silence. "But guess what, Dad. They accept Negroes and Jews and everyone else," I shouted in triumph. He sounded so relieved. His beloved son could return home.

And return home I did, at Christmas. And by that time, with the passage of just under one semester of college, my multi-race, multi-religious, far-left-leaning pacifist fraternity brothers had turned me into everything my father (and mother) detested. And I lorded all of my newfound One World United liberal views over them the entire Christmas holiday. God, was it a miserable time. It was like the McLaughlin Group every night at the table, except it wasn't as sweet and reasonable as the McLaughlin Group. All my dad wanted was for me not to discriminate. What he got was a brand new little Commie.

We, of course, laughed a lot about this years later when I was settled comfortably back in the middle of the political spectrum (and my dad also moved more to the center from his far-right turf). But I tell this story for the benefit of any parents whose home-for-Christmas sweeties have turned into political or religious monsters. Have some wonderful conversations. Be patient. And remember, Christmas isn't easy.

20

On Your Toes

Christmas isn't easy. It's that time of year again to give. God, don't you hate it? Your mail is infiltrated with guilt-begetting greetings. There's the charity that encloses the packet of return-address labels with your name brightly printed on them. It has made an investment in you; how can you not return the act of good faith? The churches, the nonprofit institutions, the charities all line up in your mail like so many outstretched hands. Why, oh why, did the Internal Revenue Service ever pronounce them deductible?

And then there are the folks out here on the streets. Where do you start? The Salvation Army? Do you give to the homeless man on Wabash Avenue or the homeless woman on State Street? If so, to how many of the penniless do you give and how much? And when you are trying to find change in your purse or pocket, do you ask the homeless to hold your $150 in gift packages you have just purchased for your family or friends?

I recently spent some time in Manhattan where I encountered more homeless street persons in one day than I see in Chicago in a month. I found myself resisting the temptation to give anything to these people. At first, I was simply overwhelmed, and then I hardened into a stare-straight-ahead-and-don't-pay-them-any-heed-modern-big-city pedestrian. I was fully equipped with all the rationalizations. They'll only spend it on booze. I already give to institutions that deal with the homeless. My tax dollars should take care of this problem. My spare change or dollar bills wouldn't make a difference in their lives anyway.

A few days after I returned to Chicago I awakened one night with a terrible spasm of guilt. I hurt more than I can tell you because I walked past all those desperate human beings with nothing more in my heart than denial.

It's not the first time I have been awakened in the middle of a deep sleep with memorable pain. When I was a high school boy in West Virginia I used to kick extra points for our football team. I remember the first cold night game we played and what happened after I returned home. It was about two o'clock in the morning. I was awakened by a terrible pain in my right leg. My right calf muscle had flipped out of place in a spasm of unforgettable pain. I had to pound that muscle back into place. I continued to suffer those spasms over the years when my leg was exposed to the cold or when I hadn't slept enough, and I would stretch and throw my calf muscles out of place. Award-winning pain.

Switch the scene now from West Virginia in the 1950s to our new apartment in Chicago a few years ago. The man of the house in the previous owner's family was at least two inches taller than I. He had left his shaving mirror in the shower I was to use. Whenever I used the mirror to shave I had to stand on my tiptoes to see my face. I'll get a new shaving mirror and place it so I won't have to make like a ballet dancer when I shave, I thought. But, being the lazy soul that I am, I postponed buying a new mirror. I continued to stand on my toes to shave.

You guessed it. No more calf muscle spasms! Just standing on my toes for a little more than a minute a day did whatever nature deemed necessary to strengthen those calf muscles.

What did I learn from this little exercise in unintended consequences? I learned that even minimal exercise of muscles on a daily basis can make them a bit stronger. And I learned that the benefits of certain actions—including ones that seem uncomfortable—cannot be planned or anticipated.

And so maybe we can use this holiday season to begin to stand on our moral and ethical tiptoes and flex our giving muscles a little. Maybe we won't be too rational about it. Maybe we'll just exercise the act of giving. Who knows, maybe it will become a habit. Who knows, maybe it will ease the pain of those spasms of guilt that come in the night. Who knows, maybe it will set an example for others. Who knows, maybe if we can give to an outstretched hand at the holidays, we can find it in ourselves to offer even greater gifts throughout the year. On your toes, everyone!

The Thing of It Is (and Other Gripes)

21

∾

The Thing of It Is — Part I

The thing of it is ...

- Ryne Sandberg of the Cubs looks an awfully lot like Mayor Daley to me.
- Waiters always ask me "Is everything okay?" just when my mouth is full.
- Whatever happened to 40 percent bran flakes?
- Interviewees should always be on the alert when the questioner begins, "With all due respect ...".
- Do you realize that we live in a nation whose national anthem begins with the words, "Oh, say, can you see ..."?
- People who recklessly zoom out of a parking space directly into the path of your car, risking life and limb, invariably drive about a block and then park again.
- All those paper clips in my paper clip bowl seem to mate overnight. When I reach in to pull one out, they are always entangled with each other like sleepy lovers.

The thing of it is ...

- I am filled with terror when I have to write my signature on the tiny white strip on the back of a new credit card.
- People drive me crazy when I answer my own telephone by saying "John Callaway" and then they say, "Is this John Callaway?"

- I can almost always correctly guess the general tone of a viewer letter by the appearance, typeface, and other linear particulars of how the envelope is addressed.
- Most newspaper photographs of national and international leaders are boring and do nothing to advance either the story or human knowledge.
- President Bush's dot, dot, dot, telegrapher's style of informal speech sounds a lot like someone who dictates a slew of notes and memos every day. I guess that makes him some sort of dictator (only kidding, folks).
- It is so thrilling when the gasoline company computer sends me a message at the top of my bill congratulating me for paying my account so promptly. Who says this is a heartless world?
- Having a gout attack isn't nearly as painful as having to explain to everyone what gout is and how a gout attack comes about.
- Why are adult bookstores called "adult" when they are anything but?
- The incessant repetition of the winning lottery numbers at the top of the radio news is a bore.
- Some of the nation's most astute, veteran media critics still refer to news coverage as "film" when they mean videotape.
- They ought to put a wall around country clubs that discriminate; call them bigotry museums; and let schoolchildren come around on trips to look at the bigots.
- If I receive another sweepstakes notice telling me I've won a big gift, I'm going to scream.
- I miss buying 33-rpm records. Heck, I miss buying *78*-rpm records.
- No-fat, sugarless frozen yogurt is the greatest discovery of this or any other century.
- My mother called people who played golf "golfists," and she pronounced White House (as in Washington, D.C.) The White *House*. God, I miss her.

- Ninety-five percent of the stuff I see at summer art fairs does not even remotely appeal to me. I can't afford the remaining five percent.
- Great newspapers aren't newspapers any more. Oh, they have news in them, but essentially they are "problem" papers. They report on the problems and expectations of how those problems can be resolved. The *New York Times'* slogan should be, "All the Problems That Are Fit to Print."
- It drives me nuts to waste twenty-nine cents on a stamp every month to tell the book club I don't want one of its books this month. Thank goodness they didn't let the local cable company get away with that "negative option" stunt earlier this summer.
- Walter Laqueur was right when he wrote in the *New York Times* recently, "Academics tend to be wrong as often as the rest of mankind, though on a higher level of sophistication."

22

❦

The Thing of It Is — Part II

The thing of it is...

Few things on the road are more dangerous than a beer truck double-parked near the corner, thus forcing you to edge out into traffic not having a clue as to who is coming the other way. I can't remember the last time I saw a beer truck parked that wasn't double-parked.

My serious health-enhancing advice during this frigid season is for those of you who suffer from chronic sinus infections. Dip a cotton swab into a bottle of mineral oil and then swab each of your nostrils once before going into the cold and once before bedtime. I have been following this advice for the past year and it is the first year in my adult life that I have avoided sinus infections. The oil provides moisture for the nostrils, which helps prevent the dryness in which infections develop. I pray that President Clinton will heed this advice, as he seems to suffer ongoing sinus problems.

Remember my previous advice: If you suffer from calf muscle spasms, stand on your toes for a minute or so each day. No more spasms.

William Schneider, the CNN political analyst, has a brilliant definition: A "political base" is made up of those people who are for you when you are wrong. Sounds like a good definition of a family.

Bylines bug me. I want to know more than the name of the writer. I want to be able to call up a data base that will tell me enough about the writer's life to know what his or her experiences are and what his or her biases might be. The longer and more interpretive the story or review, the more I want to know about the writer. This information will become more and more available to us as more and more of us turn to computer data bases to accompany our reading of newspapers and magazines.

The most underexamined statistic in our political discourse is the number of Americans who don't have health insurance. Some say there are thirty-five million uninsured, others say it is closer to thirty-eight million or more. Who are they? Eli Ginzberg of the Eisenhower Center for the Conservation of Human Resources says, "Most of the uninsured are children or young adults who use physicians and hospitals rarely." Maybe they use physicians and hospitals rarely because they have no insurance. Maybe we could afford to provide them with health insurance if we didn't spend so much on subsidies for upper income employees.

The thing of it is ...

We still refer to "albums" even though the "record" companies now produce CDs and tape cassettes. Veteran media writers often write that a news camera crew "filmed" an event when they mean that the crew "videotaped" the story. Similarly, the British often refer to radio as "the wireless." Marshall McLuhan was right when he suggested that in this fast-moving world of media we often are reluctant to use the current terminology—we lean back on the old.

That is why I often will refer to a special broadcast of my program as a special "edition." It is no more an "edition" than a newspaper is a "broadcast."

There are more than 325,000 automated teller machines in operation throughout the world.

Why do the "corrections" columns in newspapers so often fail to make clear what the original mistake was?

The thing of it is ...
 People enrage me who don't know how to leave a telephone number. Instead of saying that the number is 531-4465, they will say that the number is 5314-465. Simply drives me nuts.

One of every five adult Americans is functionally illiterate. Good luck, Mr. President.

I feel economically illiterate when I read newsletters containing phrases like "an anticipated secular inflation rate." Is there a religious or theological inflation rate? Heck, it took me years to figure out what a "nominal" interest rate is.

If all the satires based on television programs were removed from the skits on "Saturday Night Live," the program could be reduced from its current, endless, mediocre ninety minutes to a good, crisp fifteen minutes. It is a shame that the world of comedy is dominated by younger performers. Lack of real-life experience forces many young comedy writers and performers to rely on the one huge force that informs their lives—television.

Media commentators who refer to "media" as singular make me want to tear out what little hair remains on my head.

Do you think you are something of a fraud? If so, you are not alone. The *New York Times* reports on studies that show that 70 percent of the American people have felt themselves to be a fraud or an imposter for at least one period of their lives. The studies report that "the conviction that one is a fake may be prevalent in as many as two in every five successful people in all varieties of careers."

Don't stories like that make you proud to be a human being?

23

⌒

Off-Air Questions for the New Year

Permit a man who makes his living asking questions on the air to start the New Year by asking a few questions off the air.

- Why is it I can remember everything about a given day forty years ago, but I can't remember if I put on deodorant after taking a shower?
- Do you agree that people who talk too much about how often they fly ought to be convicted of "jet brag"?
- Aren't you glad we didn't live in Virginia in 1610 when they had a law that imposed the death penalty if you missed church three times?
- Why aren't dry cleaners open until eleven o'clock at night?
- Isn't it true that any system as inherently, deliberately complicated as the property tax assessment system is inherently, deliberately dishonest and unfair and ought to be scrapped?
- What if the rest of us had to live like actors and audition for our jobs every day or week?
- Is there any way to get a fountain pen repaired without sending it away somewhere for three months?
- If you thought they went too far when they started putting

perfume and cologne scents in magazine ads, how do you feel about direct mail VIDEOS?

- Does it follow that men who now wear earrings will soon wear makeup?
- Does anyone stand around the piano with friends and sing anymore?
- After the Judge Thomas confirmation hearings, did you change the way you pronounce the word *harassment*?
- Do you have as much trouble keeping your eye on the road and tuning a digital car radio as I do?
- Wouldn't it have been a gas to watch John McLaughlin moderate the Lincoln-Douglas debates?
- Will I ever take the time to read the weekly food sections of the daily newspapers?
- Is there really anything safe about sex?
- Do most public radio news anchors sound as bored and superior to you as they do to me?
- Why is it that I never seem to get around to watching any TV programs I videotape?
- If, as Johnny Carson once noted, the shortest unit of time known to man is the difference between the time the light switches to green and when the car behind you honks, then does it follow that the longest unit of time known to man is that between your asking your waiter or waitress for the check and the arrival of the check?
- Will we ever get it through our noggins that all of the citizens and experts who complain that the politicians are corrupted and the political system is paralyzed by special interests forget that we, the people, are the special interests?
- Have you noticed that trying to clip an article out of a newspaper some days lately is like trying to cut through cardboard?
- Did you know that there are more than 900,000 tax-exempt organizations in the United States?

- Why can't I remember the last time I poured a guest a glass of whiskey in my home?
- Is it okay if I oppose the death penalty for every offense except those people who market goods and services through automatic telephone dialing?
- Now that authoritarian socialism is pretty much dying, can we go to work on corporate authoritarianism?
- Isn't a most needed discovery to develop the ability to provide movable grass playing surfaces for domed stadiums?
- Did any of the more than one million persons who bought the novel *Scarlett* actually read the thing all the way through?
- Will I ever finish Norman Mailer's 1,310-page *Harlot's Ghost?*
- Would you agree that the maddening impersonality of most corporate voice-mail systems is a strong indication that the company cares more about short-term savings than about customer and human relations?
- Isn't it pathetic that the best way to learn geography in a memorable way is to fight a war?
- How many hundred years will pass before American magazine editors cease putting a Kennedy on their covers?
- Has there been a scarier news story lately than the one about the new Soviet trading company that is trying to sell underground nuclear explosions for incineration of toxic wastes and "other commercial uses"? Hey, buddy, can you spare a bomb?
- Did you know that the correct pronunciation of Pulitzer as in Pulitzer Prize is "pull'-it-zer"?
- Why is it the older I get the more I clean my eyeglasses?
- Why does it seem perfectly appropriate that I affix an Abbott & Costello stamp to the parking ticket I'm mailing?

24

~

Buy American?

The broadcast began this way:

"Good evening. I'm John Callaway. Welcome to "Chicago
Tonight." My granddad bought American cars and they ran and
ran. That was before World War II. My dad bought American
cars and they ran and died and ran and died. I bought American cars and every one of them was a disaster. The left front
wheel fell off one while I was making a turn. The steering wheel
fell off another. Frequently they stopped running just as I would
begin a long vacation trip with my wife and children. I spent
enough time with car mechanics to claim them as dependents
on my income tax returns. And so it was with a sense of regret,
but with great, earned anger that five years ago I broke down
and bought a Japanese-made car. And it has run and run. After
five years, I had to have the alternator replaced. That's it. That's
all. But now I see newspaper ads saying that it's time to fight
back against the Japanese and buy American cars—that if we
don't start buying American again there won't be any American car companies left not to buy from."

I can't remember the last time an opening essay to one of my
"Chicago Tonight" broadcasts brought so many angry letters and
calls.

One viewer wrote:

"When I heard you say you bought a Honda five years ago, it turned my stomach. It's people like you who have caused this Depression. I consider your ilk traitors when our nation is in trouble...."

I don't know what upset me more: being an ilk or a traitor. Buddy, can you spare a firing squad?

And then another big fan of mine weighed in:

"... I am now a Callaway basher and hope enough people join me so that you will become unemployed and you can drive your Honda to the unemployment office for a handout from the American government."

These writers and almost all of the others who objected to my purchase of a Japanese car had something very important in common with the American car makers I used to help support with my purchases of their lemons. There was not one iota of acknowledgment in their letters about the substance of my experience with American cars. No one said, "Wow, you really suffered personal and financial hardship and even risked your life in those American cars. I sure hope you'll consider buying American now that American cars are getting better but I surely understand why you might be a little gun-shy about American cars." And, as I mentioned on that program, not once in all of the years I was buying American cars and spending half my time getting them repaired did I ever hear the manufacturer of those cars or the salesmen of those cars say, "We're sorry. We sold you a lemon and we truly regret it." Nor did I hear them say, "Here's some compensation for all the grief we caused you and millions of other American car buyers." It didn't surprise me that I didn't hear from the automobile companies or the salesmen because had they been savvy enough to be in touch with their customers about their cars, they would have been savvy enough to build better cars in the first place.

The reason that I finally, reluctantly, broke down and bought a Honda in 1987 after renting, leasing and buying American cars for decades is that I finally took the advice of several of my friends who said deciding how to buy a car was a very simple matter if reliability is important to you. All of them said that if the reliability reports in *Consumer Reports* started to show that American cars were as reliable as Japanese cars, then by all means, buy an American car. And so I scrutinized the reliability reports (among other factors) of the U.S. versus Japanese cars in the 1987 *Consumer Reports* and guess what those reports showed? That not one American car I might have been interested in purchasing had any kind of reliability record worth mentioning. And guess what. *All* of the Japanese cars that I was thinking about buying had *excellent* reliability records. So I bought a Honda and it turned out, by a factor of about one hundred, to be the most reliable automobile I have ever owned.

Now, does this mean that all American cars are unreliable? Of course not. One of my angry viewers wrote, "Our Oldsmobile has 40,000 miles and has not had one problem. Not even a minor one." I trust that is entirely true, but the 1987 *Consumer Reports* on Oldsmobiles' reliability indicated that Olds' reliability couldn't begin to match Honda's, all exceptions aside. I wasn't about to reject *Consumer Reports*' overall findings in 1987 as I had ignored them in past years. And to the editors of *Consumer Reports* and to the people who make Honda automobiles, I say a great big, warm, huggy "Thank you" for all of your good work. You have made my life safer, happier and more productive.

Final thoughts: *Consumer Reports* says that the new American cars are getting better and better in every way, including reliability. But they also report that Japanese cars, on the whole, are still more reliable than American cars. I have such good personal feelings about Honda that I will give serious consideration to buying another Honda in a year or two. And until I get some kind of apology from American car makers for decades of shoddy products, I personally may never buy American again.

To those of you who think that is traitorous of me, I have one reply: If it weren't for the hundreds of thousands of you who bought

Japanese cars, Detroit never would have come to its senses. American cars will get better and better simply because they have to get better in order to compete with Japan and other foreign producers. The most loyal American of all was the one who sent the wake-up call to Detroit. And one last question for some of my angry viewers: Would you check what TV manufacturer you watched "Chicago Tonight" on so that you could get angry with me for buying Japanese?

25

~

Light Up For Rights: The Least a Non-Smoker Can Do

As one who cheers for the underdog and admires people who take on controversial causes with their chins out, I have to tip my hat to the good folks at the Philip Morris Companies (Kraft General Foods, Miller Brewing Company and Philip Morris USA).

Don't you just love the full-page ads they've been taking out in magazines and newspapers featuring huge pictures of your favorite heroes and mine—people like Father Theodore Hesburgh of Notre Dame and Solidarity leader Lech Walesa and Benjamin Hooks of the NAACP—endorsing the U.S. Bill of Rights in behalf of Philip Morris and the National Archives?

Doesn't it make you feel more secure knowing that the makers of Marlboros and some of the world's outstanding moral figures both are full-square behind this great crusade in behalf of the Bill of Rights? Doesn't it make you proud to be an American? It makes me damned proud. Proud enough to want to break out a case of Miller Lite and celebrate.

But my problem is that I don't have any right to celebrate yet. I don't even feel that I have earned the right yet to call that special 800 number and get my free parchment reproduction of the Bill of Rights like the more than two million Americans Philip Morris says already have called.

The fact is that so far I haven't given Philip Morris the kind of personal support it deserves. Citizens died protecting the Bill of Rights. Philip Morris, at great sacrifice, is spending millions of its hard-earned dollars on these print ads and that special television spot campaign trying to educate Americans about the first ten amendments to the U.S. Constitution. My commendation of Philip Morris here simply isn't enough. I've got to take some concrete action in support of it.

I am so proud of Philip Morris and its campaign that I am going to risk my life in its behalf. Even though I know that trying to persuade anyone to smoke or be in favor of smokers' rights was the last thing on the company's noble mind when it decided to fund this campaign, I am going to start smoking its cigarettes.

Now, in case you don't think my public announcement pledging to take up smoking Philip Morris tobacco products is a significant risk or social commitment, let me confess something to you:

I have never smoked a cigarette in my life.

Yes, as a teenager, I dangled a cigarette or two from my lips while trying to imitate Humphrey Bogart (and while some of my high school classmates were finishing their first or second packs of the day), but I have never actually smoked a cigarette. I'm not sure why. Maybe it is because my newspaper editor father was always coughing as he worked his way through two or three packs a day. Maybe it was because I frequently had to empty and then wash the many ashtrays my newspaper reporter mother filled with her two or three packs a day. And I should add that it is not because I am a particularly virtuous person. I have never smoked a "regular" cigarette, but I can confess that a couple of decades ago I "experimented" a few times with reefers. So I am not a virgin in these matters.

But now it is time to smoke an actual cigarette like a man. A Marlboro man. It's time to risk lung cancer, throat cancer, heart disease and everything else those lily-livered surgeons general of the United States keep associating with cigarette smoking in order to support my new and, I hope, good friends at the Philip Morris Companies.

I know I am not a big enough celebrity or a hero figure for Philip Morris to print my picture in full pages of paid advertising in the nation's leading magazines and newspapers. But I hereby pledge that if Philip Morris will join me in a news conference, I, John Douglas Callaway, will smoke a Philip Morris cigarette in full view of reporters, photographers and television camera crews as a health-sacrificing act of support for the campaign for the U.S. Bill of Rights. At the same time I will, with a perfectly straight face, tell those assembled reporters that I am certain the Philip Morris people are not using this campaign as a back-door approach to smokers' rights.

Yes, if Father Hesburgh, Lech Walesa and the other heroic figures can sacrifice their good names and reputations, built painfully over decades of hard, selfless work, in behalf of the Philip Morris Bill of Rights crusade, then the sacrifice of my own good health for the cause is the least I can do.

26

⁓

The Content Imperative

Imagine the following conversation:

"Mr. Updike, Mr. Sonny Mehta is calling."

"Thank you, put him on."

"Hello, John, how are you?"

"I'm fine, Sonny, how are you?"

"John, I know you are busy, so let me get directly to the point. If we can get a book from you by July, we will be able to put at least 200 people to work. We'll have everyone from lumbermen cutting down trees to copy editors editing copy. Think of the resin producers, the ink manufacturers, the paper cutters, the graphic artists, the binders, the packers, the shippers, the salespeople, the bookstore clerks, the tax collectors, and all the others who become involved when a book is published. In this slow economy, New York City surely would appreciate anything you could do to create 200 new jobs. I know the mayor and the governor would both be most grateful. And you should know that we are going to be talking with Norman Mailer and Joan Didion to see if they both can produce books for us by the end of summer."

"Sonny, count me in. Anything that John Updike can do for the economy, John Updike will do. Don't worry about a thing."

"John, thanks so much. I knew we could count on you."

Anyone familiar with the creative process of writing a quality novel knows that the fictional conversation I have constructed between novelist John Updike and Sonny Mehta of the Alfred A. Knopf publishing company of New York is ridiculous.

The publication of a novel surely creates jobs, and the writer may, indeed, find himself at least partially motivated to write because he wants to pay for the roof over his head and put food on the table, but everyone who is serious about the publishing of fine writing knows that good writers don't imagine vivid characters and think up great stories in order to provide lumbermen with jobs. It works in precisely the opposite manner. The writer writes because of the organic artistic integrity of the storytelling process and if jobs are created as a result of that process, then fine, so be it.

I thought of this often when I heard Chicago's Mayor Richard M. Daley repeat his mantra of "jobs, jobs, jobs" when asked why he favored the development of a huge family entertainment and casino center for Chicago. It also reminds me of the days when Jane Byrne was mayor of Chicago and tried, along with some of the Loop establishment business leaders, to develop a world's fair for Chicago in 1992. As I recall it, the reasoning behind the development of such a world's fair was always the same—it would be a tremendous economic development strategy for the city. It would mean, to use the current mayor's words, "jobs, jobs, jobs."

There was only one thing missing in Mayor Byrne's great push for a world's fair—and that was what the central organizing principle or creative idea would be for such a fair. If that central idea had been offered first and a huge amount of committed activity had supported the idea, then the jobs and all of the other subsequent activity would follow naturally.

Everywhere you look there is evidence of this "bass-ackward" approach to things. You can tell instantly when a magazine is designed to exist for one and only one purpose—and that is to serve as a vehicle to carry advertising. You can also instantly recognize a magazine that is designed to meet the editor's high standards of editorial integrity and content. Ironically, it is the latter kind of magazine that almost always ends up selling the most advertising.

You can also see this phenomenon, which I call "the content imperative," in action in politics. You know instantly when the only motivation for some political action or some campaigns is to win election or re-election, as opposed to those great campaigns that are waged to bring new vision or leadership or badly needed reform to government.

A young performer once told me that the greatest moment in her artistic process occurred when she was told that she had been chosen for the role. That is a sign of immaturity. That young performer, I hope, will grow up to know that the moment-to-moment content and artistry of playing the role and growing in the role are the greatest part of the artistic process. Jobs are fine, roles are fine, but content and purposefulness must be at the center of any great enduring enterprise.

And so, ridiculous as this may seem, the casino development argument would have been much more powerful to me if its proponent had dared to express why casinos are an existentially powerful requirement for our times. He could have said, "We live in times of utter complexity and bewilderment. More than ever, we are faced with layer upon layer of reality in our lives and thus, more than ever, we need to find escape into mindless, even somewhat risky entertainment. Yes, we can be criticized for seeking escape, but, my fellow citizens, I argue that we need new and brilliant modes of escape." At least, then, there would have been a rationale for the content of the casino activities. Without that, the rationale of jobs creation simply isn't compelling enough. Content is imperative.

27

⌒

View from the Future

So here we are, at the beginning of not only a new year, but also a new decade, the last of the twentieth century. It's a time that makes a middle-aged columnist's thoughts turn to the next century.

I don't know why I bother with the future. It is all too clear that I'm already out of date. Two months ago in this space I wrote a small minuet of complaint about all of the untidy complications of trying to pay the monthly bills while wrestling with envelope windows, untearable perforations, and unwieldy account numbers. A twenty-first-century reader lasers a quick response: get hip and use electronic bill paying.

And so, I've been wondering a lot lately how out of date I am and perhaps most of us are. What is it, I've been wondering, that our children's children's children's children will look back on in 2090 and say, "How could they possibly have tolerated that?" Or "Didn't they know any better than to do *that?*" I do think they would scornfully laugh at me if they knew that I typed this column on an IBM Correcting Selectric III and that had I written it six months ago, it would have been composed on a middle-twentieth-century manual typewriter. Like ancient, man.

But I wonder how they will feel about The Big Issues. We look back on an institution such as slavery or the fact that women didn't have the vote and wonder how perfectly enlightened folks such as George Washington could tolerate such societal behavior. Historians now provide reasonable answers to why things were the way they were then, but to us modern freedom lovers, it seems all so incredibly unacceptable.

In order to obtain a highly unscientific reading of the "How will they look back at us in 2090?" question, I started quizzing people wherever I ran into them, the first group run-in being in a Soldier Field skybox during the first half of the Bears-Rams game. Unexpectedly, delightfully, I found myself sitting next to a most unlikely sporting event seat-mate—none other than **Mortimer Adler,** the octogenarian philosopher, author, and education reformer. Dr. Adler told me that future generations will wonder how we put up with our presidential-congressional form of government. He predicts that we will change to a parliamentary form of government perhaps as soon as the next quarter century. But Dr. Adler hopes we'll act sooner on what he thinks is another urgent problem. "Unless we take presidential campaigns out of the hands of those who control television, we'll never have a good president again," he shouted over the cheers of Bears fans.

Chicago attorney **Newton M. Minow,** the former chairman of the Federal Communications Commission, ignored the Bears long enough to tell me that he thinks future generations will look back at us and say, "Why did you tolerate welfare? Why didn't you provide jobs for people?"

My skybox seminar continued with **Donna Shalala,** then new chancellor of the University of Wisconsin at Madison (now secretary of health and human services). I intercepted her as she tried to make her way to the hot dogs at halftime. She told me that she thinks the model of a teacher standing in front of a classroom full of students will be history by some time in the twenty-first century. "Learning will be different. It will be multi-media. Students will interact with computers and with faculty thousands of miles away."

A few nights later, at the annual Emmy Awards dinner (please tell me those will be a thing of the past by 2090 or much sooner), I found myself sitting next to political scientist **Dick Simpson,** the former Chicago alderman. Said he in response to my query: "One hundred years from now people will look back and wonder how we could tolerate nuclear weapons."

In subsequent days, I received answers from the following friends and colleagues:

Vernon Jarrett, the *Chicago Sun-Times* columnist: "They will wonder why we made such a big deal out of a person's skin color. And if we haven't come to terms by then with the race question, we will have failed as a civilization.

David E. Moncton, Argonne National Laboratory scientist who works on the Advanced Photon Source: "They will have trouble understanding why we didn't recycle. They will know that we as individuals knew better than to use and throw away Styrofoam food and drink containers, but that we went ahead and used them anyway."

Dr. Glenn Paulson, director of the Center for Hazardous Waste Management of the Illinois Institute of Technology and IIT Research Institute, put it another way: "They will say, 'You left us with nothing.'"

Since I was concerned about what future generations of children would say about the way we live now, I decided to poll my own two daughters. **Ann Hampton Callaway,** a New York City–based cabaret singer, lyricist, and composer: "Future generations will ask why we stifled the truth about UFOs. And they'll also wonder why we indulged in a 'throw-away culture.'"

Liz Callaway Foster, the Broadway singer: "I hope they will look back with compassion and say, 'If only they knew what we know now, they could have conquered AIDS and cancer so much more quickly.'"

As for me, I hope we will be embarrassed by our disputes over the sanctity of the American flag. Our future generations will live in such a global and planetary interdependent environment that patriotism will be viewed as an exercise in nostalgia, not unlike swapping old baseball cards. And I do think, with my friends, that they will view our possession of nuclear arms and our waste of natural resources as crimes against humanity, even as we now view the practice of slavery generations ago. And my prayer is that we may leave our children's children's children's children's planet in such a condition that they will still be able to say at this time then, what I say to you now, "Happy, Happy New Year."

28

⮾

Selective Memories

Are you having trouble getting the Cold War out of your system? Do you think we can find a cure for the common Cold War symptoms we've been nursing for more than forty years? If you're like me and were brought up with good, solid indoctrinations against the Commies, this tearing down the Berlin Wall stuff isn't easy to swallow. No one prepared us for change *this* rapid. I attended two different in-depth conferences on the future of U.S.–Soviet relations during the mid-1980s, and the most optimistic view of possible deep change in the Soviet system was voiced by a softhearted journalist. He gave the Communists about fifty years to mend their ways. All the other "experts" present thought it would take closer to one hundred years if ever. That kind of foreign affairs analysis makes me wonder about attending conferences with "experts," but I must admit that it is much easier to cling to old ideas than to accurately predict the future.

I'm still not over Pearl Harbor. I can vividly recall the fear my sister and I experienced upon hearing the news bulletin on the radio. I was only five, and I didn't know where Pearl Harbor was, but I knew something awful had happened. My Pearl Harbor phobia did not deter me from experiencing my first serious love affair with a young Japanese woman, and it didn't spoil my very pleasant visit to Japan two years ago, but I still cringe at the prospect of military cuts that might leave us sleeping at the switch again. So I forgive, but I do not forget.

Closer to home, Alderman Ed Burke now knows what it is like not to be forgotten *or* forgiven. Black committeemen in the Cook County Democratic Central Committee voted against Burke being slated for Cook County Board president because they remembered his unbending opposition to so much that the late Mayor Harold Washington proposed during the Council Wars years.

And yet Alderman Luis Gutierrez (now U.S. congressman) was more than willing to join those who supported Richard M. Daley's campaign for mayor, even though many of those supporters were steadfastly against the historic remapping for Chicago's wards—the remapping that finally brought representation of his-panics in the Chicago City Council. Why was Gutierrez, the reformer, able to put aside past differences with Daley support-ers? Undoubtedly because he feels he can do more for his people (and who knows, even for himself) by going with the Daley major-ity. Memories are fine, a sense of historical justice is good, but jobs power, and constituent service may be even better.

When Chancellor Helmut Kohl of Germany ended his visit to Poland last November, he laid a wreath for the victims of Auschwitz. In a book for visitors he wrote, "The warnings emanating from this place must never be forgotten. Unspeakable hurt was inflicted on various peoples here, but above all on European Jews in the name of Germany."

Robert LeRoy says he was reading his *Chicago Tribune* the morning of November 15 when he saw an AP Laserphoto that showed young former East Germans placing lit candles among the cobblestones of Leipzig to protest past police brutality. LeRoy, who came to this country in 1949 and became a citizen in 1954, says the irony of that picture was almost more than he could bear.

He told me that it was on April 21, 1944, that he and other pris-oners were taken from Auschwitz and brought to Leipzig where they were forced at gunpoint to dig up the cobblestones of the city square and then put them back. Five prisoners were killed by the Nazis, he says, during this forced labor exercise, as citizens of Leipzig stood by and laughed at them amidst the blaring of the oompa oompa band.

Seeing that picture, he says, "was like putting darts in my heart. I felt so abandoned." What hurt LeRoy so much, he says, was that the young people placing the lit candles in the cobblestones probably had no idea of what had taken place in that very spot forty-some years earlier. They have not been taught the horrors of the Holocaust. "They protest police brutality, but they do not know their own brutality of the past." Robert LeRoy thinks those young demonstrators in Leipzig are innocents. He says he only regrets that "they have not been taught in their schools about the Holocaust and that East Germany made no reparations to Israel."

LeRoy is saddened, but he is not bitter. He passionately hopes that this generation of East German youth will now be able to learn of their nation's past. He recently took the time to tell his own children and grandchildren about his experience at Auschwitz. He recorded himself for two hours with a video camera and gave a tape to each of his children and grandchildren.

But what is it, finally, that we should expect to learn from history? What should we remember and what purposes should those memories serve?

A friend of mine, a distinguished professor of American history, was once asked in a seminar if he believed George Santayana's saying that "those who cannot remember the past are condemned to repeat it." My friend replied that he believed almost the opposite—that those who are most obsessed with the past may be the most inclined to repeat it. How then, he was asked, do we deal with history? I loved his reply. He said that our study of history should be something like a good psychoanalysis. Get in there and study the hell out of your past, somehow get it integrated into your understanding while at the same time getting it out of your system, and then don't dwell on it every time a problem in life arises. Use what you know about the past and mix it in with what you know about the present. Add a dash of common sense, and you're all set to confront the future.

Words and Pictures

29

⌒

Words to Live By

I was out of work for the first time in my adult life. The local magazine I had helped edit had folded. I had less than one hundred dollars in the bank and a wife and two young daughters to support. I was scared. In the midst of my depression, an old friend telephoned his condolences. He said that he knew I would probably think it was a crazy thing for him to do, but that if I had no objection he would like to read a poem to me over the telephone. He said he just wanted to cheer me up a bit. He took less than a minute to read, in his memorably gruff and growly voice, a few stanzas. I don't even remember what the poem was, but I will never forget that it made me feel much better. I have always considered that telephone call one of the loveliest gifts of friendship in my life.

A few years later, I found myself down in the dumps again. What purpose, I wondered, was there to life? Sensing my grief, a friend gave me what turned out to be a gift I shall always cherish—a paperback edition of the late Ernest Becker's *The Denial of Death*. Becker described his book as "a bid for the peace of my scholarly soul, an offering for intellectual absolution." *The Denial of Death* is a mesmerizingly brilliant coming to terms with nothing less than the meaning of life—an exquisite synthesis of Becker's thinking about the work of Sören Kierkegaard and the theories of Sigmund Freud, Carl Jung, and Otto Rank. Becker tried to take the very best he could find from every area of human science and religion "to avoid moving against and negating any point of view, no matter how personally antipathetic to me, if it seems to have in it a core of truthfulness."

Becker argued that we need to drink in all of the psychology and knowledge of human sciences we can find, but in the end we need to be of faith—we are not just biological and psychological, but theological beings as well.

Becker reminded us that while all of us walk around consciously or unconsciously fearing death, we also carry with us a life-affirming desire to lead heroic existences. "I, heroic?" you might reply with a laugh. "No way. I just want to work nine to five, pay my taxes, take care of my family, keep the lawn trimmed and increase my bowling average a point or two. No heroics for me, Mr. Becker." And Becker would have gently informed you that the life you have just described is, for you, heroic. It is the chunk of life you have chosen to bite off. If you have chosen correctly you may be better off than the poor souls with talent who don't bite off enough and stew in their own unrealized creative juices or the poor souls who don't have as much talent as they think they have and end up falling on their faces while reaching for the stars.

When I finished reading *The Denial of Death* in my days of anguish, I came away with a better appreciation of life's necessarily paradoxical nature and my need never to stop my search for faith. What a lasting gift that book has been for me.

About a year ago the telephone rang. It was a friend from California. "Have you read Kazuo Ishiguro's *The Remains of the Day?*"

"No."

"You *must* read it."

Another perfect gift from a friend and one not unrelated to Becker's *The Denial of Death*.

As *The Remains of the Day* opens, it is the summer of 1956 and we meet Stevens who, like his father before him, is a butler in the first rank of English butlers. He is in the twilight of his long career at Darlington Hall, the two-century-old estate of the late Lord Darlington, who once employed twenty-eight servants. Now Darlington Hall has been purchased by Mr. Farraday, a back-slapping, jovial American who has closed off many rooms in the house and reduced the staff, headed by Stevens, to four. Stevens is standing on the stepladder dusting the portrait of Viscount Wetherby when Mr. Farraday suggests to him that while he is on a return visit to the United States, Stevens take his Ford and enjoy the countryside for a few days. This little trip will be more than a chance for Stevens to get away from the estate for a few days. It will be a journey of inner discovery for him and for us.

Stevens knows what his station in life is—what heroic chunk he has chosen to bite off. He knows, as he learned from watching his father before him, that the responsibility of a butler of the first rank is to be the personification of "dignity in keeping with his position." If there is a tiger resting under the dining room table just before company is due, you don't panic. Reflects Stevens, "The great butlers are great by virtue of their ability to inhabit their professional role and inhabit it to the utmost; they will not be shaken out by external events, however surprising, alarming, or vexing. They will wear their professionalism as a decent gentleman will wear his suit: he will not let ruffians or circumstances tear it off him in the public gaze; he will discard it when, and only when, he wills to do so, and this will invariably be when he is entirely alone. It is, as I say, a matter of 'dignity.'"

Dignity has been everything to Stevens, dignity at a price of self-deception and personal denial that he at last begins to acknowledge as he motors through the countryside toward a possible reunion with Miss Kenton, who once was in his employ and who may have offered him something more than his "dignity" then would have allowed him to contemplate.

The passage of Stevens' reflections that I quoted gives, I hope, an idea of the perfect "butler's English" which Ishiguro (who was born in Nagasaki, Japan, in 1954 and has lived in England since 1960) has achieved in Stevens' narrative. This voice is sustained perfectly for the entire 245 pages of this small masterpiece. *The Remains of the Day* is a sublime literary achievement and gift from Kazuo Ishiguro. I only wish Ernest Becker could have lived to read it.

30

∾

The Final Word

At first it was amusing. I had heard about it, but had not actually listened to it in operation until a friend gave us one for Christmas. It is called "The Final Word"—a black plastic-encased device that looks something like a miniature battery-operated shaver. But it doesn't shave. It swears.

With the press of a button on the side, a robotic male voice, sounding more vexed than angry, issues four expletives in short, staccato two-word bursts. The first is an assertion that is grossly biologically impossible, however deeply felt. The second is the word "jerk" preceded by the most commonly employed sexual adjectival curse of the day. The third is a command to perform a most unappetizing and unsanitary act and the fourth and concluding message is an oath, which has become so commonplace that it has lost most of its power to wound.

I brought it to my office and impatiently waited for the right moment in an editorial meeting to press the button; the right moment being that inevitable time every week when either a great idea of mine is soundly rejected or I wish to perform the same diplomacy on a colleague. My timing was off. A colleague offered an idea that I loved but knew would not be approved. I pressed the button offering the most commonplace oath, but the group wasn't sure what it had heard or from where the words had been uttered. But one staffer laughed so loudly that he overrode what the group was to have heard with my second press of the button. With no little embarrassment, I put the device back in my briefcase, only to overhear, later in the day, another one being put to use in some distant hallway where people were cackling with apparent glee.

I am told that more than a half a million of these surrogate potty mouths have been sold in recent months. I suspect that most people have used them at the wrong time in the presence of the wrong people and now deeply regret having pushed the button. That would make for a most interesting product liability suit. "I didn't say it, Your Honor, the machine did."

As for myself, I don't need a battery-operated profanity machine. I do quite well on my own, thank you. And I am quite weary of it. Maybe I'm just getting older, but recently I have found myself feeling streaks of self-loathing because of all the dirt that flows so freely from my mouth. The other day, for example, one of my colleagues brought her baby to our editorial meeting and I found myself loudly invoking a string of four-letter words to describe a situation when suddenly I remembered that I was in the presence of a baby. I hope the child was too young to understand what I was saying, but I felt that I had committed a form of child abuse and that it was intolerable.

My addiction to profanity, like most disorders, has its roots in my childhood. I am an Adult Child of Parents Who Cussed. These loving, otherwise highly intelligent parents of mine were hard-drinking, hard-cussing newspaper people. Growing up in my home was like being raised in a newspaper city room—it was more fit for sailors than for children. My roommates at college were also habitual cussers and my bosses at the City News Bureau of Chicago, where I began my reporting career, were world renowned for their command of invective. Every newsroom I have worked in since has carried on the tradition of foul-mouthedness. If the late B. F. Skinner was even partly right in asserting that we are the products of our environments, then I possess an easy cop-out for my intolerable use of foul language.

And it really is intolerable. There is the author Salman Rushdie, poor soul, living under a continuing Islamic death sentence for the allegedly blasphemous things said and thought by characters in his splendid, elegant novel, *The Satanic Verses*. My blasphemies are ten-thousand-fold greater in volume and hold not a trace of redeeming value, may I burn in Hell.

The esteemed *New York Times* sage Russell Baker wrote recently that the use of colorful vulgarity "confers glamour nowadays." As evidence, Baker asks us to see Eddie Murphy films, Nick Nolte films, or just about any other film playing these days. He asks if this can explain President Bush's threat to Saddam Hussein to punt him in his buttocks.

If this is true, then I wish to announce my withdrawal of any aspiration to glamour. But I do not aspire to become a prude. I possess no hope at all of being able to purge myself completely of this low habit. And I know that with this public confession I am at least a step ahead of those of you who would not be caught uttering an oath in public but who, behind the sound-proof confines of your two-ton driving machines, release your true aggressive/defensive personalities and shocking streams of obscenities at anyone who dares to cut you off on the road or tailgate you for a few miles. Come now, acknowledge it. Behind the wheel we are almost all monsters and if there are any saints among us, pure in heart and mind, it is that one in a million driver who does not indulge in obscenity when his life is threatened on the road.

No, all I aspire to is the gradual reduction of volume and greater selectivity of my unclean speech. I want to be like a forty-five-year-old relief pitcher whose fast ball is so long gone that when he comes in with one it really is a shocker. Otherwise, profanity is a curse and I say to Hell with it.

31

❦

The Time of Your Life

The telephone rang one day last June. It was an emergency. A scholar scheduled to deliver an important graduation speech later in the week at a local university had fallen ill. Would I be able to fill in at the last minute? I was asked. "Sorry," I replied. "I'm out of town that day."

I must confess that I am not enamored of graduation speeches. Not possessing a college degree, I confess that I've never had to sit through one, but it is true that from time to time I am asked to deliver one. It's not fun.

Graduations at colleges frequently are held on weekends, thus cutting into serious Cub-watching and golf-flogging time. Usually it is hot, and I break into a sauna-like sweat the minute they dress me in one of those thermal robes from Hell and one of those funny hats with the tassels that unerringly massage my cornea with unbelievable accuracy. And let's face it, the about-to-be-graduates aren't particularly interested in hearing your pronouncements on the Possibilities of the Future. They're interested in fleeing the premises as quickly as possible so they can begin earning big bucks to pay back the million dollars they owe in student loans. Some may even wish to watch the Cubs or flog some golf.

Still, I feel guilty about turning those people down. So, I've taken some preventive action in case the phone rings again this year or any year in the future. I have taken the liberty of writing a

special, all-purpose graduation speech, which any surrogate is free
to borrow and read in its entirety. The great thing about this speech
is that it lasts less than five minutes. No fee is required—just mention my name and tell them that while I'm out here watching the
Cubs or flogging the golf ball, I wish them all well. Here it is:

Dear friends, forgive me if I begin by telling you what time
is. It is precisely (insert time here) p.m. on June (insert date
here) in the year (insert year here). I hope the relevance of that
announcement will become apparent shortly.

Commencement speakers frequently note that we do not
know what the future holds for you graduates. And to the extent
that we cannot predict depressions or wars or auto accidents,
those speakers are correct. But if the actuarial tables have any
validity, then one can pull out one's calculator and venture forth
with some very specific estimates of what your future might be.
So let me tell you a few things about what you are likely to be
doing with your lives assuming that most of you are now around
twenty-one years of age and that you are going to live to the age
of seventy-five.

You have 54 birthdays, 54 Fourth of Julys, and 54 World
Series left (does that mean 54 more broken hearts for Cub fans?),
and 54 more years to file taxes. You have 27 more congressional
elections and 13 more presidential elections to endure.

You have 19,723 more days to live. That's 473,352 hours in
which to live it up right. And how will you spend those 473,352
hours? Let me count the ways.

If you sleep for an average of 7 hours a night, you will snooze
away 138,061 hours or 5,753 nights or 15.75 years of those 54
years left.

If you retire at the age of sixty-two and you are fortunate
enough to find work for at least 38 of the 41 years you will live
until your retirement, and if you work 7 hours a day, 5 days a
week, 48 weeks a year, you will have worked for 7.25 years of

those 54 years. And if you watch only 2.5 hours a day of television you will have spent 49,307 hours or 2,054 days or 5.67 years watching the tube.

Assuming you average 3 meals a day and you spend only 1.5 hours at the table, you will eat away 3.33 more years of your lives consuming those 59,169 meals.

If you spend at least 30 minutes a day brushing your teeth, shaving, bathing, cutting and painting your nails, putting on makeup, taking off makeup, etc., you will employ an additional 9,862 hours or 410 days of your precious life primping and preening and cleaning.

If, during your remaining 38 years of work, you spend only 40 minutes a day commuting to and from work—and you'll be blessed if that's all the time you spend—you will use up 6,019 more hours or 251 days of your life.

Add in 2 hours a week for shopping, 15 minutes a day or 1 hour and 45 minutes a week waiting for everything from elevators to your spouse to Godot, and 4 hours a week on other maintenance activities, such as doing the dishes, repairing the car, warding off creditors, visiting doctors and psychiatrists, etc.—total that and you've spent 907 more days or 2.5 years of your life.

Okay, let's pause a minute and add it up. So far, with just the basics of sleeping, eating, working, maintenance, and TV, you've used 318,441 hours of those 473,352 hours remaining in your life, 13,268 days of your 19,723 days left on earth and 36.33 years of your 54 years. Roughly 67 percent of your life has been consumed, and we haven't even spoken yet of time with family and friends, time to pray and worship, time to travel, time to write the great novel, paint the great painting, raise the great child, or time for making love.

Therefore, I take my leave with two hopes for you. One is that you will make a conscious effort to make something as special as you can out of every one of those so-called ordinary or

mundane minutes of your life—eating, waiting, repairing, commuting. And I hope you take the remaining 154,911 hours, 6,454
days, or 17.75 years of that invaluable "free to do what you will
with it" time and make every effort to listen to your soul, and
dare to take chances and employ your personal gifts in such a
way as to make a gift to the world. My fondest wish for each of
you is that your deepest wishes come true.

32

We Are What We Read

Let's start this month with a ten-part quiz.

1. Is there any proof that eating chocolate makes a person's face break out?
2. Which are better for you, "natural" or synthetic vitamins?
3. Which eggs have more food value, brown or white?
4. What percentage of U.S. imports is produced by American companies abroad?
5. How many persons worldwide have died of AIDS since 1981?
6. How many persons have died of measles since then?
7. How much did the U.S. Justice Department spend to prosecute the Iran-Contra case?
8. How many persons living in Mozambique have been chased from their homes or forcibly removed from their villages in civil strife in recent years?
9. What is TIROS 7 and what does it do?
10. When the word "wigwag" is used as a verb, what does it mean?

Let's indulge in some immediate gratification and go directly to the answers.

1. No.

2. There is absolutely no difference.
3. They are identical.
4. Twenty percent.
5. 72,504.
6. Fourteen million.
7. $7,792,849.
8. Four million.
9. It is a television observation satellite that helps meteor-ologists track and forecast storms.
10. To flag someone home.

Now some of those questions and answers may not thrill you enough to call your best childhood friend in Alaska and share the excitement (although I was stunned at the number of measles deaths), and the point of the quiz was not to prepare you for SAT exams but to reveal to you the seemingly unlikely source of the information—what you and I commonly call junk mail.

Doesn't junk mail make you proud to be an American? My favorites are the 315th offer to sign this and protect every card in your wallet now and forevermore and the weekly notice that you have "won" a sweepstakes certificate for $200. (The certificate allows you to squander another $200 to $300 on a set of jewelry rejected by the home shopping network or a $27,000 set of imitation, genuine fake something-or-other luggage.)

One night I was tossing one piece of junk mail after another into the wastepaper basket (mine actually is a wicker basket) when I realized that not all junk mail is junk. (The people who send it tell you that it's direct mail.) Some of this stuff actually is passingly interesting. For example, the answers to the first three questions in the quiz are from the people at Tufts University Diet and Nutrition Letter who want me to subscribe to their publication. (I, a fatty who doesn't want to remain fat, subscribed.) By the way, please write to them, not to me, if you truly think chocolate makes your face break out or if you are convinced that "natural" vitamins are superior to synthetics.

The answers to the next four questions on imports, AIDS, measles, and Iran-Contra were contained in a subscription pitch from *Harper's* magazine. Each month, *Harper's* publishes a datamonger's delight of a feature called the Harper's Index, which reveals everything from the percentage of Americans who say their feet are ugly (13 percent) to the percentage of Americans who cannot name any member of Bush's cabinet (81 percent). We subscribe at the office, so I passed on receiving *Harper's* at home.

The tragedy of displaced persons in Mozambique was reported in a request for funds from the American Refugee Committee (I sent a check). The explanation of TIROS 7 was contained in a handsomely designed and illustrated sales brochure for *Encyclopaedia Britannica* (I already am a proud owner of a set). And a subscription offer informed me that the word "wigwag" not only means "to flag someone home" but also is the title of a new literary publication that promises "direct, personal, honest, funny" writing. (I mailed my request for the premier issue; I'm a sucker for the promise of good writing.)

Most junk mail is direct, but much of it is not personal, honest or funny. Some of it is so crude and unpleasant that it makes the word "junk" seem generous. But the direct mail people should know that some of us appreciate some of what they send us. However, if you wish to rid yourself of junk mail, I found the solution in a useful little book called *Complete Trash—The Best Way to Get Rid of Practically Everything Around the House* by Norm Crampton (Evans, $8.95).

Crampton recommends that you write to the Direct Mail Marketing Association (6 East 43 Street, New York, N.Y. 10017) and request that your name be added to the next quarterly edition of the do-not-mail list that is circulated to 20,000 or so mail-order companies. Or you can call (212) 689-4977 and ask that your name be removed from the mailing lists.

As for me, I'll continue to slog through the catalogs and come-ons and wait with cheerful anticipation for the first copy of *Wigwag*.

Note: Some of the quiz answers are, by now, out of date. And by the way, *Wigwag,* unfortunately, went out of business.

33

~

Hands Off My New Yorker

Yes, the New Year is upon us and we're supposed to look forward to exciting new developments in our lives and in our world, but the fact is, we really hate to change. Yes, we nod our heads in solemn agreement with the feel-good speakers who tell us that the art of good living is learning to adapt to change and being prepared to endure the pain and experience the pleasure of personal growth. All of this self-motivation piffle is based on the hilarious premise that we are in charge of our destiny.

Our destiny is that the weather changes three times before we get home from work. Our destiny is that just as we had grown fond of the 1,300-page summary of the 1986 "tax simplification" code, they've gone and messed with the tax rates again. Our destiny is that a leader we once supported is now our dearest enemy. Our destiny is that today it is all right to drink decaf coffee, tomorrow it isn't and the next day it is again.

All of this change helps explain why some of us cling so irrationally, so desperately, to particular cultural institutions. It is why some people can't believe—won't believe—Elvis is dead. We may laugh at them, but Elvis is someone they cherished so much that they don't ever want to lose him. To them, Elvis is eternal.

We all have our Elvis—dead or alive. Our Elvis is a cultural institution we probably formed an attachment to earlier in our lives—an attachment we simply can't bear to part with in the midst of so much change that showers down upon us.

My Elvis is *The New Yorker* magazine. Yes, *The New Yorker.* I have collected almost every issue of *The New Yorker* since 1958. I have stacks of them stashed away in costly storage. I am a *New Yorker* freak.

Now you might say that the Elvis metaphor doesn't hold water. Elvis is dead and *The New Yorker* isn't. That depends on your viewpoint. There are those who say that *The New Yorker* was in critical condition, if not dead, during the last years that its great editor William Shawn ran the magazine. Long articles became interminable. Story selection was less than timely if not substantially irrelevant to the lives of the readers. And even more threatening, those of us who are magazine readers changed. We found ourselves spending more time with publications featuring short articles, italicized data, and snappy graphics. We found it harder to spend time reading book-length articles about subjects we didn't need to know much about. Movie reviews ran on and on, Roger and Gene didn't.

But when Shawn was eased or forced into retirement a few years ago, I and a lot of other *New Yorker* zealots feared that the new owners would import an editor who would defile our precious publication. Where else could we read the superb reportage of John McPhee, the lovely book essays by John Updike, and the hard-hitting, if sometimes breast-beating, essays in the "Talk of the Town"? Would the new editor throw out the cartoons?

Our fears were not realized. Robert A. Gottlieb, who had run the distinguished publishing house of Alfred A. Knopf for eighteen years, succeeded Shawn as editor. He proceeded to carve out a lot of editorial dry rot and sharpen the editor's pencil, but he did not tamper constitutionally with the great institution he inherited. The reportage is still long, but it is long in the service of understanding complexity, not feeding the author's ego. The foreign coverage of *The New Yorker* under Gottlieb's leadership is superb.

The investigative pieces, such as Paul Brodeur's work on the health hazards posed by high-current and high-voltage power lines, are among the best in the magazine business. The addition of a table of contents to the magazine was long overdue and the inclusion of multi-page advertising inserts has not for a minute distracted readers from the excellence of the editorial content. If only Gottlieb would establish a letters column, I could join Elvis and die happy. Or is it live happy?

The survival and editorial growth of *The New Yorker* is just short of miraculous. Given our short attention spans, it would be no rational surprise to see *The New Yorker* die. But if *The New Yorker*'s editorial integrity were greatly compromised, I would be on the front lines of those who would protest.

There is a lesson here. To those whose unhappy fate it is to find themselves presiding over an assignment to change a cultural institution that is mismanaged and out of date and out of touch, beware that you are walking in a cultural fundamentalist mine field. Those who fell in love with the doddering institution are probably blind to its deficits, its outdatedness, and its clogged cultural arteries. Those loyalists are probably for the most part very astute, change-oriented persons who would not for a minute tolerate the atrophy of their own business or family affairs. They probably are "with it" people in every respect but the one cultural "Elvis," which they will eternally support.

Most of us are at least one part cultural fundamentalist because of all the crazy, unending change in our lives. We want one last cultural breast to suckle. Take that away from us and you have an angry baby. Robert Gottlieb showed us how to change the bathwater without throwing out the baby.

Note: Since Tina Brown was named editor of *The New Yorker,* the changes in the magazine have been much more radical. It is not *The New Yorker* I grew up with, but in many ways the changes she has wrought, while disturbing in some instances, have made the magazine entirely more readable. As one who uses foul language I took a certain perverse pride in the old *New Yorker*'s civility, its puritanism. And there is a gossipy quality to some of the new *New Yorker*'s pieces which would fit better in Ms. Brown's previous publication—*Vanity Fair*—than in *The New Yorker*. But Ms. Brown has given the magazine a sense of excitement and a vitality which are, to me, irresistible. Her editing reflects a reality that I hate to admit, but must: it's not so much that she has changed *The New Yorker*, as that we as readers have changed (we have little time to read a constant diet of interminable excerpts from book manuscripts in a weekly magazine), and her editing of the new *New Yorker* acknowledges the new reader. So in a way she has thrown the baby out with the bathwater, but the baby somehow made a safe landing and is, with Ms. Brown's radiant, robust guidance, growing up quite nicely, thank you.

34

⁓

The Monthly Statement

It is a sweet dream. The governor is there. The mayor. The post-master general of the United States has flown in from Washington. The chief executive officer of the College of Surgeons is present. The top officials of Commonwealth Edison are there, beside themselves with joy. The proceedings are broadcast live on a special edition of "Geraldo"!

I am being honored for an achievement previously thought to be unattainable. No one imagined it could happen in our generation. Sure, we sent men to the moon. Yes, we legalized flag burning. Truly, we are a great people.

But who honestly dreamed that in our lifetime an individual human being, working entirely alone, underwritten by no research grant, subsidized by no government funding, employing no surgical instruments or microscopes, using only his bare hands would—without one tiny tear, missing not one single perforation—actually succeed in making a perfect separation of a Commonwealth Edison return envelope from the envelope packet holder the utility company provides for its customers?

I know, it's a laughable dream. Forgive my monumental naiveté. No one I know or you know has ever successfully separated one of those envelopes from the packet holder. No one ever will. I can now reveal that I have been reduced to using a huge pair of scissors to cut along the perforations. Yes, I cheat.

The remainder of this column can be better experienced if you read it aloud in your best Andy Rooney imitation.

Don't you just hate those creditors who make you detach a flap containing an advertising message before you can seal the envelope? Have you ever bought anything advertised on one of those flaps?

Don't you just hate all the instructions they impose upon you on the back of the envelope?

- Write your account number on your check or money order.
- Write the amount paid on your remittance document(s).
- Return your remittance document(s) with payment in this envelope.
- Make sure the REMIT TO address on the remittance document is displayed in the envelope window.
- Do not send cash through the mail.
- Do not staple statement to your check.
- Do not enclose correspondence with your payment.

I have some instructions for these creditors:

- Please keep the number of digits on the account number to under twenty.
- Please do not use pretentious jargon such as "remittance document(s)."
- Please feel free to steal cash from anyone stupid enough to send it in the mail.
- Please discontinue use of envelope windows and thus increase American productivity or leisure time by 50 percent.
- Please feel free to let us write anything we want to write and enclose it with any check we send.

And another thing. It isn't enough to work hard and earn the money to pay the bills. It isn't enough to sit there and write check after check, making entry after entry in the checkbook and hoping to God it will balance some year. It isn't enough to detach the advertising flap. It isn't enough to write your account number on the check and then again on the return envelope (I sometimes feel as if I were being kept after school and ordered to write my account number on the blackboard one hundred times). It isn't enough to figure out which way the top portion of the statement fits into the return envelope so that the return address somehow ends up correctly placed in the envelope window. By now you may be exhausted, frustrated, and penniless. But it isn't enough. There's one more tack, friends. See that little box over there under the amount due? And see that printed instruction next to the little box? You know what it says, don't you? It says, "Please indicate amount enclosed." Do they want an indication or do they want the exact amount? If they've billed me for $40.95 do they suppose that I won't pay $40.95? Suppose I write a check for $40.25, won't my check be the amount that really counts? Wouldn't the $40.25 on the check be the true "indication" of what I've sent?

I've got to go now. I'm feeling a little dizzy after licking all of those envelopes and stamps. I've got to finish reading my Illinois Bell *Telebriefs* with the one millionth reminder that starting November 11, Chicago suburbs currently in the 312 area will receive the new 708 area code. I've got to finish reading the Peoples Gas explanation of its bills. Love those therms.

And I've got to write a thank-you letter to Citibank Mortgage in gratitude for its coming up with a new, vastly improved windowless return envelope.

You all be sure to write now and "indicate" if you've had as much fun paying your bills as I have. Please don't staple your stories to the envelopes. And have a nice month.

35

❧

Do Ad Limits Exist?

I love a good commercial. When the boss gathers his salespeople around him and lays on the news that one of their major clients has just fired them, I stop, listen and watch. There he is, walking around that huge bullpen of an office handing out United Airline tickets so they can cut out the phoning and faxing and get back to basic person-to-person business the way they used to do it. Now I'm totally involved. I want one of those United tickets and I want to help good old Ben win back that account. The spot lasts only a minute, but it contains within it the story line upon which a good novel could be written and a moral upon which a business could be reinvented. I hope whoever wrote that spot will write another one telling us, no, *showing* us how Ben and his people did once they started selling face to face. I care about Ben and his people. I care about the principle of person-to-person communication. So do you. That's why the spot works.

You might think that public television people shouldn't love commercials, but let me tell you that when they bring up the sound loud and clear on one of the underwriting spots at the beginning of "Chicago Tonight," I swell with pride because I know in my heart of hearts that television—public television most definitely included— is a commercial medium. Television without commercials is like a ballpark without billboards. You may not like them, but they are part of the landscape, and they help pay a lot of the bills.

Much as I love a good TV spot or print ad or clever billboard, I must confess to what I'm sure you've found to be a most unattractive character flaw—I am utterly fascinated with the most wretched excesses in the world of advertising. It is as though I were telling you that I love great athletic competition and then confessed that I can't take my eyes off pro-wrestling on TV. I am hooked by tasteless, exploitative advertising the way some people (not any of you readers, I'm sure) are unable to resist staring at the blood and debris of auto accidents.

Yes, I thrill to late-night car dealer spots and make meticulous notes of the latest styles in sport coats the car hawkers wear. And who can ever forget the experience of driving through miles of lovely farms and pine trees along the road and coming upon that land of a million and one billboards called the Wisconsin Dells? Who can ever forget Tommy Bartlett and his water show bumper stickers?

My favorite current form of wretched commercial excess is the corporate sponsorship of "moments" such as the *Tribune*'s Roundtripper replays of Cubs' home runs. I'd like to take this concept of corporate sponsorship of moments just a step further:

Ted Koppel: Sir, my next question, which will deal with the underlying structural relationship between the banking industry and the savings and loan industry, is brought to us this evening by the proud makers of ...

If sponsorship of individual questions on news and public affairs programs becomes a hit, it could then logically progress to corporate underwriting of newsmakers' answers. This not only would enhance the broadcasters' coffers, but also would advance the cause of public understanding because the respondents would be given a merciful moment to think of an answer while the commercial sponsorship of that answer was being broadcast.

I have thought for a long time that the 1990s would herald the onslaught of "live" commercials in "live" news programs and specials. This development paraded off to an impressive start with a

former Miss America polishing her nails in a live spot during the
seventieth Miss America Pageant in September. Even Bert Parks
couldn't compete with that.

Think of the possibilities. With hundreds of convicted mur-
derers facing execution, each of these events could be televised
under corporate sponsorship. Depending on the form of execution, it doesn't take a lot of imagination to know which chemical,
utility, or fiber company should sponsor these "live" death events.
Wouldn't it be great?—This death is brought to you *live* by...?
Contingency sponsorship could be sold in case of a last-minute
stay of execution: This reprieve moment is brought to you by the
makers of....

Presidential and other political news conferences and events
could be sponsored live by those companies that specialize in helping us with our vocabulary and grammar, with immediate replay
of the public official's (or broadcaster's) mistakes along with the
recommended corrections.

Lawyers, who long ago gave up the pretense of dignity that
accompanied their silly ban on legal advertising, could really get
into the ad biz whole hog and start broadcasting live from police
stations and drug clinics, touting their ability to achieve reduced
charges on everything from drug-inspired homicide to drunken
driving. Not to be outdone by their professional brethren, surgeons could take their eyes away from the sutures long enough to
look up into the teleprompter on a live camera and make a dramatic pitch for emergency medical services at greatly reduced rates
at such and such a hospital.

And, what the heck, if those forms of live commercials aren't
exciting enough, I'll suggest to my bosses that we in public television try something new and put on live broadcast periods in which
we actually ask people for funds and tell them live on the air how
much we've raised so far. Okay, I'm sorry. I know that's carrying
the live advertising idea just a wild and crazy step too far.

36

⮂

America's Fuzziest
Hotel Room Videos

However the narcotics use and perjury trial of Washington,
D.C., Mayor Marion Barry turns out, one thing is clear: our
United States government, which can send men to the moon, does
not know the first thing about how to make a quality undercover
videotape.

The pictures purporting to show Mayor Barry and his "friend"
allegedly smoking crack in a Washington hotel room are fuzzier
than an alcoholic's tongue and the sound is cloudier than a day in
London. Whoever made those tapes wouldn't stand a chance of
having his or her work accepted by "America's Funniest Home
Videos," however laughable the end product.

If we the people are going to depend on Uncle Sam to rid the
streets of dope fiends and government bribe-takers, we had better start demanding that the government either send its video tech-
nicians to school or go back to old-fashioned testimony from
witnesses who can speak with clarity and credibility in court.

If you saw the videotape of the Barry raid on the news or on
Ted Koppel's "Nightline," could you possibly have understood
what Barry and his friend were saying without the use of super-
imposed words on the screen? Of course not. Is it all that difficult
to mike a hotel room so that the words can be heard clearly? Not

at all. Talk to any good local radio or TV engineering staff and they'll tell you in a minute how they equip their undercover investigative reporters.

It's not just the Barry trial. Remember the pictures and sound in the Chicago Incubator "Mole" investigation of bribe-taking in city government? It was so awful that it made one ashamed, I'm sure, to be seen is such a lousy production, not to mention being guilty of the crimes.

I'm not kidding about that. When charges were brought against some Chicago police officers not long ago, one of them called me to complain about how unfair the prosecution was. As he ended his beef, he asked to add one more observation. He went on to say that, as a law enforcement man and a citizen, he was very concerned about the poor quality of the tape the government had made that showed his allegedly corrupt action. He said he felt that if the government goes after you, the least it can do is produce a high-quality tape that will stand up in court.

And pity some of the poor people used to do the government's undercover work. I remember interviewing a Greylord courts scandal undercover agent who told of sweating through long days of lugging around a bulky, barely concealable audio tape recorder under his jacket. He nearly went crazy with fear that the recorder would show through his suit and get him bumped off. We may enjoy seeing Dick Tracy and his two-way radio wristwatch at the movies this summer, but Uncle Sam's FBI is still making scratchy 1920s-like motion pictures that just barely qualify as "talkies."

The only defenses I can think of for the government's performance in this area is that it doesn't have enough money left over from the savings and loan fiasco to rent decent tape and audio equipment, or it deliberately makes the pictures awful so they'll be believable to juries that otherwise might think the government had gone "Hollywood" with slick productions.

The irony is that this shameful video performance is produced by a government whose CIA can bug a hotel room thousands of miles away with an orbiting satellite camera that can show grass growing between the sidewalk cracks in Havana. This is a government whose executive branch excels in staging events with the most memorable "photo op" video backgrounds.

George Orwell would be ashamed of our law enforcers if he could have seen the Marion Barry trial footage. Big Brother, he would have to conclude, is turning out to be a technological clod. The pictures and sound are so bad that they make me wonder whom we are to suspect of being on dope—those on the camera or those behind it.

37

❧

The Mail Animal

On "60 Minutes," humorist-commentator Andy Rooney showed us what he does with his mail, his many boxes of mail. He stacks those boxes away in storage. Thanks so much for writing.

By now, nearly everyone knows that Oprah Winfrey's corporation, Harpo Productions (Harpo is Oprah spelled backward), owns her syndicated TV talk show, her restaurant, and her production house. What you may not know is that Harpo was started as a corporate entity as a way of (in addition to station relations and public relations) handling the more than 2,000 cards and letters that pour in to Oprah's office each week (a staff of six handles much of this mail, and Oprah herself answers at least 200 letters a week).

Mike Royko and other columnists discard much of their mail, but retain the most hostile letters as set-ups for their witty and/or vitriolic replies—printed on days when they want to get out of the office early or when they can't think of anything else to write which would elevate your intelligence or your blood pressure.

Members of Congress have staff people who do little else but respond to complaints and inquiries about everything from social security to lack of national security.

I have Susan Godfrey. God knows she's efficient enough to command an army with one hand and raise a family with the other, but let's confess it now: Ms. Godfrey and I are overwhelmed with mail. She opens it and delivers it to me. I read it and stack it in neat (ho-ho) piles and when I get time (ho-ho) I sit down at my typewriter and answer it (no, I do not dictate—many of us ink-stained journalistic wretches never developed a talent for that) and then Susan photocopies my reply and attaches it to your original letter for my files and then she types the envelope and sends it on its way to our mail room and from there with the help of God and the U.S. Postal Service it makes its way eventually to your home or office or prison cell or hospital bed or love nest or wherever.

Your mail attacks us on about a dozen fronts: signed comments on our latest "Chicago Tonight" programs ("the absence of an introspective black panelist was glaring and at least regrettable"); and unsigned cards and letters in the very finest crayon available ("you are afraid to ask 'Fast Eddie' and Daley questions"); personal letters sent via WTTW such as the one a friend wrote who saw my daughter Ann Hampton singing at Maxim's in New York recently; letters and notices inviting us to cover everything from the latest civic dinner to the opening of a new mall or theater; mail with recommended reading (Thomas Hunneman's *The Economic Constitution of the United States* or the Annual Report of the Institute for East-West Studies); letters proposing programs for "Chicago Tonight" (five-part series on pornography, a project on the homeless, an interview with an author who thinks professors don't teach much anymore); letters proposing investigations which would take months; invitations to yours truly to speak, moderate, play celebrity golf, host a cultural event, participate in an auction; and a whole host of letters with résumés and work applications.

Will I ever catch up with those of you who wrote about our coverage of the mayoral election? Maybe by the time we start covering the next one in 1991. What about the ton of mail we received on the flag display at the School of the Art Institute—will I get those letters answered by the time the school schedules its next festival of outrage?

You see, "Chicago Tonight" mail isn't just your "love you" or "hate you" garden variety mail that so many television programs receive. Many of you who write hold strong philosophical positions about issues and you take several pages to set out your position. Some of you are technically expert in subjects we have aired and you send background reports containing hundreds of pages for us to read and analyze. Some of you even send book manuscripts and unproduced plays for us to read.

So, if you haven't received a reply yet to your letter or your proposal or your threat or your manuscript, please be patient. Susan and I are working on it. In the meantime, please accept this column as a kind of acknowledgment and thank-you. Many thanks.

38

❧

Knock 'em Dead

Back when they were both alive, Mayor Richard J. Daley and John Cardinal Cody would meet secretly once a year to talk over common problems—schools, finance, race relations. On one supposedly surreptitious rendezvous they elected to walk by Lake Michigan to share their burdens of high office. As they walked and talked, a gust of wind suddenly blew the cardinal's precious red cap way out into the lake. Mayor Daley knew how much the cap meant to the cardinal and so he walked out onto the waters of Lake Michigan and retrieved it for the archbishop, who was ever so grateful.

Unbeknownst to either man, a reporter for the *Chicago Tribune,* crouching behind a nearby park bench, had witnessed the entire episode. He knew he had a great scoop and he raced back to the *Trib* to write his big story. Sure enough, the next day the *Trib's* front page was ablaze with the following headline:

DALEY CAN'T SWIM!

Did you find that story amusing? Have you ever heard it before? You surely have heard it if you have heard some of the speeches of Chicago attorney and former FCC chairman Newton Minow. And you surely have heard that story if you have heard certain of my speeches in recent years. I know, because I borrowed it—with full credit—from Newt. I don't know where he got the story, but being the meticulously ethical man that he is, I am sure he gives full credit to *his* source. If you want to make Newt's day or my day, tell us a new story that can be used appropriately to begin a public talk. Those of us who find ourselves on the rubber chicken circuit are as desperate for a new, amusing, introductory story as a junkie for a hit.

My all-time favorite lead-off story is one meant to illustrate that cynicism has no bounds. I came across it in a *New York Times* Sunday magazine article about the "new philosophy" several years ago.

It seems that the world's greatest philosophers were meeting at their annual convention in London. These were the "new" philosophers—men and women who explored the nuances of linguistics as opposed to the traditional philosophers who dealt with such trivial questions as the meaning of life. At any rate, the highlight of the meeting featured a talk by a new philosopher who was to present what would be the earth-shattering, front-page news findings of his forty-year-study of language. Most of his presentation, to be candid, was highly technical and boring. But knowing that the world's news media were in attendance with dozens of video cameras set to shoot, he made sure that his conclusions were stated in language that any layman or news reporter could understand.

"And so, ladies and gentlemen, after forty years of study of more than 116 languages and 3,112 dialects from every corner of the earth, I found that in some of those 116 languages and in some of those 3,112 dialects a double negative is a negative.

"And in my forty years of study of more than 116 languages and 3,112 dialects throughout the world, I have found that in some of those 116 languages and in some of those 3,112 dialects a double negative is a positive."

Now all of the philosophers and media people were on the edge of their seats. Every camera was running. The moment of the great finding had arrived. "But, ladies and gentlemen, in my forty years of the most rigorous scholarship, travel and study of the more than 116 languages and 3,112 dialects known to mankind in any and all of its cultures down through the ages, never ever did I find that a double positive is a negative."

There was a solemn hush in the hall and then from the back row a voice was heard to mutter, "Yeah, yeah."

Sometimes when I tell that story the laughter is thunderous and continuous. Sometimes there is utter silence—they don't get it. I want to crawl into a deep, dark hole.

That's how I felt when I addressed a huge religious assembly in Louisville several years ago. I had been giving a lot of talks to churches and my opening story was about the editor of the old *Chicago Daily News* who wanted no lead sentence longer than seven words. Without telling you the whole story I can tell you the punch line was, "Jesus. The body of an unidentified young woman was found washed ashore at North Avenue beach today." I had been greeted with laughter at church after church with that story, but in Louisville, some three thousand ministers and their wives sat in stony silence when I finished the story. I can't tell you how utterly painful it was to get through the ensuing one-hour lecture. Later, a church official told me that under no circumstances would those ministers laugh at what they thought was the taking of the Lord's name in vain. A good lesson for a young speaker.

Public speaking can have powerful, lasting consequences. About twelve years ago I was the lead-off speaker at a suburban women's club. Just before I entered from stage right, someone said to me, "Knock 'em dead, John." I opened my talk with a long, convoluted story involving the differences between the right side of the brain and the left side of the brain. I won't bore you with the details except to say that most audiences—particularly older audiences—find the punch line to the story devastatingly hilarious. I know the first time I heard it in Texas, my group didn't stop laughing for five minutes. The punch line of the story is: *It means you have an extraordinary interest in* (long pause) *SEX.*

As usual, my audience went bonkers with laughter. But I noticed that a few minutes after the giggling had subsided and I was into my serious remarks, paramedics entered the hall and removed a woman who appeared to have fainted. She was easily in her mid-eighties. It turned out, as I was told later, that she died of a heart attack suffered while laughing at my story. She literally died laughing. And so I ask people who invite me to speak never, ever to tell me to go out there and "knock 'em dead." I too often do what I'm told.

Over There

39

❧

Making Change in Japan

Snapshots, impressions, and notes from a recent trip to Japan: Headlines in a Tokyo English-Language Newspaper That Most Reminded Me of Home:

> STUDENTS READING LESS, POLL FINDS
> DEALING WITH UNRULY CHILDREN
> PUBLIC ENNUI GREETS SCANDALS

Juiciest Data Learned in a Seminar: We were told that the value of the land under the Imperial Palace in Tokyo is worth more than all of the land value in the state of California. That doesn't get to you? Try this: we were also told that the value of real estate in Japan is twice that of all the land in the United States! This seemed to be confirmed by an article in the *Wall Street Journal,* which said that one square meter of a certain property in downtown Tokyo was valued at $250,000. How would you like to be the assessor for Tokyo?

Why I'm Looking for a Good $50 Wash-and-Wear Wrinkle-Proof Suit: The charge for pressing and dry-cleaning one two-piece suit, one blazer, and one pair of trousers and for washing and ironing three shirts came to 6,449 yen, or $47.77, at the hotel.

What I Learned About How Much I Value *The New York Times:* At that same big Tokyo hotel, I wandered to the newsstand to buy a copy of the Monday (no, *not* the Sunday edition) *New York Times*. The price was 1,400 yen, about $10.70. I declined, thank you.

Moment That Made Me Feel Younger Than Ever: When we were apologetically told that the Buddhist temple we were about to see was "only" about 360 years old.

Most Interesting Choices Offered: Walking toward a Shinto shrine in Nikko, our guide pointed to holes in a wall and told us that if we wanted our wish to come true, place one stone in the hole; if we wanted marriage, place two stones in the hole; and if we sought divorce, place three stones in the hole. They didn't give us time to put any stones in the holes.

Moment I Knew American Culture Would Triumph Eventually over Japanese Know-How: When I saw every available seat taken in a huge downtown Tokyo McDonald's by young Japanese kids wolfing down Big Macs and fries.

Best Definition of Emphasis in Japan on Group Conformity: A Japanese scholar told us, "In Japan, if you are an individual it is like a nail that is hammered down."

I Have Seen the Future and It Scares the Heck Out of Me: While touring the Nissan Motor Company's huge plant in Tochigi we saw *500 robots* in action on one part of the body assembly line. Three thousand different parts are installed in a 900-meter line. Of the more than 13,000 employees who work at Nissan's Tochigi plant, 1,200 families and 2,500 unmarried workers are housed in compact quarters at the plant. The day shift works from 8 a.m. to 5 p.m., with assembly line workers getting two ten-minute breaks in addition to an hour for lunch.

Most Memorable Sight in Japan That I Didn't Expect to See: After spending the night at a mountaintop hotel in Nikko, as our bus carefully negotiated the hairpin turns back down the mountain, we saw rather large monkeys staring at us from the mountainside.

Most Disappointing Sight in Japan That I Saw: In the resort area of Nikko, a precious national park in Japan, we saw a shockingly huge amount of litter scattered along the roads. Tokyo seemed much cleaner by comparison.

Greatest Improvement in Japanese Life Since Our First Visit in 1985: Maybe it was just the time of year or maybe we just lucked out, but the pollution in Tokyo seemed much less than it was six years ago. And the cab drivers seemed to have settled down to a nice, steady approach to life.

Greatest Changes Coming in Japanese Society: According to scholars and government leaders who briefed us at our seminars, the younger generation is tiring of the insane twelve-hour day, seven-day week grind necessary to qualify for Japan's elite universities—schools which too often provide little more than a four-year holiday once you've broken your back to gain entry. Women are tiring of the third-class citizenship they suffer inside the big corporations and the fifty cents they earn for every dollar a man earns in a comparable job. Japanese firms are quickly ending the "lifetime guarantee" of work for their employees, who more and more are taking up the American pastime of job switching. Younger Japanese employees are tiring of two-hour "sleep while you stand" commutes into Tokyo and the long hours at work after they arrive. Japanese companies facing huge labor shortages may have to ask the government to qualify the long-held policy of strictly limiting foreign workers.

All of this impending social change in Japan makes me think of the retired government official, Naohiro Amaya, as quoted by David Halberstam in his new book, *The Next Century:*

> For forty years we were single-minded in our purpose. We were the greyhound chasing the hare. Now the hare that we chased has disappeared. So who are we and what are we after the hunt? What is our purpose in life?

To my Japanese friends, I say, "Good luck in your quest for the answers to those questions, and if you find them, will you please fax them to us right away."

40

☙

From Russia with Fears and Tears

Here are some personally unforgettable moments, lasting impressions, close calls, and memorable quotations jotted down from a recent trip first to Moscow, then to Tashkent, the capital of the central Asian republic of Uzbekistan, and then on to the hauntingly beautiful Moslem city of Samarkand.

Unforgettable Moments and Lasting Impressions

- Standing just outside the Russian parliament building (the White House) and seeing where the barricades had been erected after the historic August 1991 coup. Across the street stands a ragged band of demonstrators who now want to restore the monarchy in Russia!
- Riding a tour bus through the streets of Moscow, which are nearly empty because few people can afford gasoline. There are no little old women in babushkas cleaning the streets with brooms. The parks are shabby and overgrown. The great ballet and circus performances we watch are in halls half-filled because Russians can't afford a night out on the town.
- Seeing Red Square in person for the first time and realizing that it seems so small and unthreatening compared with

the TV pictures of old which showed all the guns and tanks and cold warriors standing up there on the review platforms.

- Visiting a farmer's modest home in a collective outside Tashkent and realizing that about the only piece of furniture in the place is a television set.
- Walking into the Moscow International Airport and seeing my first Russian whose eyes reflect all of the misery, defeat, and depression of the Russian people, past and present. He is young and blond and wears a shabby military uniform that looks three sizes too big. He doesn't stand, he slouches.
- Looking at the soiled, washed, and re-washed rags being used and reused as bandages in the Moscow hospital.
- Seeing the incredibly bejeweled thrones, coaches, and carriages of the tsars on display at the Armory, the oldest of Russia's museums. One clergy vestment is said to have 150,000 pearls. The woman who made it is said to have gone blind. A colleague whispers to me, "Now I know why they had a revolution."

Close Calls

- Drunken members of a wedding party in Samarkand attack some of the members of our group, punching one woman in the stomach, kicking another and stealing the wallet of still another. What an ugly welcome to what is one of the most beautiful cities in the world.
- A state security police official in Tashkent seizes the passport of one of my colleagues after he had videotaped a meeting of political opposition party leaders. He is questioned interminably until it is clearly established who was running things in Tashkent. His passport is returned eventually and our knowledge of police state politics leaps beyond what we had found in books and seminars.
- On our Aeroflot trip back to Moscow from Samarkand we taxi down the runway and stop. The self-serving crew gets

off, goes into town, buys fruit at the bazaar and finally comes
back to the plane! The washrooms on that plane are as filthy
as those in a prison camp.

- A swarm of Gypsy women explodes up out of a subway station stairwell and begins to surround me. I come to my
senses and shout "nyet, nyet," and they run away. Most are
very attractive young women but they will strip you of all
belongings in a minute.

Memorable Quotes

- From members of the Russian parliament with whom we
talked:

    "Our society is dying. Pardon me for being so dramatic."
    "We know it will take several decades for real reform. We
    don't have a dictatorship in mind. We want things working."
    "Bolshevism is a state of spirit. Whenever you want to address
    a complex problem and solve it overnight, turn to bolshe-
    vism." "If our government had to resign because of the econ-
    omy, we would have a different government every month."
    "We can't afford to buy coffins for our dead. We bury them
    now in plastic bags."

- A newspaper editor in Moscow: "Freedom of the press here
is not well protected by the law. The Russian state still owns
the printing presses. Some restraints are sure to be
introduced."
- A young female student in Tashkent: "I have a child, but
no husband. I like my situation. An Islamic state here would
be a nightmare for me."
- A man in Samarkand who has invited us to his father's home
for dinner: "Once I paid a half a ruble for this piece of bread.
Now I pay eight rubles. My income has not gone up a ruble."
- An Islamic leader in Tashkent: "We don't wish to establish
a religious state, but where the state fails, religion moves in."

- A Japanese-Russian woman who runs an investment company: "We don't have people who really believe in private property. The average Soviet wants his meager ration instead of being willing to take a risk—even a modest risk. Those who get rich are despised."

So what are my conclusions? At a big academic conference ten years ago on the future of U.S.–USSR relations, there was consensus that the Communists would control the USSR for the next one hundred years. So much for academic and government powers of prophecy. But getting rid of the Communist party is one thing. Changing a mind-set that is dependent on authority and despises individual initiative is another. The younger generation in Russia is more market-oriented. But at least twenty years are needed to make the new revolution in Russia something more than a slogan.

41

~

South Africa—
The Landscape of Tragedy

Sometimes the most obscene human tragedies play out against the most beautiful landscapes. I remember being astounded at how lovely the summertime countryside was around the Nazi concentration camps, as depicted in the PBS documentary film *Shoah*. I had always carried newsreel black and white pictures in my mind of the horror of Auschwitz. Similarly, when I visited Germany for the first time, I expected to hate it. Instead, I was enchanted by most of the people and the lush landscape. My prejudices received a good thrashing.

My preconceptions about South Africa were, ironically, quite different. The dirty little secret is that since I was a kid I have been in love with the majestic beauty of Cape Town and the lovely beaches of Durban as depicted in geography textbooks and magazines. As an adult who moderated public affairs discussions about the brutal, killing effects of the South African policy of apartheid, I felt guilty about my personal love of the South African landscape. As a golfer, I felt even more guilt about wanting to play ocean-side courses in a country that was systematically dehumanizing its overwhelmingly black majority population. I felt a bizarre kind of political incorrectness.

And so I carried pens and notebooks, not golf clubs, on my recent visit to South Africa. If I had the space in this column, and

I don't, I could tell you all about our visit with the unemployed black men who stand around all day in the barracks-hostels of the townships outside Johannesburg, or the thrill of being only a few feet away from Nelson Mandela as he spoke in Orlando Stadium in Soweto to angry youthful ANC supporters who had been chanting "Kill the Boers, kill the farmers" only minutes before his arrival, or the conversations we had with members of parliament and cabinet ministers in Cape Town, or the memorable, long session we had with the king of the Zulus, or the chilling words of resistance spoken to us by a former South African head of Military Intelligence who said his country was on the brink of civil war.

But it is not the conversations with the officials that remain most vivid in my memory. What stays with me is Gertrude, a Zulu woman who supports the Inkatha Freedom party, which is locked in a deadly battle with Mandela's African National Congress. Said Gertrude, matter of factly, "If the ANC wins, I will be the first person to be placed under house arrest or to be executed." She knows something about political violence. Her previous home was destroyed by firebombs.

Not more than a mile from Gertrude's home, we talked with Robert Nutli, who recalls that his brother Sam, an ANC supporter, "was murdered on September 29, 1991 ... he died because he was anti-apartheid." His mother steps to the porch and utters one sentence, which speaks to everything we saw in black South Africa—"We are suffering."

I talked to a businessman who had returned to Johannesburg after living with his family for several years in Atlanta. After establishing that his business was not doing well at all (South Africa's economy has been pulverized by its racism and by international sanctions), I asked him why he had come home to South Africa. He said he was optimistic that the elections to be held next April would put his country on the road toward democracy and economic rejuvenation. His wife, like the general with whom we had talked, countered that South Africa was on the brink of civil war.

At another informal gathering, I spoke with a white magazine photographer who said he had become fed up with the violence and racism of South Africa and had fled to London for several years. He complained that South Africa's apartheid system had destroyed any sense of cultural and intellectual life in the country. He simply had to get out. "Why, then," I asked, "did you come back?"

He said he came home because he missed "the craziness of South Africa, the beauty of South Africa." He pointed out the back door and said, "Not more than a mile from here is the most violent area in all of South Africa. People are killing each other over there even as we speak. But I missed it, all of it, and so I came home."

I think that if I lived in South Africa I would have left it and then come home to it. The haunting beauty of the view of Cape Town from atop Table Mountain, the sugarcane fields of Natal, the Indian Ocean lapping onto the lovely cityside beaches of Durban, were more compelling even than my picture-book images of South Africa. But if I did come home to South Africa I would know that I was coming home to tragedy. I would know that even if elections are held next April and Nelson Mandela comes to power, decades of apartheid have rotted the social fabric of South Africa, deeply wounded its economy and left millions of blacks unschooled, unemployed and angry. South Africa as Yugoslavia is not unthinkable, nor Cape Town as Beirut.

Sometimes the most obscene human tragedies play out against the most beautiful landscapes.

42

⌘

The Media and the Presidential Campaign: What Happened to Foreign Policy?

Because I ask the questions on my "Chicago Tonight" program, I have little opportunity to indulge in long analysis of politics and public affairs. And so I use the occasion of a public speech to get off my chest some of the things I can't say at any length on camera. What follows is a talk I gave at a Chicago Council on Foreign Relations meeting held at the University Club in Chicago on December 15, 1992.

The short answer to the question raised by the title of my talk is "not much." Thank you and good night.

But that would be a seriously misleading answer. In fact, I am prepared to say that, in defiance of all conventional wisdom, this election in many ways was very much about foreign policy.

An aside about the title of this talk. I want to say that, with all exceptions noted, and meaning no disrespect toward our hosts, and acknowledging my one intense and long-time interest in international matters, I do sometimes feel that the term "foreign policy" almost qualifies as an oxymoron. International events are subject to so much unpredictable change that the notion of having a policy seems almost dangerously self-indulgent and self-deceiving. I know that a nation can have general principles to which it tries to adhere in foreign matters, but there are so many exceptions to the application of these general principles that sometimes I wonder what the general principles were in the first place. Anyway, there is much to be modest about in the use of such solid-sounding phrases as "foreign policy."

But here is my more detailed answer to the question "What happened to foreign policy?" in the 1992 presidential election.

First of all, George Bush very much depended on his record in foreign affairs and military affairs as the cornerstone of his candidacy and even though we all know now that the issue was, as we say, "the economy, stupid," it is, in my view, completely understandable that George Bush should pin much of his hope on his record as foreign affairs specialist and commander-in-chief. One does not achieve a 90 percent approval rating in the presidency, even for a few months, and not take that quite seriously. And all political strategy aside, George Bush was entirely sincere when he presented himself as being the superior candidate because of his long foreign and military service to this country. In fact, it was the sincerity of this view which, in my view, got him into so much trouble with campaign focus.

And even though his campaign managers finally moved Mr. Bush toward a domestic focus (one that was hastily conceived and insincerely, that is to say, not believably, articulated by Mr. Bush), the president continued to emphasize his foreign affairs and military experience, particularly in the debates. His "whom do you trust" focus in comparing himself with the governor of the small southern state of Arkansas was simply too much for Bush to resist. He simply didn't understand that most Americans do not now particularly care about "what happens when that phone call comes in the middle of the night." Most Americans fear that the bad news call in the middle of the night will be about the Tokyo Stock Market, not nuclear attack. Bush knew that the Cold War was over, but he didn't know that the American people were in no need to celebrate its end, if you define "celebration" as an act of good-faith voting for the people who presumably had something to do with its end. There was something unseemly about Mr. Bush's taking so much credit for something as complex as the End of the Cold War. First, Mr. Reagan probably deserved the kudos (if anyone were going to get them) and second, most Americans now think that the Soviet empire was decaying of its own weight and while they were and are willing to give a fond nod to Mr. Reagan and maybe even Mr. Bush for a role in the drama, they no longer are interested in this particular chapter of history unless they are defense-related workers who are losing their jobs because the threat of world hostilities has receded.

But let it be clear that the media wrote and broadcast about this particular Republican conundrum and that it very much had to do with foreign policy. It simply was foreign policy of the past, as opposed to the particulars of the foreign policy of the future. Bush stated simply and directly that there would be international crises in the future—he chose not to enumerate them or speculate about them—but he consistently referred to this possibility and to the advisability of returning him to office so that there would be a steady hand on the ship of state in the event of such crises.

As for Governor Clinton, it could be said that he based his entire campaign—and that it was accurately and faithfully reported by the media—on a foreign policy concept of immensely important dimensions. However clichéd, it, nevertheless, is all the more important. The concept simply stated is that the regeneration or reconfiguration of the U.S. economy was our number one objective politically, economically, educationally and socially.

And Clinton, not at all unaware of the international burdens of the presidency, did not deliver his "come home to America's interests" message in isolationist rhetoric or with isolationist intent.

On the contrary. Always, he couched his strong domestic regeneration message in two contexts:

1. America cannot be a successful global player, much less a prevailing superpower, unless it develops a much stronger educational and economic base at home.
2. America's economic regeneration must be achieved within the complex challenges of the global economy.

My guess is that a computer analysis of Clinton's rhetoric would find the word *global* appearing as often as the word *America.*

And so these were the major international themes of the Bush and Clinton campaigns and they were more than adequately expressed and repeated and reinforced by the candidates and the media. And most voters absorbed these broad messages, in my view. And the voters correctly perceived Ross Perot as being more protective on trade than Bush or Clinton, but they also saw his budget deficit emphasis and his ideas about the U.S. economic retooling challenge as being profoundly internationally contexted, much as Clinton's ideas were internationally contexted.

And so, if your concepts of foreign policy permit a discussion of the Cold War and the necessity for continued military strength and crisis management skills, and if your concepts of foreign policy are broad enough to include Clinton and Perot's "Let's get ready to compete in a global economy," then it could be said that this campaign, conventional wisdom to the contrary, was actually centered in a very important way on foreign policy and with a most sophisticated global view.

Remember, there was much talk and debate about how to compete against Japan—how much longer should we pay for the defense of Japan and Germany.

There was incessant discussion of how much the defense budget should be cut and how should it be cut so that we don't spend as much but still retain highly sophisticated and mobile armed forces which can meet the needs of nationalist explosions and terrorists bearing nuclear surprises.

There was a robust discussion of how many troops should be brought home and why and when and from where.

There were ongoing debate and discussion and media coverage of how much more we should do to protect U.S. workers and our environment before finally embracing the North American Free Trade Agreement.

And, of course, there were major foreign policy speeches, background papers and party platforms so that the candidates, especially Bush and Clinton, could say that they had spoken to many of the foreign affairs issues.

And for its part, the national press could point to significant reporting on any number of international issues during the time the campaign was in gear—the ongoing struggles in Russia and the remnant Soviet state, the civil war in what once was Yugoslavia, the continuing drama of South Africa, the decline of the Japanese economy, the anxieties and drama of the European Community, the near collapse of John Major's government in Great Britain, the ominous economic and political unrest in Germany, the aftermath of the Gulf War, the ups and downs of the Middle East peace talks, the development of more free market economies in Mexico and India, the continuing turmoil in South and Latin America, the national referendum in Canada, and on and on. The clip files on all these subjects from stories written and broadcast during the campaign year would bulge.

And yet, unlike years when there was a great, overwhelming, sometimes violent debate on, say, Vietnam, or "How Hard Should We Be on the Menace of Communism," there was no "country-specific" or "region-specific" or even "enemy-specific" debate in this presidential campaign—unless you agree that the "enemy" this year was the unproductive, uneducated, unprepared American.

And if you are among those who see presidential campaigns as rich opportunities to engage in highly visible debates and discussions which can serve to educate the public, and if you were among those who hoped and prayed that our 1992 presidential election would give rise to a robust discussion of possible U.S. policy initiatives or considerations toward Russia and the other former Soviet republics, Africa, South Asia, the EC, South and Latin America, the Middle East, then you must be sorely disappointed in the candidates and the media in the campaign. Nor did we take the opportunity to have a great national debate on the dozens of brilliantly articulated issues and questions raised in Vice President-elect Al Gore's richly stimulating and controversial book about global environmental questions.

And it should be said that if we were having this discussion tonight at the Chicago Council on Race Relations, or the Chicago Council on Crime Issues, or the Chicago Council on Women's Issues, or the Chicago Council on Agricultural Issues, or the Chicago Council on Dismantling the Cold War Economy, or the Chicago Council on Urban Issues, or the Chicago Council on Space Issues, or the Chicago Council on Oceanic Issues, we would not be satisfied with the broad sweep of the 1992 presidential election as presented by the candidates and the media.

It is interesting to note that, in the end, even the high-marquee issues such as abortion and family values did not play either Peoria or the precincts of Chicago and other big cities.

As Mayor Daley would say, this campaign was about "jobs, jobs, jobs." And that sounds parochial if you are interested in a highly sophisticated discussion of South Asian policy or the complexities of how to try to help Russia. But, as a matter of fact, the focus on jobs was itself a highly sophisticated focus. People know that from jobs comes income and that income brings the kind of things that enable people to live more humanly and with more fulfillment. And people know that jobs can be interesting and vital. And they know that jobs are now created and lost in a highly complicated, constantly changing global context.

And so, in a way, the focus on jobs for the future is the most

sophisticated possible foreign policy, global sort of issue and discussion. And Clinton and Perot led us in that discussion. People
by the millions stuck with Perot's flow chart infomercials. And
people by the millions followed Clinton's teach-ins in Little Rock.

I want to add that while I think the 1992 presidential campaign was about jobs, and all that I've said that jobs mean in the
global economic, political and social contexts, I do not think the
problem Bush encountered was simply the current unemployment rate of 7-point something. In fact, objective economic data
during the campaign showed several quarters of economic growth,
low interest rates, low rates of inflation, and manufacturing growth
of 2.6 percent for a period in which the Japanese and Germans
were experiencing declines in manufacturing growth.

It is true that some of the job loss was more dynamic in the
past two years than in the huge lay-offs of the early 1980s when
Reagan's unemployment rate was much higher than Bush's this
year. It is true that when a white-collar communications worker
gets laid off the word and the fear spread in a way that is more
explosively communicable than when a steel worker on the south-
east side of Chicago gets laid off. That was a dynamic, however
unfair to Bush, that hurt him.

But I think that when people said they were voting on the economic or jobs issue what they really meant was that they see the issues
of economic regeneration in the global context as being long range
and highly complex. Therefore, they wanted someone in the White
House who demonstrated an on-the-ground, working, day-to-day
concern and feel for those long-range and complex issues. The voters—two thirds of them—felt that both Clinton and Perot were on
the case, so to speak, and that Bush was out to lunch, so to speak.

There were some other foreign policy aspects of this campaign
that should not go unnoted. It was a terrible and, in the end, unproductive thing for Bush to have asked James Baker to resign as secretary of state to come back and run the White House and the
campaign. It was too late and, to aggravate the error, Baker's first

response to the challenge he so reluctantly assumed was profoundly un-Baker-like. He went on vacation. By the time he returned, the Republican National Convention was half over and all the Pat Buchanan, Pat Robertson, Dan and Marilyn Quayle damage had been done. And considerable damage was done.

And then there was the Baker-Bush attempt to paint Bill Clinton as a Communist collaborator; a 1950s act of political desperation that failed and failed so quickly that anyone who doesn't think the Vietnam War is over should think again. I really think that, in a sleazy kind of symbolic way, the attempt to get Clinton on the Vietnam War and the failure to get him are a kind of end of that war.

And then all of the reporting of and congressional investigation into the possible Bush role in Irangate didn't help the president's campaign. And there were substantial reporting of and congressional attention to the Reagan-Bush administration's incredible back and forth policies toward Iran and Iraq during the Iran-Iraq war. New Dimensions of Foreign Policy Tilting and Jilting were made apparent.

And, ironically enough, all of this came back to haunt Bush on an issue he thought he controlled—trust. His failed end game with Saddam Hussein; his transparent lying about Irangate; his failure to show any leadership, even to educate, on the complexities of Russia and the other former Soviet republics; his willingness to sacrifice the progress of the Middle East peace talks by removing James Baker from State were all reported by the media, hammered home by Clinton, and particularly Al Gore, and thus became a significant part of the last weeks of the campaign.

And so, while we will think of this as a presidential campaign in which foreign policy was largely ignored, we will be wrong if we do so. Foreign policy of the past, the end of the Cold War, the failure to demonize the Democrats with Vietnam, the globalization of our economics and the raised consciousness of our globalization of our economics, the global environmentalism of Al

Gore—all of these and many more aspects of the campaign had to do substantially with foreign policy.

I look forward to Clinton's leading nationally and internationally televised seminars on the complexities of trying to help Russia; on what the colonial and post–Cold War consequences are on the Horn of Africa, and on the kinds of post–Cold War unintended consequences that John Mearsheimer (University of Chicago professor of political science) has been writing and talking about with respect to Eastern Europe. I hope that Clinton will educate all of us as he himself is educated about the complexities of these and other issues.

What we in the media and Clinton and others in the leadership need to do is to communicate not so much a sense of definite policy about these regions, nations and issues, as a sense of complexity about them. If we can tuck an overview of complexity away on one side of our brain while focusing specifically on improvements about certain policy matters, foreign or domestic, on the other side of our brain, we will begin to forge a modern context of politics which takes note of the problems generalist leaders face in a world of specialists. We need to manage expectations, not just nations.

Reflections on Chicago

43

❧

Chicago Is Not a Shining City on a Hill

Remarks for the Michigan Avenue Forum of the Fourth Presbyterian Church on February 6, 1989.

Chicago is not "a shining city on a hill." It is a post-colonial city which was built on a swamp, burned in a fire, reborn in a spasm of inspired, inventive greed, developed and run by an Irish politburo, overwhelmed by a southern immigration, split asunder by the death of a boss, stunned and slightly freed by a black revolution, caught short by another heart attack, left wanting by eight years of federal neglect and now finds itself in the media fed the mis-premise that its destiny is somehow to be determined by the questions asked of the candidates who now present themselves for mayor. I have no questions for the candidates, and that is good, because the handlers of the campaigns, who decide what will and what will not be permitted in the debate format, do not permit the moderator, yours truly, to ask any questions.

No, my questions are not for the candidates. My questions are for the voters, for the people of this city of swamps, fires, sky-scrapers, futures exchanges, racial polarity, disgraceful public schools, wonderful theater, prison-like projects, Michigan Mile shopping and the rest of it.

My first question, why have 400,000 of us chosen not to register to vote? How dare we not register to vote? Next, why have so many of us who have decided to vote been content with political leadership which assumes that our vote is worth only a garbage can or a similarly low-cost political favor which is no favor but merely a municipal service which should be ours as a taxpayer but which is delivered to us only at a patronage-bloated, contract-manipulated inflationary cost? Why do we complain about a city that collects only one in five parking tickets? Why did we get the ticket in the first place? Why were we not a part of the body politic which demanded decent mass transit so we wouldn't have to drive and park illegally? Why didn't we pay the ticket voluntarily instead of asking that the city be efficient in its collection?

Why do we leave it to white politicians with children in parochial schools to decide the fate of our public schools?

Why do we vote for aldermen who do not account for their $18,000-a-year expenses and who are not required to acknowledge possible conflict of interest when voting on zoning matters? Do we think a mayor can control those aldermen? How can he do that when we have given him a majority which likes things the corrupt way they are?

Why do we not attend the PTA meetings? Have we truly earned the rights and responsibilities about to be vested in us, with our new school councils? Why do we pay off the clerk of the court or the harbor master?

Why did we permit our aldermen to hold up all of Harold Washington's appointments when there were no real public policy disagreements at issue—not even race was at issue—only the control of a very few municipal jobs for each alderman or committeeman?

Why do we continue to send legislators to Springfield who represent districts that desperately need greater education funding but who follow the House Speaker's instructions to cut down tax increases which could provide those funds?

Why do we demand that our leaders do something about drugs when we gulp down alcohol, kill ourselves with cigarettes, watch our children take drugs, let them watch us take pills, and watch television seven hours and ten minutes a day?

We are a crisis-driven, pain-avoiding, denying society. Most of our medicine is taken after the fact of the heart attack, the liver failure, the lung cancer.

We spend thousands for surgery; we spend peanuts on prevention. That is our medicine; that is our politics.

But wait a minute, millions of Americans now exercise regularly. Millions of Americans pay attention to what they eat. Most Americans don't, but millions do. Could that same rationality be applied gradually to our politics in this city?

Would it be possible for some aldermen to vote on something that might not be comfortable for them in the short run, something like scattered-site housing in their ward, but that would help the city in the long run? If the mayor has a citywide project in mind but can't get a majority to vote with him unless he gives them certain jobs and perks and committees, would it be possible for him to go public with this knowledge and let us float a patronage bond for him so he can make his necessary payoffs so we can get the housing built, the jobs retraining center developed, the schools functioning again? Could the next mayor hold a city council meeting in the projects? Could the next mayor ask the state legislative committees on education to hold their hearings on the west side of Chicago? Could the next mayor work very closely and continually with Jack Kemp and Bill Bennett on housing and drugs, and not wait for them to hit town calling names?

Why do I ask these questions of we the people in this city? Because we the people in this city have gone along for decades with the lowest possible expectation of our leaders. The editorial writers and reformers may ask for greatness, rationality, fairness, and far-seeing vision from our leaders, but we the people must be the leaders. If we believe adequate government and adequate city life are a fixed ticket, a dead-end job with no real responsibility at City Hall, another missed PTA or civic meeting, another drink, another night in front of the tube, we are hypocrites beyond description if we think a mayor will make a difference.

Some excellent questions will be asked at the Channel 11 debate Tuesday evening. When you watch the debate, think what your own answers would be; think what you'll need to know and what you'll need to do in order to help lead the next mayor and the next city council of Chicago. Without your leadership, without *our* leadership, it will be business as usual at City Hall.

44

~

Chicago's Mayor Daley: On Camera and Off

I used this speech before the First Friday Club of Chicago on April 7, 1989, to comment on what it was like to interview Richard M. Daley, the new mayor of Chicago, and to talk about some challenges facing him.

Richard M. Daley, in person, is a charming, reasonably well-spoken, conversationally interesting and intelligent person. That's off camera. That's at dinner with him or even with him in the studio before the cameras are turned on. A likable, almost sweet, decent sort of person is the way he comes off. And if you know his wife, Maggie, you've got to trust your own sense of his sweetness, likability and decency. In other words, if he's good enough for a great woman like Maggie Daley, he must be pretty damned good.

Daley *on* camera, however, is a portrait of resistance, denial, argumentation, and premise destruction. You ask a question about his campaign contributors, he asks you a question about your corporate underwriters. You ask him a question about the racial climate in Bridgeport, he asserts that you live in a community better off than his. You ask about what value his state's attorney's experience is when it comes to dealing with the complicated issues of education and housing and he blurts out that he was a good state's attorney who did not abuse his power and who did not subpoena you even though he could have. You remind him that it is he who is running for mayor, not you the broadcast interviewer, and he sharply retorts that you, the broadcast interviewer, can wield immense power night after night and therefore you have these retorts coming.

You know that because he won't give the light of day to any of the premises of your questions you are going nowhere in the interview. You hear the words "no, no, no ..." as the opening to his answers. You hear the insane giggle and you wonder what's funny. You know that in a broadcast sense, you are going absolutely nowhere with this conversation, that you look like a jerk, that he looks like a guy who has just cleaned up on you in the schoolyard and you know that this is not a positive experience for the candidate, the interviewer or the audience, except that part of the audience which is sick and tired of interviewers beating the hell out of their subjects and are pleased to see the tables reversed at least this one time. And even the interviewer feels some affection toward his assailant after having encountered the like of Alderman Larry Bloom, who decided for mayoral campaign purposes that he would play the total bottom-kisser to the press, particularly the television press, and carried little blue cards with him into the studio with little reminders to be pleasant while on camera. You wince at the memory of that kind of obsequiousness and patronizing behavior. And you wince at the memory of Tim Evans, whose responses in an interview nearly put you to sleep with their gaseous elegance.

So those of us who make a living talking to politicians and other leaders on the air will not have a happy time with young Mr. Daley. He is not happy talk. The only way to deal with him is to do exactly as he would have you do, would respect you if you do, and that is to report on what others say he will do as mayor. He will take office knowing that he will appoint a boat full of competent professionals who will give only the most unrelentingly, unforgiving opponents reason to criticize them. He will delight in the opportunity to reach out to all parts of this community because he knows that in 1989 and 1990, not only is it the smart and necessary thing to do, it is the right thing to do, even if you appear on camera in interviews to represent a personality type who is incapable of reaching out even while mouthing clichés about the need to reach out.

Daley and his campaign managers must be given credit for several important successes in this campaign, successes which were not lost on the voters:

If a candidate can honorably and usefully be judged in part by the people he picks to run his campaign and the manner in which that campaign is run, including the ability to raise money, then Mr. Daley must be given an "A", and the voters sensed that.

Mr. Daley voiced a simple theme, a cliché, but nevertheless a welcome cliché, and that is: The fighting in this city must stop and we must come together and move forward to address the issues that afflict us all, regardless of race or station in life. It takes a certain courage by the managers and by the strategists and by the candidate to keep with that cliché. Courage because the cliché contains so much truth. Courage because it can backfire on you if you stumble into personal attacks or negative thrusts, which any campaign is tempted and enticed to do.

Mr. Daley has now established himself as the all-time champion of saying that he was talking issues when what he did was say that he was talking about them even though he simply was listing them. The news media, particularly commercial television nightly news, let him get away with that night after night after night after night. I've never seen anything in political hocus pocus which could remotely match it: locally, regionally, nationally or internationally. His media people and managers took everything Lee Atwater taught Reagan and Bush and one-upped them by eliminating the Willie Horton kind of negatives. He didn't need them and wouldn't have been inclined to permit them to be used in a tele-vised campaign, even though he has the personal capacity to mug interviewers up close.

Why did the media and the voting public let Daley get away with this sound-bite candidacy? I'll tell you why. There was no stand on the issues that Daley took that wasn't reasonable to the general public. He's for school reform, more accountability in the classroom, less bureaucracy downtown at the board of education, spending some money to help train the school councils, and not willing to show his cards yet and come out in advance for a state income tax increase to support schools. You may not agree with all of that, but it is a reasonable and honorable set of positions to take. You're against crime, so is he. You think the traffic tickets and water bill collections should be efficient? So does Daley. You think there are too many city council committees? So does he. You think minorities ought to have their fair share of government? So does he. You think the new mayor shouldn't fire everyone at City Hall when he takes over; you don't like bloodbaths. Neither does Rich Daley. He didn't do it as state's attorney and he says he won't do it as mayor. Even without showing up for the general election debate at Channel 11, Daley has made all of this clear in short speeches and sound-bites. Add to that six million dollars for TV commercials which were masterpieces. Lots and lots of that money for organizing in the precincts. Add to that the incredible restraint in attacking his opponents. Add to that a campaign schedule that was busy enough to get to most parts of the city and modest enough to save the candidate's energy and not fray his considerable tem-per. And add to that an opposition that was badly split and, as Mike Royko wrote, confused the needs of a campaign with the strategies of a movement, and you've got a Daley landslide.

There is one great ironic ingredient in this election. One that stands out as a contradiction of the conventional wisdom that, in Chicago politics, the professionals never forget and they never for-give. Well, they may never forget, but they do, indeed, forgive, or at least they come over and join forces with those who previously worked against them. And I'm not just talking about the few blacks who were so angry that they came out for Vrydolyak.

I'm talking about Alderman Luis Gutierrez, a man Daley had opposed for alderman. Gutierrez comes out for Daley, even though Daley had not spoken out and supported Harold Washington's greatest and most noble and most cherished crusade, the historically important effort to obtain a city council remap which would bring equal access to blacks and hispanics in this city. I'm not one for holding grudges, and I've never been one who thought Harold Washington's coalition was pure and reformist, but I thought one critical political act that should be honored was the effort to remap. And I thought that anyone who wasn't for that remap deserved to be punished. Not punished forever, but punished at least once at the polls so that the statement would ring true and clear: we may disagree on school policy, we may disagree on housing or crime or community development, but by God, the one thing we ought to hold as a true political litmus test in the 1980s in Chicago is, where were you on the remap? Did you speak out? Did you support Harold Washington? All people of all races and parties should have stood up on that, I thought, just as I thought all people of all parties should stand up for voting rights for blacks in the South in the 1960s. Voting rights should be particularly precious to constitutional conservatives and to ethnic groups which themselves have suffered discrimination in past years. Pardon me while I drown myself in my political naiveté. Luis G. went with the winner. When Luis G. went with Richard D. I knew the ballgame was over, even if Gene Sawyer threw his arms around Tim Evans in the general election. Does that make Luis Gutierrez a political hypocrite? I doubt it. He wants for himself and his people the power that comes with signing up with a winner after you've gotten the vote. In fact, some politicians would argue that Alderman Gutierrez took his newly won enfranchisement in the city council as seriously as it can be taken by going for the power. There are real needs in his neighborhood and they are needs that might not be met by idealistically clinging to those who helped you come to power in the first place. Sometimes you don't leave the dance with the person you entered the ballroom with, and sometimes that works out all right for all parties concerned, however embarrassing it is the night of the dance. And sometimes it doesn't work out and there are hurt feelings and a real sense of loss for years.

I was most fascinated to read a quote from Rich Daley the other day in which he said that city workers would be expected to do a day's work for a day's pay, and that the old patronage days are over. I think he really will try to make that happen, within limits.

I think Rich Daley and the people around him know that big cities are in so much trouble that there just isn't that much room for fat. I think they will have little patience for people who don't want to make the government more efficient. Again, I know my naiveté is showing, but I was just dumbfounded when I talked with aldermen who opposed Harold Washington and asked them what substantive issues they based their intractable opposition to him on and they acknowledged that it wasn't issues. It was that Jacky Grimshaw hadn't ladled out to them the six jobs they wanted or said they had been promised. Not two million dollars. Not a stand on principle. A lousy six jobs. If that's what the price is, why don't we acknowledge it now and float a patronage bond issue every year for the few million in payoffs that will take these creeps off our backs and let us address issues in city council instead of their lousy, stinking, piddling six jobs.

Some Final Thoughts:
If you want to judge the Daley administration, watch what people he appoints and retains and watch what those people do. Don't worry about what Daley says.

Daley should reach out to all communities but he should not patronize them. It would be true to his character, in my view, not to patronize them, although patronizing is in the eye of the beholder and many blacks would see the choice of Cecil Partee as state's attorney as patronizing while I would not necessarily think that is fair. Given that he has only two years, Daley should go berserk showing that he is interested in the schools. He should be seen in the schools day and night, and, while he has been criticized for sending his children to private schools, he could turn that around by seeing to it that the people he appoints to the school board apply some of the lessons of the private schools to our public schools, particularly in increased classroom accountability and decreased central bureaucracy.

Daley should make good on his promise to get us all involved in highly visible things like city clean-up.

He should steal Walter Netsch's idea and get different areas of the city to create wonderful occasions in their park systems and invite people from all over the city to see what they've come up with.

He should strike quickly on his plan to cut way down on the red tape involved when you want a building permit, increase office hours and service.

He should be seen with Vince Lane in the projects and he should spend time with Vince learning what he is doing and getting involved with it in a highly visible way. Otherwise, he may be beaten in a race for mayor by Vince Lane someday. Keep your eye on Mr. Lane, friends.

He should make himself available to joint broadcasts on stations like WBBM and WGCI-AM. He should encourage Channel 11 to resurrect its "Chicago Feedback" show where we took five cameras to Daley Plaza and let Mayor Byrne field questions from citizens groups in prime time.

He should honor his father, who really loved Chicago and American cities, and spend enough time in Washington to be perceived to be the new, great champion of American cities.

He shouldn't sign on to any new taxes until he can prove to the people that he's cut school bureaucracy fat, City Hall fat and has something going that's earned our respect so that we can give it our sweat.

He should name a high-visibility commission (a trick his father was a master of) and shoot for a five-year plan to begin to deal with the multi-billion-dollar unfunded pension crisis that is looming.

He should gather us all in prayer that we avoid a recession that will doom his administration as it might doom any city administration in the short run.

He should—and this will go against his grain and his father's example—acknowledge mistakes when he makes them. He should remind us that our goals should be high and our expectations modest and our efforts untiring.

45

❧

Streetwise Chicago

When Chicago Sun-Times *reporters Don Hayner and Tom McNamee asked me to write the foreword to their book on the history of Chicago street names, it gave me an opportunity to indulge in some memories of my own about walking Chicago streets. As one who now drives around the streets more than he walks (other than my lakefront three-mile speedwalks) I miss having the feeling of freedom to walk almost anywhere in Chicago, a feeling I exercised in the first years I worked and lived here. One reference in the following essay seems sadly dated. I had suggested that a street be named after Chicago Cubs baseball star Andre Dawson, then an icon in this city. Alas, Dawson was traded to the Boston Red Sox and the performance of the Cubs in recent years has not inspired anyone to name streets after them.*

Fancy it.
   "My darling, I'm now going to take you someplace you've always wanted to go."

"Where is that, dear?"

"Don't ask. Just trust and come with me."

And off you drive. Where do you go?

Down Memory Lane. Literally. It is on Chicago's Far North-west Side. More precisely, in the terminology of Chicago's streets grid (or is it street grids?) you drive to 5146 N, from 8000 W to 8158 W. That will take you down Memory Lane.

I've been walking and driving Chicago's streets and reporting from them since 1956, and I didn't know there was a Memory Lane. Now, thanks to this instructive, historically helpful, fre-quently whimsical volume, I came to learn that Chicago has a Memory Lane and many other streets, avenues, boulevards, places, and roads that I (and I'll bet you) didn't know about. In this urban geography, mystery-history story, our passionate street sleuths, McNamee and Hayner, are amazingly, almost perversely, fanati-cal in tracking down the whys and hows of street names. Even as this Foreword is being written, they are begging their editor for more time so they can make one last stab at discovering the ori-gin of that Loch Ness Monster of Chicago street names—Agatite Avenue. Will they ever sleep peacefully until Agatite yields to sci-entific, historically documented consensus?

But they can rest well now that we know that Beaubien Court (120 E, from 150 N to 186 N) is named after "Jolly Mark" Beaubien, an innkeeper, ferryman, fur trader, and "truly wicked fiddle player." And we can relax now that we know that Beaubien was the father of twenty-three children and that his brother, Jean Baptiste Beaubien, fathered twenty children, and that between the two of them (and their incredible wives) they produced more children than the entire population of Chicago in 1829.

Now be warned that, despite all of the superb scholarship and investigative journalism that resulted in the Beaubien revelations, the explanations for some of the street names end up being less than enthralling. To go back down Memory Lane: "More than likely, the whimsical man or woman who named this street was inspired by the saying, 'a stroll down Memory Lane.'" But if I know McNamee and Hayner, they probably spent a month double-checking to see if it was possible that an ancient Indian or alderman or real estate developer's last name wasn't "Memory."

This book is nothing like the first street guide I was issued as a cub police reporter for the City News Bureau of Chicago in June of 1956. That was the "little black book"—*Leonard's Street Guide*. Only with *Leonard's* in my pocket could I survive the transition from walking the few maple-lined streets of my small hometown of New Martinsville, West Virginia, to chasing fires and murders in the countless big-city streets of Chicago. *Leonard's* just told the name of the street and how far north it was and how far east to west it ran. This volume is a feast, but not terribly movable unless you happen to have a coffee table in your automobile.

As a young, practically penniless newcomer to Chicago, walking city streets was my pastime. I got to know the hustlers, Gypsies, and street walkers of South Wabash, the Italian street fairs at 23rd and Oakley, the bargains on Maxwell Street, the slums of 63rd and Woodlawn, the seemingly endless ethnic diversity of Devon. I walked the length of West Madison Street years before the riots of 1968 turned it partially into a no-man's land. I walked all the way up and down Chicago's lakefront. As a police reporter, death and destruction on the streets burned their names into my consciousness: a murder-suicide on Flournoy; a terrible multiple-fatality fire on Dorchester; an el crash at Wilson Avenue; the tear-gassed streets of the Democratic convention of 1968. I became street-smart.

But this book is street-wise. In digging for why Chicago's streets have the names they do, the authors provide us with a series of historical developments and personal sketches that add up to much, much more than a street guide. And we really get a sense of the self-interest which built Chicago—it is no small fact that a huge number of our streets are named after real estate developers. I can hardly wait for the naming of Rubloff Drive. You can bet on it.

And we learn that people take their streets seriously in this town. McNamee and Hayner remind us that a twenty-year court battle ensued over the changing of Crawford Avenue to Pulaski. Some people still call it Crawford.

A personal note: It was just the week before that 1968 Democratic convention in Chicago that I covered the story of the defacing of the new Dr. Martin Luther King, Jr. Drive signs that replaced the signs for South Park Avenue. And I was stunned to learn in this book that in the first six months after a one-mile stretch of 43rd Street was renamed Pope John Paul II Drive (to commemorate his 1979 visit in Chicago) that twenty-three of the new street signs were stolen!

This book has inspired me to offer one modest and one ambitious suggestion to our city fathers and mothers. My modest proposal: if you want to rename a street without igniting huge controversy, try something like Dawson Avenue (3432 W, from 2800 N to 2962 N). It was named, we learned from our authors, for John Brown Dawson, a barber, Methodist minister, and real estate operator of the 1860s. Who would object if we someday hold a ceremony and update the naming of Dawson Avenue in honor of Cubs' star Andre Dawson? My ambitious proposal—do away with vanity addresses so that the fire department dispatchers will quickly know were to send their units when people are trapped in high-rise fires. In doing away with vanity addresses such as on Michigan Avenue, provide new names for the various streets that are created in the huge new downtown developments. What the hell, name one Rubloff Drive.

We really are serious about street names, but mostly this volume is just great fun. The late Sidney Harris, who wrote those famous "things I learned en route to looking up other things" columns, would have gone wild with this book. I'm sure Sidney knew (but I didn't) that Academy Place was, and still may be, the city's narrowest street (ten feet wide) and that Grand Avenue was called "Whiskey Point Road" when it was an Indian trail. Oh, for the joy of broadcasting a live mini-cam news report from Whiskey Point Road!

Well, I've stalled as long as I can. Maybe McNamee and Hayner have by now discovered the true origins of the name Agatite Avenue and have phoned it in to their editor. If they succeed, I hope they both have streets named after them.

46

⤳

The New Colonialism

Maribeth Vander Weele's book about the tragedy and promise of the Chicago public school system is a brilliant study of what I call the new colonialism. Unlike the traditional colonialism which, however brutal and exploitative, built nations and civilizations on the backs of the poor and disenfranchised, the new colonialism isolates its victims in inner-city ghettos and results in the building of little more than jails and prisons that are refilled with thousands upon thousands of young, mostly minority men, who become discards from the dysfunctional plantation called the Chicago public school system.

The overseers of this new colonial plantation are the men and women of the Illinois General Assembly who bear the responsibility to create, fund and maintain a Chicago public school system that functions in at least a modestly successful fashion. The vast majority of these men and women do not have children in the Chicago public schools—and this includes those who are in the leadership from the city of Chicago, not just those legislators who live in the safely removed, mostly affluent white suburbs.

In other words, unlike the original slave masters and colonial overseers, most of these new colonial leaders do not even live anywhere near the plantations they are charged with running. And, bitter irony, these plantations of today are not as well run as many of the original estates. These minority kids are mostly out of sight and out of mind of their modern masters. They become visible only when they are killed and become the subject of front-page Chicago newspaper stories and even then the frequency of youth homicide is so great that many otherwise caring readers tune out after a while to the relentless accounts of child killings in Chicago.

Who are these new colonial masters? They are the black politicians who fight Chicago Housing Authority Chairman Vincent Lane's attempts to clean up the lethal environment of the "projects." They are the white suburban and downstate legislators who sustain a tax system that permits a wealthy suburb to invest $10,000 or more a year in the public education of kids who come from the most advantaged homes while investing half that amount in the Chicago public school system where 80 percent or more of the students come from homes under the poverty level. And the new colonial masters are the legislators in the city who, for obvious political reasons, support all of those who have an investment in resisting changes in union work rules which add millions and millions of dollars in school spending—dollars which otherwise could be spent on all the services and materials a deprived plantation school system so urgently needs. And these are the legislators who, when finally reluctantly agreeing to support changes in work rules, do so only while borrowing money now to pay for school operating expenses, thus once again loading up the Chicago public school system with a debt which inevitably will create a still worse financial crisis.

These new plantation managers think they can get away with their crimes. What they don't spend on education for inner-city schools, they try to make up for in spending on prisons for the human effluent of those schools. Those kids could go to Harvard for a year for the amount of money spent on keeping them in prison a year. These absentee leaders will tell you that they won't spend another dollar on the Chicago school system until it's cleansed of corruption and bureaucratic waste. But these are the same off-plantation managers who will support national political leaders who thought nothing of maintaining a huge wasteful military-industrial complex, a modern intelligence empire that consumes twenty-nine billion dollars a year, an agricultural subsidy scheme for the richest farmers and a middle-class welfare provision in the tax code called mortgage and real estate tax deductions. This sounds like a diatribe against the Republican leadership nationally, but it is not. The Democrats have and continue to do more than their share in perpetuating the new colonial subsidy for the great middle class. We all are on the take. And the kids in the inner cities be damned.

Maribeth Vander Weele blows the whistle on all of us. No one escapes her urgent, passionate, meticulous reporting. Her exposé of the colossal hypocrisy of the Illinois General Assembly's approach to school reform is both hilarious in a Menckenian way and heartbreaking. Unlike the state of Kentucky, the Illinois legislators did not accompany their school reform legislation with the necessary funding to ensure a shot at success. And unlike their Kentucky counterparts they did not establish an auditing and inspections system which would deal with the very bureaucratic corruption of which they never ceased to complain. In other words, they established school reform in such a way as to work for its failure. And believe me, many of these legislators want school reform in Chicago to fail so that they can confirm their worst prejudices, of which race is prominent.

As one who has been reporting on and discussing Chicago public school issues since 1957, I can admit to my own prejudices. I admit that when I finished reading this book I was overwhelmed by the multiplicity and complexity of the issues which need to be addressed and which frequently are not being addressed. I admit that I am sometimes reluctantly skeptical about even the best efforts of all of the corporations and foundations and other civic volunteer groups that have poured millions of dollars and thousands of hours into trying to help pull the Chicago public schools out of their quagmire. My skepticism is based on the notion that all of the hard work, good faith, real money efforts of these fine people only let the people who

really should be doing the work and the financing off the hook—
our legislators and ourselves, the taxpayers.

But skepticism aside, this book tells the enthralling story of
the politically revolutionary idea of giving power to people in hundreds of local schools so that they might begin to take destiny in
their own hands and improve their schools and save their children. This story gives great meaning to the contention that all politics is local. And at the same time, the story of Chicago school
reform truly is global. Anyone in Russia or Eastern Europe wondering how the roots of democracy are nourished should read this
book. Those roots, as this book makes clear, are fragile, as fragile
as trying to teach committed, but barely literate parents how to
use Roberts Rules of Order in a local school council meeting.

I write this not long after returning from a trip to South Africa.
Just as decades of state-sponsored apartheid may be coming to an
end in that country, the new government will be handed a generation of unschooled, unemployed, black youth. South Africa's
major cities are surrounded by black townships filled with these
gun-toting angry young men. Ask yourself how you would like
finally to win the right to democratic elections and then be handed
that time bomb as a reward for winning.

Maribeth Vander Weele, in heartbreaking detail, shows us the
time bomb we are building in our inner-city schools. Her account,
in my view, is entirely fair and balanced even while, I am sure, it is
fueled by an anger that no sensitive front-line reporter could deny.
The concrete suggestions that she asks our leaders to make in order
to ensure the success of the valiant efforts at Chicago school reform
must be followed or failure is guaranteed. As the world watches the
drama of Chicago school reform unfold, this book should be used
as a primary source of information on who the players in this drama
are and as a straightforward accounting of the complex educational,
social, political, racial, financial and historical ingredients of this
drama. For all of those who need an investigative and analytical tool
with which to press the case for school reform, this book is required.

47

⌒

Reflections on Herman Kogan

When the veteran Chicago newspaperman, author, historian and radio/television commentator Herman Kogan died in 1989, I was asked to speak at his memorial service at the Newberry Library in Chicago on April 14. I include first those comments, then my talk on June 2 at the Chicago Bar Association's first annual Herman Kogan Media Awards. I miss Herman more than ever in the relatively barren media landscape of Chicago.

You did not have to be Herman Kogan's best friend in order to feel the force of his personality and the impact of his life. Your own life was better off if you read what he wrote or listened to what he had to say on the air or had the privilege of his personal company for even a few minutes or a few hours. Even the briefest encounter with Herman could stay with you for the rest of your life.

Evidence of this is contained in a letter I received two days ago from my friend, Tom Hollatz, the former *Tribune* photographer who now enshrines geese and other beautiful objects with picture-taking from precincts in Boulder Junction, Wisconsin. Writes Tom: "Neil Milbert, the track writer, and I represented the *Tribune* at an Aaron Cushman media tennis event. Neil and I had a couple of glasses of champagne prior to the match—all in good spirit, of course. Our opponent was an 'old man' named Herman Kogan and his partner. Mind you, Neil and I are twenty years younger than 'old' Herman. The match began. We chuckled to each other that 'we'd cream' the *Sun-Times* guy. Our red *Tribune* T-shirts expanded with a pre-ordained victory pride. The bottom line— the 'old guy' Kogan and his partner killed us. I still wonder after all these years if we ever won a game. Never have I observed such a fire and intensity. I, too, salute his memory."

I was talking with Donal Henahan, now the distinguished music critic of the *New York Times,* who once wrote for Herman on the wonderful Panorama arts section of the *Chicago Daily News.* He said that as an editor, Herman's great gift was as a stimulator and a catalyst. "He got you juiced up and running," said Henahan. And then he reminded me that for years under the "14 W" formula under the late, great Stuffy Walters, *Daily News* writers were forbidden to construct sentences of more that fourteen words, resulting inevitably, of course, in the legendary lead sentence—"Dead. That's what Harvey Frobish is." But Donal Henahan says Herman came around to him one day and uttered to him the unthinkable. "Donal," he said, "you know it doesn't hurt to write a sentence *longer* than fourteen words." I can see Herman's sly grin now.

When I was a young man in this town, just out of the City News Bureau and over at CBS, I searched for mentors—people in the journalism racket who knew what it was to cover murders or fires but who had larger truths to report and concern themselves with. It wasn't long before I discovered Herman Kogan. I didn't become a buddy of his; he was in the big leagues and I was but a pup. But I would make it my business to read what he wrote, talk with some of the younger writers he edited and encouraged—in other words, to follow along in the wake of this totally unpretentious, humanly available great man who seemed to me to be a nurturer in a business filled otherwise with cynics, drunks, headline-chasers, non-readers, and womanizers. My own newspaperman father was hundreds of miles away and I needed a father-figure inspiration. There weren't but a handful and Herman was one of them and he was a standout.

Then one day several years later I had the pleasure of inviting Herman to work with us in public television. It was our old Public News Center—the children's crusade of Chicago broadcast journalism—eager, overly serious, intense, fumbling, somewhat pretentious, inexperienced, deeply caring, fun-loving and experimental. (For what is regarded by most as a failure of a television series, those aren't bad things to recall about it, are they?)

Anyway, Herman was one of our dozen commentators. When he showed up in our downtown studios I felt as if the captain of the ship had arrived, as if someone who was true at the center was in our presence. Herman, with his warmth, his deft scalpel of prose, his engaging smile, was everything television commentary should be and, with few exceptions, was not and is not. Herman wasn't slick, wasn't self-promoting, wasn't cute, wasn't grudging, wasn't nitpicking, wasn't theatrically bombastic, wasn't any of the things we've come to know and abhor about so much of television. Herman was a working newspaperman, critic, author and artist who walked across the bridge to our Michigan Avenue studios and delivered well-written, well-reasoned, straightforward, frequently humorous essays about the things he cared about—delivered in that lovely, resonant voice that conveyed the believability he personified. I hope for all of our sakes that television as a medium can some day rise to the level of Herman Kogan.

One personal footnote. One day, after the Kogans shuffled off to New Buffalo, Michigan, I received a letter from Herman. It was warm and it was respectful, but it kicked butt. "I don't know where you and the others came up with it, but the pronunciation is not MAY ORAL. It's mayoral. Please, John, do not contribute to this destruction of the language." I immediately corrected my pronunciation and even after Rick (Herman's son, who is the TV critic for the *Chicago Tribune*) wrote about the continuation of the use of the pronunciation MAY ORAL, I still hear too many of us using it in all of its pretentious intonations.

Herman's care for language is more than a footnote. It goes to the essence of who he was and what he stood for. We speak in our journalism of endangered species. Herman Kogan was such a rare gift of a man. I felt with Herman's passing the loneliness I felt when my own father died, when Edmund Wilson died. Who amongst us working stiffs will protect the tradition of letters and art? We mourn not just the loss of Herman Kogan, but also the loss of the tradition of intellectual, literary and artistic passion and expression tempered with street wisdom and city-room common sense and good humor. We mourn not only for Herman and his family, but for us and for our civilization.

48

❧

The "Profession" of Journalism

Remarks at the Chicago Bar Association's
First Annual Herman Kogan Media Awards, 1989

I'm deeply honored to be asked to speak at the Chicago Bar Association's first annual Herman Kogan Media Awards. I am honored not because I'm in love with awards but because anything I am asked to do in association with Herman Kogan's name and Herman Kogan's legacy is a privilege, however undeserved, for me.

I said my personal piece about Herman Kogan at the lovely memorial service for him at the Newberry Library on April 14 and I do not intend to use this time for another eulogy. I think if Herman were here he would agree that it's time we get on with it and use this occasion to take care of some business. But I do not think he would object if I use this occasion to comment on a few issues that should be of concern to journalists and lawyers and to all citizens who care about the things which Herman Kogan cared about and about which we should all care.

There is an irony which I see and which I want us to think about in the presentation of awards by a bar association organization to journalists. Journalists should particularly be aware of the irony. (No, the irony is not that an organization representing an institution which the press often investigates and sometimes exposes should turn around and congratulate the press for meritorious work. That is no more ironic than the press printing or broadcasting editorials, columns or commentaries which call attention to particularly meritorious work of the bar or the courts.) The irony which I see and which we don't often acknowledge is that a group of professionals—the bar association—is choosing to give awards to non-professionals. Non-professionals, you say? How dare you call us professional journalists "non-professionals!" Everyone who wins an award here today will see himself or herself every bit as professional as the lawyer who presents the award and the organization sponsoring the award.

We who are journalists may act professionally, but we are not in what normally is considered a profession. There are no educational requirements for entry into our workplace—nothing required, that is, by law—and there are no certification tests for admittance. We can't be certified even if we wish to take the test. (I note that some journalists are so hungry for certification that they make an end run and obtain a law degree and perhaps gain admission to the bar. Good for them.) We have no official peer review that scrutinizes our professional behavior or sanctions us. We depend on voluntary acceptance of national journalism organizations' codes of ethics, and we feel more bound to and/or threatened by the guidelines of our own commercial or non-commercial institutions than anything else, short of libel laws and public disapproval. In other words, we are crafts people who aspire to professional behavior in the absence of professional certification and professional discipline even as we toil in the vineyards of the only commercial enterprise specifically protected by the Constitution.

So what does that have to do with awards? Or with irony? Simply this: even though we journalists some days can't get any work done because we are so busy dealing with award presentations or award acceptances or drinking away the depression that accompanies losing a much-coveted award, we really tend to forget that awards, however exploitative or arbitrary or undeserved they *some-times* can be, are, at their best, devices intended to convey some sense of professionalism in an occupation which is not a profession in the sense that law and medicine are professions. And so the irony is that the law profession is trying to help the journalism craft be as professional as it can be in the absence of the usual professional norms and standards.

So you might say, okay, awards are a minor part of an informal process of professionalism for a non-profession which seeks to be seen as professional. We all know that. I don't think we in journalism really see it that way. I think we believe that we are a profession even in the absence of the professional standards lawyers and doctors must meet. I think we look at these awards as public relations shots which help our careers, our salaries and our relations with the boss even as they fill a shelf or two at home. We don't really take awards seriously as professional certification (1) because we know there are so many phony awards and (2) because we either don't care about professionalism or arrogantly and incorrectly assume we have it.

I recently spent five years in a part-time position in which we gave out awards. (I have since returned to direct the program.) These were cash awards amounting to more than a million dollars in five years to journalists who were accepted into the William Benton Fellowships Program in Broadcast Journalism at the University of Chicago. And we gave those Fellows more than another million dollars' worth of free tuition, seminars, trips abroad and other educational niceties. Those who won the fellowships were most grateful and constantly report back to us that the months they spent away from deadline pressure at the University of Chicago have added immeasurably to their ability to be professional journalists. But you should know that their employers were not always so grateful. Some employers would not let go of their people even for six months or nine months. Other employers were begrudging about giving their reporters or producers a leave of absence. Why? "Because the ratings sweeps period is coming up and we need you here." "If I, the news director, can be fired if we get another bad ratings book, how can you possibly expect me to let you, one of my best foot soldiers, go off to the University of Chicago for several months of scholarship and reflection?"

One of the things that I learned during my years as director of the William Benton Fellowships Program is that those who applied for the fellowships and those who won them, were deeply, urgently, almost desperately serious about being professional and about being taken seriously as professionals. Those who worked for commercial operations lamented that their managements all too often used them in *infotainment,* ratings-seeking approaches to news which diminished them as professionals and as human beings. These were and are mid-career journalists who were keenly sensitive to the fact that they worked for a constitutionally protected business which hid behind constitutional protection when necessary and which avoided responsible journalism in the pursuit of higher audiences and revenues. Imagine what it would take for the managements of American broadcast operations to be professional enough to see the value, the long-term value, of mid-career education for their journalists. I can only hope that the Benton Fellows of today become the managers and owners of media tomorrow so that we can watch them test their professional and intellectual ideals against the rigors of the marketplace forces.

I mention the desirability of ongoing education as an aspect of professionalism on this occasion because, as Richard Christiansen so eloquently noted at the Newberry Library memorial for Herman Kogan, Herman not only was a newspaperman, broadcaster, author, critic and editor; he also was a teacher. He was an educated man himself in the very richest sense of the word *education*—well schooled at the University of Chicago and steeped in the experience and knowledge of the institutions, people and streets of this world. And like any great professional, he was a master teacher, a giver, a leader who made those around him want to do better and be better.

Herman Kogan was that rare journalist who knew that men

and women alone are not enough; that we need institutions in our lives. He knew more than most journalists the role institutions play in professionalism and in the stability of our lives generally in the republic. It may have been his book on the first century of the Chicago Bar Association, or his book on the history of Marshall Field's, or his books dealing with the history of this city of Chicago, but Herman Kogan dedicated a major part of his life to the proposition that institutions are worth investigating, celebrating and remembering. That, in my view, is worth remembering during this week when we saw the institution of the House of Representatives of the United States shellshocked by the resignation of the Speaker and of Congressman Cuelho. There is a sort of everyone-for-himself-or-his-party thing going on in Washington and it may not be good for a country which is diverted enough already from the serious discussion and contemplation of public policy. And the press must ask itself what grades it gives itself on its role in reporting on ethical questions in Washington. Are we pleased professionally that we ask a United States senator if he has been unfaithful to his wife?

So, to summarize, the best of journalists, the people you honor today, are known as real professionals ... real "pros" even as they labor in a field which can't be called a profession because of the constitutional protections which prevent government certification. We can give and receive awards. We can go back to school. We can improve our company's ethical standards and practices book. We can make our national journalistic organization guidelines more binding. We could even give rebirth to a National News Council. But in the end, given the freedom we are saddled and blessed with, it will be the Herman Kogans of this world who will make us more professional, better read, more sensitive to the role of institutions, better equipped with the gift of simple, straightforward language— the last attribute being one I hope lawyers will also cherish.

There will never be another Herman Kogan, but I hope the example he set for all of us who survive him will help foster the values he exemplified and the excellence he achieved.

49

⁓

Call It Blue Leather ...
10 P.M. News in Chicago

*This piece was assigned after Herman Kogan's son,
Rick, the TV critic for the* Chicago Tribune, *wrote a
scathing essay on the putrid state of the 10 P.M. commercial television newscasts in Chicago. Since the 10
P.M. news is an institution locked into the schedules
of millions of Chicagoans, Rick Kogan's commentary
caused no little stir. The editors of the* Chicago Journalist, *a publication of the local branch of the national
Society of Professional Journalists, asked me to comment on the 10 P.M. news squabble.*

About seventeen years ago, when we were struggling with
the development of the Channel 11 Public News Center as
an alternative to local commercial news, my boss Bill McCarter
and I had many discussions about what was and what wasn't
"news." Bill wanted to present something on Channel 11 which
had relevance to viewers but which did more than show them
pictures of murders and fires and reported more than ball scores
and weather.

During one of those conversations, McCarter said to me, "You know, what I saw last night at ten o'clock on Channel 2 wasn't really news. I don't know what you would call it, call it anything you want—blue leather—but it wasn't news." And then he went on to say that the CBS News special that came on at 10:30 that night on the sentencing of some Watergate burglars, with detailed reportage and analysis, seemed to him to be the real "news" broadcast that night on WBBM-TV. Bill McCarter was on years ago to the fact that the 10 P.M. "news" isn't the news. And that was at a time when, in my view, the ten o'clock news was in much better shape than it is in Chicago today.

McCarter saw what came on at ten o'clock more as a kind of "family" half-hour program where, at that time, Big Brother Bill Kurtis and his little brother Walter—a cute scamp of a kid—would tell us some items in such an engaging way that we could get to sleep and get up again tomorrow and get through the day. He saw the personality-driven presentation as a kind of "comfort station."

Yes, the phrase "ten o'clock news" is an insidious oxymoron like "presidential debates." There are a few exchanges at presidential "debates" and there is some news on the ten o'clock news, but that's not the point of the ten o'clock news.

The point of the ten o'clock news is to provide a family of performers who will present infotainment compelling enough to provide an environment where a huge number of high-priced commercials can be broadcast. These commercials will enable the company-owned network stations to continue to be the cash cows they have always been and continue to be for the revenue-starved parent networks. Any journalistic seriousness and excellence which appear on those programs do so only at the mercy of personality and entertainment values that will make attractive environments for those advertisers.

Therefore, if you think of the ten o'clock news as a commercials festival which provides a big boost for the local GNP and employment for hundreds if not thousands of "journalists" and advertising people and others who labor in the vineyards of television production, then you will have internalized the right way to view what is on at ten o'clock.

It will only get worse before it gets better. I said that the company-owned stations were cash cows. That is still true, but less true than some years ago when they ran profit margins of 35 to 40 percent or higher. Now, as viewing of networks declines, the viewing of network-owned stations also declines and the pressure is on to do anything necessary to grab viewers from the competition. Enter Bill Applegate at Channel 2 with his tabloid news format.

Nobody does it better than Applegate. His sense of flash and trash news is every bit as good as any of the old Hearst newspaper editors. I hate to live in a city without a really hot tabloid newspaper. I miss the *New York Post* and *Daily News*—the *Sun-Times* is by comparison a truly mature, responsible and public policy-oriented newspaper.

So, at a time when you can get your news straight and sober from CNN, all-news radio, the *Tribune,* the *Sun-Times,* the *New York Times,* the *Wall Street Journal,* MacNeil/Lehrer, etc., who wants to moan about Channel 2's "top story" breathless format? Only if you are the relative of a victim of something like the West Side gas explosion and are run down and run over by Applegate's terrifying field reporters do you have a right to complain. Otherwise, you are absolutely free to switch to the relative sanity of what Channels 5 and 7 now present on their ten o'clock programs, if you haven't had the good sense to watch WGN-TV's excellent nine o'clock news first. My heart goes out to Bill and Linda who have to be the front people for Applegate's tabloid approach, but I'm sure that discomforting situation will be resolved some time in the future and Mr. Applegate will be able to entertain us with front men and women who really believe in his brand of first-class sensationalism. In many respects, Applegate is the only honest operator at ten o'clock. His brand of news is perfect for the values of that hour and he shouldn't apologize for it or be asked to apologize for it. By the way, there is a bit of irony here. In the midst of his huffing and puffing approach to news, Applegate usually manages to put together a team which is very adept at covering late-breaking spot news. If it is important that you get your news first—and for most of us, it is *not* important—Mr. Applegate's troop often delivers. He and they also tend to deliver higher ratings.

Yes, Rick Kogan is right on target. The ten o'clock news is dying. It will go on for years, but significant numbers of us huddled masses who used to watch it religiously are opting out. As Kogan says, most of us watch it out of habit, not out of some real need.

It is heartbreaking to see some forms of journalism disappear. Those great photographs in *Life* magazine in the 1940s had an editorial and artistic integrity that theoretically could have lasted for centuries. The old *Life* magazine didn't die because it wasn't fundamentally wonderful. It died because we changed. With the advent of television we no longer stood by the door looking at the cream rise out of the frozen milk bottle on the front porch while waiting for the postman to bring us the latest issue of *Life*. We may someday witness the passing of great magazines such as *The New Yorker,* where book-length reporting somehow survives.

But isn't it good that while we may have to suffer the decline and fall of some journalistic forms we loved and respected, others, like the ten o'clock news, will not be inflicted upon us forever. We will someday view those old ten o'clock news programs in the Museum of Broadcast Communications and we will either laugh, or cringe with embarrassment, or both. And to all of those who have to produce and report on those programs and try to fit reality and complexity within their unforgiving confines, my heart goes out to you—I did it once and am overjoyed to be relieved of doing it now. May you all be liberated soon.

50

❧

Reflections on Chicago, August 1968

In 1968 I helped lead WBBM radio into becoming the second CBS-owned radio station to switch to an all-news format. We could not have chosen a more timely year in which to go all news. Martin Luther King and Robert Kennedy were assassinated that year, the USSR invaded Czechoslovakia and the anti-Vietnam and hippie movements collided with old-time politics at the Democratic National Convention in Chicago. Most major radio station news directors would, appropriately, have stayed inside the station and directed their news-gathering efforts from a desk. But Van Gordon Sauter, whom I had appointed managing editor after having hired him as a national correspondent, asked me, given my twelve years of street reporting in Chicago, to hit the streets and report the convention from as many perspectives as possible. It was the most complex, frightening assignment of my career—a career which had included coverage of several race riots. Ten days after the convention, on a

Sunday evening, I obtained station management approval to broadcast what in those days was an almost unheard of thing—a thirty-minute essay with no sound bites. It received a very big response from listeners, pro and con. I remember years later that every time I would interview Mayor Harold Washington of Chicago, he would tell me before the program that my essay on the Democratic National Convention of 1968 was his favorite piece of radio and would I please give him a tape of it. I regret that I never was able to find the tape and give it to him before his untimely death.

Several years ago, in a hiatus of a few months from my labors here at CBS, I was associated with a local magazine that sought to report the life and times of the city of Chicago. The editors and writers of the magazine spent quite a long time debating and re-debating what they thought the image—the identity of purpose of the magazine—should be. And thus we spent a corresponding amount of time arguing over our various perceptions of what the city of Chicago was in reality.

I can recall one long session in which one faction of the group argued that basically the city of Chicago was a provincial, unsophisticated, uncultured, brute political force-dominated city which deserved nothing more than continual exposé, satire and put-down. Others contended that Chicago was an especially beautiful city with human resources and institutional achievements that desperately deserved to be confirmed and affirmed.

And then there were those meek and timid among us who saw the city as a complicated, beautiful, ugly, lovely, brutal, swinging, square and otherwise undefinable assortment of human beings and their works. I, for example, was reckless enough to confess before that highly critical accumulation of editorial minds that I was hopelessly in love with the city but that my affection for Chicago was so miscellaneous, so off-beat, so personal that it escaped me how we could ever translate that love into any particular, unified, definable editorial policy. How could you tell a reader that his was a great city because you dearly loved to walk down Wabash Avenue on a Saturday night listening to the sound of a trumpet emanating from a girlie joint mixed with the sound of an elevated train overhead? Everybody knows trumpets are too loud, girlie joints aren't nice and the elevated an outdated, congestive, unmodern form of transportation. It would become all too clear to our readers that if that were an example of my love for the city, this magazine was in deep trouble.

How could you ever affirm an editorial policy that would include in it your deep feeling of affection for sergeants at the Englewood station who, despite what would be viewed as their inherent racism and insensitivity, still opened themselves up to you as human beings with great needs and great possibilities? How could you create a slick, modern, sophisticated magazine and still celebrate the things and people in your experiences in Chicago who were not slick, modern and sophisticated? The barn boss at County Jail. The traffic judge on the take in the Central Office building at 321 North LaSalle. The gruff starter at the first tee on the Waveland Municipal Golf Course. The guy who got coffee for the boys in the County Building Press Room—his name was Frank. The girl who walked holding hands with you in Grant Park. The bartender on Oak Street who was heralded as America's foremost critic of class B and C movies. The crazy county official who was so delightfully defensive when you even said a cheerful "Good morning."

These human beings and a thousand others were my Chicago. They were my reason for staying here year after year while others opted for suburbs and exurbs. But I was stumped as to how you could create a magazine editorial identity on such a mixed grab bag of perceptions, emotions and experiences.

Well, that part of my story tonight is academic because for one or a number of reasons the magazine failed. But during the past ten days I thought of those editorial identity arguments we had many times as I heard journalists who had spent anywhere from a lifetime to only a week in this city define it in a single lead sentence as sick ... or brutal ... or a police state. No complications, no millions of different personalities and experiences serve as a brake on their perceptions. It is all clear to them. Chicago is rotten. From 138th Street on the South to Howard Street on the North to Pueblo on the West to good old polluted Lake Michigan on the East. Rotten.

Well, I too have called this city rotten. You come in off the street from a slum fire that kills four babies and their mother and you want to cry "Rotten!" What is it that permits persons to be consumed in fire? What human beings and what systems abound? Upon reflection, they are the same human beings and systems that have provided millions of the living with opportunities for health, employment, free expression, fruitful experience and nearly unlimited development. And, sure, the city was a police state to me the night I wanted to inspect the ruins of a burned-out building but the cops and firemen wouldn't let me in. I muttered about curtailment of free inquiry and was quite angry with the authorities until the ceiling of the first floor of the building collapsed ten minutes later and I realized that the so-called police state cops had saved my life.

And so on this Sunday evening, ten days after the conclusion of the Democratic National Convention in Chicago, the controversy continues to simmer and flare and you're either against Mayor Daley and his cops or you're 100 percent behind them. It's either a police state like Prague or the world's greatest city with the world's greatest newspaper.

I know that it's going to be a long, cold winter alone, but you'll excuse me from all that company.

Let me recount for you what I saw prior to and during those days of the Democratic convention.

And let me confess to you that this report will not be the whole truth and nothing but the truth. Within the limits of human perception of one reporter that is impossible. And within the limits of what is described as conventional decency it is impossible. That is to say that the foul and unacceptable language used by demonstrators, police, reporters and others will probably be reported to you in later years in fiction if not now in fact. We would not bother to inform you of the obscenity absent from our reports except that to understand the impact of the verbal horror of these days and nights you almost had to be there.

Thousands used publicly, and sometimes in unison, words previously reserved for abundant and often cheerful distribution in locker rooms, back alleys, rest room walls, modern novels and private conversation.

The uniqueness of it all was to be seen not in the words themselves but in the mindless, hateful, irrational brutality of the public unleashing of them. As in the Bunyan story, it was as if the previously frozen air had thawed in the stink-bomb and tear-gassed nights and the words revealed themselves in all their graceless form and content.

And it must be said that even with the swinging of nightsticks, the screaming of those struck, the blood pouring out of a gash in a policeman's head, a demolished squad car back window and countless other memories of actual violence of the days and nights of convention week, the passionate use of words and symbols, the metaphors that abounded are starkest in recollection.

For example, on the Saturday night before the convention began we drove to the far South Side and confirmed reports that Dr. Martin Luther King Drive street signs had been defaced by white paint on several blocks of the predominantly white neighborhood between 107th and 114th streets.

On the Sunday night and afternoon before the convention we spent several hours in black belt communities around 42nd and Cottage Grove and recorded the voices of many who spoke of hav-

ing little or nothing to do with the powerful events that would
shake Chicago and the world in coming days. Many expressed the
feeling that what happened in the Amphitheater was irrelevant to
their lives, to their problems or to their possibilities. The recollection of that grim witness of mere words is still as powerful to
us as the more obvious physical conflict that followed during the
convention nights. And it must be added that our conversations
and recordings of that Sunday afternoon in the black belt were not
flash-in-the-pan pre-convention reporting. They were but one
more confirmation of reporting experiences in that area over a
twelve-year period.

On Monday night, having just heard the mayor's speech about
how proud he was to hold the Democratic convention in his own
neighborhood, we decided to visit his neighborhood once again
even while the convention proceeded at the Amphitheater. Upon
reflection, the idea for that story is a bit cute, a bit contrived but
the experience of talking with people in the mayor's neighborhood that night was real and became a meaningful event for a
reporter. We talked with a wide variety of people. Those of you
who heard our tapes will recall that you heard proud people, inse-
cure people, people sociologists would term "working class," people the Kerner Commission reporters would call "white racists."
But they were complicated people. One man we talked with burst
with fairness and the desire to be understood even as he spoke
words that revealed his doubts about living peacefully with black
persons.

And who knows, maybe this man's brother or his friend had
been among those of the so-called working-back-of-the-yards class
that attended the Czechoslovakian freedom rally the previous Saturday afternoon at the Civic Center Plaza. I could recall talking
with people at that rally who saw black men as threats in Chicago,
but who came to protest the Soviet takeover of Czechoslovakia. It
was a bewildering series of recollections for those of us who rou-
tinely walk many different streets and neighborhoods of the city.

People earnestly concerned with freedom, but defining freedom in so many ways. Walking into the bar just half a block from the mayor's house and seeing the bartender harshly condemn Julian Bond and make strong comments about all black persons. But remembering even more vividly the people in that bar talking about how they didn't understand what they were seeing on the TV screen. What were those speeches about and what was everybody voting no for? And remembering what absolute pride these neighbors had in Mayor Daley.

One man spoke of the fact that he had to go to the Criminal Courts building the next day to face a burglary charge. He asserted that he was innocent but he said he held little hope for acquittal. He said he had no defense witnesses, poor counsel and thus fully expected to go to prison for at least a year. This man spoke not, however, of a police state but of what fine things Mayor Daley and Alderman Matt Danaher had done for the Eleventh Ward. And he added that he had no idea whatsoever what the meanings of events were on the screen from the televised proceedings of the Democratic convention.

I thought of this man's rather placid acceptance of his probable place in prison as I drove away from Bridgeport that Monday evening. Our managing editor had asked me to drive north to the Old Town area and join our reporters who were covering the conflict between the demonstrators in Lincoln Park and the police in the area.

My only previous experience of such coverage was the night before when I had driven into the Old Town area to report on demonstrators who had been driven out of the park and reportedly were moving south on Wells Street. At just a block north of Division, on Wells Street, the traffic in front of me stopped and soon I discovered why. Hundreds of the demonstrators were walking right down Wells Street, chanting and pounding on the hoods of automobiles, and flashing the V sign with their fingers. They pounded on my car, cursed me after seeing the press credentials and insisted that I honk my car horn. In two or three minutes the bulk of them had passed by and the rear was brought up by a contingent of walking policemen. At the time I was curious as to why the policemen were in the rear. I remember wanting them to be a little closer to the front where I had been received with such vigorous words and gestures from the marchers.

And so on that next Monday evening, having driven from the mayor's neighborhood to the Near North Side of Chicago, I parked on LaSalle Street not far from where the demonstrators were holding a traffic jam-up rally in the intersection of Clark and LaSalle streets. They apparently had been driven from nearby Lincoln Park by the police. It was well after eleven o'clock and the police were determined to enforce the park closing time of eleven o'clock.

The demonstrators milled around the intersection. Traffic was piling up. A number of the cars were honking in unison. Residents of nearby apartment buildings opened windows and complained that their children couldn't sleep because of the noise. Cherry bombs were thrown. Two police cars appeared to be surrounded by demonstrators. The police projected tear gas canisters and dispersed the mob at the intersection. They came streaming south on LaSalle Street. Hundreds ran westward toward Wells Street. Others ran south on Clark Street. It was a scene of much running, cursing, chanting, chasing.

For the better part of the next hour I observed the activities of police as they attempted to disperse and control the thousands of demonstrators who previously had been encamped in Lincoln Park that Monday evening. I was standing at an outdoor phone station talking with my office with a clear view of North and LaSalle streets. Suddenly the area would be relatively quiet. Two minutes later, dozens of the demonstrators would be chased east on North Avenue directly past me ... the police pursuing them, cursing them with nightsticks raised over their heads. The demonstrators used the strongest, most obscene language on the police. The police caught some of them and put them under arrest. The police caught others and several beat them with nightsticks and then left them on the ground.

At one point, as I stood talking with my office and police were chasing demonstrators directly past me, two officers with night-sticks looked severely at me from a few feet away. I merely stopped talking for a moment, turned toward the phone booth and watched them go on by. I had no recorder or helmet or gas mask and was dressed in a very conservative gray suit and kept totally alone as best I could while out on the street. At no time during that night while walking on Wells, North, LaSalle or Clark Street was I advised to get off the street by policemen. It was this same evening that several reporters alleged that they had been beaten by police in or near the Lincoln Park-Old Town area.

It was an evening of great confusion. I can vividly recall policemen trying to regroup at North and LaSalle and trying to decide which direction they should go next in pursuing the demonstrators. I can recall many trashcans in the area set on fire and overturned into the streets. I can remember driving down LaSalle Street at about 1:30 that Tuesday morning and suddenly seeing demonstrators chased off Burton Place into LaSalle where many of them were severely beaten by police and left on the pavement.

Those recollections of confusion and confrontation differ sharply from the experience of walking up and down Michigan Avenue across the street from the Conrad Hilton Hotel on Tues-day evening: thousands of demonstrators milling in the park across from the hotel; the police and later the National Guard standing in front of them on the sidewalk. I remember that despite the hours of provocation, name-calling, and chanting of obscenities, the police were cool and the atmosphere almost friendly. High police officials that evening said things like, "Well, let 'em stay in the park. Let 'em have their fun." That was said well after the eleven o'clock closing time. One remembered the previous nights of enforce-ment in Lincoln Park.

But the chanting of obscenities continued hour after hour into Wednesday morning and the mood changed. At a little after three o'clock, the National Guard sent in troops to replace the Chicago policemen who had been on duty for at least fourteen hours.

Late on Wednesday afternoon I arrived at the Grant Park band shell in time to hear the finishing touches of a long series of speeches by those who say this country is a basically corrupt land worthy only of a serious, basic, revolution. The tones I heard were strident, haranguing. The facts were absent in many cases and the views of the nation terribly oversimplified. The totally dark picture of the nation painted by those orators would be recalled in future days as one read or heard the totally dismal account of Chicago rendered by others.

The speeches were followed by more than an hour and a half of attempts by the demonstrators to march out of the Grant Park area. They were surrounded by the National Guard and the Chicago police. A scene of confrontation. In the midst of it I shall never forget a handsome young couple playing tennis in the Grant Park tennis courts just across the street from this setting that would become an indelible part of American history. I talked with them. They said they had both worked hard in the campaign for McCarthy but now it was time to play tennis and so they played. As they played an ice cream vendor sold his goods to spectators on Columbus Drive.

Finally, the demonstrators began to move north on Columbus Drive to try to get back over to Michigan Avenue. Thousands succeeded in doing so, but not before some arrests had been made and two more tear gas canisters used on them as they attempted to cross over to Michigan at Congress Parkway.

Once again at Michigan and Congress Parkway there was one of those ironic touches that swell up in the memory more prominently than other, more violent, occurrences. It was a little past 7:30. The sun was going down on what was an absolutely lovely August evening, one of those evenings you would have loved to listen to a Grant Park concert or walk among the flowers of that lovely place. The Buckingham Fountain was spurting in all its glory. And from somewhere appeared two young men and their young women dates. Beautifully dressed, beautiful kids. Tanned. Intelligent faces. *New Yorker* ad material. Straight out of Brooks Brothers and *Vogue*. They walked, hand in hand, right up to the National Guardsmen who formed a line blocking all movement east to west on Congress Parkway. One guardsman, himself a handsome, extremely reasonable-looking young man, apologetically told the four youngsters they would have to proceed up the cinder path north another block or two if they wanted to cross over to Michigan Avenue. They replied that they were on their way to attend Mayor Daley's concert being held that evening at the Auditorium. The guardsman nodded his head that he understood, but he was sorry—they could not cross. And so they backed off and walked north on the cinder path that runs parallel to the Illinois Central railroad. I followed them and soon found myself back on Michigan Avenue near the Sheraton-Blackstone Hotel.

By that time the tear gas that had been propelled at Congress Parkway had caught a westbound wind and had penetrated into the Hilton Hotel and into the room of Vice President Humphrey.

When I returned to Michigan Avenue the demonstrators were staging a stand-up and sit-down in the middle of the street just north of Balbo and Michigan. Rocks and bottles and nails and a wide variety of other objects were thrown at policemen. I saw one policeman's face cut open with a rock. I saw another policeman's shirt ripped off his back. I saw the entire back window of a squad car bricked out. The confrontations were rapid and violent. Missiles were thrown from the group into the police. The police charged in, made arrests. Some used nightsticks and used them vigorously. Others slammed those they arrested into police vans.

Finally, the police formed a concerted line and began pushing the crowd north on Michigan in an attempt to clear the street. The demonstrators retreated violently. When a rock hit a policeman or a policeman fell, the demonstrators cheered. It was at this point that a policeman at the rear of the police line turned around and warned those of us in the news media to get off the street at once. And so I retreated to a phone booth at the Sheraton-Blackstone to report at least what I had seen up to that moment.

Later I circled the block and could see some of the demonstrators running away from Michigan Avenue down streets like Jackson. The officers chased them and some policemen again severely struck with nightsticks those they caught.

Later, thousands of demonstrators recongregated in front of the Hilton Hotel and remained there until dawn.

On Thursday afternoon I arrived back in the Grant Park area in front of the Conrad Hilton shortly after four o'clock. As our car circled the area it finally pulled up at Ninth and Michigan where we could get a good view of the demonstrators who had encamped on the small hill which supports the statue of General Logan. At this time a most curious event occurred. A plainclothesman who identified himself as William Murphy began taking notes on the identification of our vehicle. I asked him why and he replied it was because he had seen someone leaving the vehicle carrying fascist signs. I reported to the officer that no such activity had occurred and that he was seriously mistaken. However, he kept taking notes on the automobile—which happens to be an unmarked WBBM mobile unit—and I returned to a live broadcast which had been scheduled from the unit at that very moment. After the live report, I discussed the matter further with the policeman. I gave him my business card, and offered to discuss his allegations either there on the spot or at his earliest convenience. He then said that there were no allegations being made and that he was acting only on information that someone else had given him. He then walked away into the huge crowd gathered on Michigan Avenue. He took with him an old press vehicle credential which had been in the mobile unit.

A few minutes later we walked over among the demonstrators in the park and listened to them as they cheered the arrival of Senator McCarthy. It was here that Senator McCarthy was to make his major address following his defeat the previous night at the nominating convention. The senator opened by welcoming his people and government "in exile." That received tumultuous applause.

At that moment, one forgot about the violence and obscenity that so many in this gathering of demonstrators had engaged in the previous days and nights. At that moment, one was inclined to think that perhaps love and peace were the main impetus of this group. But that illusion was sharply flattened within seconds as some among them began to scream angrily at the senator when he spoke of being a part of the traditional political process in this country, when he spoke of trying to get more senators like Morse of Oregon into the U.S. Senate. They screamed at him to announce formation of a fourth political party. And he did not. Finally, the senator finished his speech and turned the bullhorn mike over to the poet Robert Lowell. Mr. Lowell read two of his anti-war poems to the thousands sitting and standing on the grass in the park that beautiful, sunny afternoon. And when that was over they united to march south out of the park to Michigan Avenue, past 12th Street on down to 16th, where they were met and turned back by a powerful force of National Guardsmen and police.

Later that evening they regrouped under the leadership of Dick Gregory and proceeded to march out of the park south on Michigan again. Mr. Gregory said he was just taking 5,000 folk home to Hyde Park for dinner. He said a man ought to be able to take folks home for dinner in a free country. The authorities thought otherwise and brought the proceedings to a halt at 18th and Michigan. I will not soon forget the scene of Dick Gregory conferring with Deputy Superintendent Rochford and National Guard General Dunn at the intersection of 18th and Michigan. Armed guardsmen surrounded them as they talked in an earnest, but entirely friendly manner. It somehow resembled the scene at a football game when the team captain is surrounded by referees who are offering him a difficult set of penalty options.

Mr. Gregory refused a compromise offer that he be permitted to walk home with a small number of persons. He opted for jail. And soon he and a large number of others were led into police vans and hauled away to 11th and State for processing. The vast majority of those placed in vans at 18th and Michigan were led there and placed into the vehicles gently.

Minutes later, however, the crowd surged forward into the line of National Guardsmen and the demonstrators were repelled with bayonets and tear gas. The authorities reported that as the crowd surged forward in the initial clash some among them sprayed guardsmen with a fluid that caused a burning sensation.

The demonstrators were tear-gassed and moved back into Grant Park. Later, from the CBS newsroom on the fifth floor of the Hilton, I observed them singing and chanting. Across from me in the newsroom, a color TV monitor showed Mr. Humphrey's acceptance speech in the Amphitheater. Downstairs the corridors of the Hilton reeked with the stench of stink bombs.

Those are just some of the recollections of this reporter who spent most of the time in the streets of Chicago during the convention.

After all of this and after having had some time to reflect on these events, I have come to at least one conclusion—there is a great deal more to be learned about the real ingredients that fueled these events.

We know considerably less than we like to think we know about young people who participated in the demonstrations, or about the many over twenty-one who participated. During this piece tonight, I referred over and over again to "the demonstrators" as though they were one definable body of human beings. Some were pacifists; others were violent. Some may have been pacifists who turned violent during the week. Some were radicals with a program; others pursued confrontation almost as an art form—passion without politics, confrontation without content—existentially winging it in front of TV cameras, almost as a tribute to McLuhan.

And the police and guardsmen? Who were they? Who are they? Just faces behind bayonets and gas masks? Just men with nightsticks raised? Are they, as Richard Rovere concluded in his *New Yorker* magazine essay this week, just men who would beat demonstrators but not beat their own neighbors if the demonstrators had been permitted to walk through Bridgeport or Back of the Yards? Can we lump them all together in their talent, their experience, their discipline? Or out of a force of more than 12,000 men are there those who are corrupt but not representative of the mass; those who are brutal but not representative of the mass? What are the hopes and fears and aspirations of Chicago policemen? What do they go home to at night? When they fail, why do they fail and when they succeed can we ever record it? Can we ever record the achievements of honorable and decent policemen or will our perception always focus on the moment of raised nightsticks?

These are some of the questions still with this reporter. They are questions that may defy answering through the media of mass communication.

The limits of conventional journalism were once commented upon by an older correspondent who also reported at this convention. His words, which were broadcast near the end of World War II, may have their application at this time in our lives. He wrote:

> Only the soldier really lives the war. The journalist does not. He may share the soldier's outward life and dangers, but he cannot share his inner life because the same moral compulsion does not bear upon him. The observer knows he has alternatives of action; the soldier knows he has none. It is the mere knowing which makes the difference. Their worlds are very far apart, for one is free, the other is a slave.
>
> This war must be seen to be believed, but it must be lived to be understood. We can tell you only of events, of what men do. We can see, and tell you, that this war is brutalizing some among

your sons and yet ennobling others. We can tell you very little more. War happens inside a man. It happens to one man alone. It can never be communicated. That is the tragedy—and perhaps the blessing. A thousand ghastly wounds are really only one. A million martyred lives leave an empty place at only one family table. This is why, at bottom, people can let wars happen, and that is why nations survive them and carry on. And, I am sorry to say, that is also why in a certain sense, you and your sons from the war will be forever strangers. If, by the miracles of art and genius, in later years, two or three among them can open their ears and the right words come, then perhaps we shall all know a little of what it was like. And we shall know, then, that all the present speakers and writers hardly touched the story.

Those are the words of a man whose own reporting during the past days in Chicago is the subject of controversy—Eric Sevareid.

The other quotation which I would like to share with you for the conclusion of this piece comes from Murray Kempton, as quoted in *Time* magazine after Senator Robert Kennedy had been assassinated. Mr. Kempton had written a highly critical profile of Senator Kennedy which appeared in *Esquire* magazine just before the senator's death. In reflecting on his attack on Senator Kennedy, Mr. Kempton wrote:

Our politicians are just too vulnerable to be thought of in the old callous way. We must see them in life as we would in the shock of death when we would be conscious only of the good in them. The language of dismissal becomes horrible once you recognize the shadow of death over every public man. For I had forgotten, from being bitter about a temporary course of his, how much I liked Senator Kennedy and how much he needed to know he was liked. Now that there is in life no road at whose turning we could meet again, the memory of having forgotten will always make me sad and indefinitely make me ashamed.

It is not inconceivable that those words have application to the treatment of cities as well as of the men and women who live in them.

The reporter or citizen who bothers to walk with the people of this city and talk with them will come away over the years with the full swell of feelings—pride, despair, anger, contentment, amusement and all the rest. And somewhere in this city, there is perhaps a novelist or a poet or a playwright who can take up these matters in proper time and succeed where flashy columns, quick documentaries, indignant editorials, oversimplified film or cute comments have failed. *This is John Callaway for Newsradio 78.*

The Problem Society

51

The Problem Society

The late James Baldwin, in one of his most memorable essays, wrote, "I am not a problem, I am a man." It was Baldwin's way of saying that he would not be reduced to the identity-smashing, dehumanizing level of sociological jargon, statistical analysis or political rhetoric. He did not want to be a part of what then, in the 1950s and early 60s, was described by academics and journalists as "our Negro problem." Baldwin demanded to be acknowledged and treated as an individual human being.

James Baldwin got his say, but he did not get his way. He, along with the rest of us, has become a "problem." We live in "the Problem Society." This is not so much a lament as a clinical description of how we often organize our thoughts about ourselves and how we organize action to develop what we perceive to be our needs. My dictionary's first two definitions of the word *problem* are: (1) any question or matter involving doubt, uncertainty or difficulty and (2) a question proposed for solution or discussion. It is the latter definition which drives most of our social, scientific and political lives today.

We can think of our society as a huge hotel called Complexity and within its thousands upon thousands of rooms reside the people of the Problem Society. In the big, basement ballrooms of Hotel Complexity thousands of people work on the major problems—war, peace, starvation, religious strife, nationalism, ethnic

hostility, post-Cold War dislocations, global warming, global unemployment, all the major health issues, racism, sexism, illiteracy,
violent crime, homelessness and economic anemia, just to mention a few.

Upstairs, in the thousands of smaller, individual suites and
rooms, the residents of Hotel Complexity work on the really specialized problems such as debating the equipment standards established by the International Electrotechnical Commission or coping
with the widespread radioactive contamination of American oil
fields. On the main floor of the hotel are located the desks where
the problem people check in and the administrative offices where
people who are elected fill the jobs of general leadership and administration. These people are most often detested by the residents—
particularly the specialists upstairs—because they have had to
campaign to obtain their jobs and they have had to ask for dona-
tions from all sorts of special interests in order to finance their
campaigns. Worst of all, these people are generalists who know
even less about problems than the generalists who work on the
major issues in the basement ballrooms.

You should see this place try to operate. Everyone tends to call
for room service at the same time, creating a sort of gridlock. At
certain times of the year, everyone tries to utilize the hotel's communication facilities at the same time and, again, there is a break-
down. The residents have become very disappointed with the
hotel's managers and are cynical about their ability to lead. The
specialists upstairs also think that the generalists who work on the
big problems don't know what they are doing because they don't
enjoy the kind of incremental success that the narrow specialists
upstairs often achieve.

If you tire of the hotel analogy, think of the Problem Society
as an air space where thousands of different-sized aircraft try to
land at an airport that is not much larger than it was at its founding. And each of those airplanes is trying to communicate with
the control tower at the same time and each plane is filled with

hundreds or thousands of customers, all of whom have direct communication to the pilot and are attempting to tell him or her how to fly the plane.

In describing the Problem Society, I do not mean at all to suggest that other times haven't been thick with problems or with change. Nor do I mean to suggest that the unintended consequences, both good and harmful, which accompany broad policy or action by generalist leaders are new.

I do argue that a greater level of complexity faces generalist leaders today than ever before, even while acknowledging that the leaders in the past faced incredible complexity. FDR and Churchill during the 1930s and 40s and Truman in the tumultuous post-World War II era dealt with extreme complexity.

What is profoundly new in our time is that the generalist leaders swim in this sea of complexity at a time when the emperor has no clothes. The cost of information is so low and the dissemination of that information is so fast that ordinary people know nearly as much as the generalist leader knows, particularly in a high-visibility crisis. When state leaders have to watch CNN, along with the rest of us peasants, to know what is happening, that is profoundly new and profoundly important. It is important because the viewer (peasant) comes to his or her own conclusions about big national or international events just as the generalist leader is trying to do the same. And the peasant either expects the generalist leadership to do something that is smart and effective, or, even worse, holds no expectation that anything smart or wise will or can be done. So the generalist is trapped between unfair high expectations and public cynicism. As a State Department official was quoted by the *New York Times* as saying when President Clinton was dealing with the Boris Yeltsin counterattack against the old-line forces' takeover of the Russian parliament building, the deaths of U.S. soldiers in Somalia, the seemingly intractable quagmire of Bosnia and the tragedy of Haiti, "Every one of these situations involves a lot of imponderables. It's not easy to define our national interests, to decide when to intervene, to see all of the consequences of intervention. *And there's no upside. You win, and nobody in the general public cares much; you lose American lives and the country demands that you pull your horns in."*

The unhappy citizen is apt to say, with great cynical feeling, "Ah, they (the politicians) don't know what they're doing." I say, descriptively, clinically and with compassion, "They (we) don't know what they are doing." When the citizen dismisses the politicians angrily, he or she means that the politicians are so greedy, so self-interested and so out of touch with reality that they don't know what they are doing. This is true often enough to make it difficult to judge when well-meaning, gifted, caring politicians honestly fail.

So what do I mean when I speak of the failure of the generalist to know what he or she is doing, for good or bad, when trying to formulate general public policy? I mean that when presidents or congresses bite off big hunks of policy that cut across many scientific, economic, social or cultural disciplines, it is as though they are pumping complex ingredients into a social fuel tank and that when the engine of real life is turned on, the fuel propels society in ways that the makers of the fuel did not anticipate, for better or for worse.

For example, in the 1960s we finally came to our senses as a nation and legislatively outlawed all kinds of behavior that was racially discriminatory. Good for us. Blacks can now vote. Blacks can now hold office. Blacks can be a part of the mainstream society. And even while we acknowledge all of the remaining racism and barriers to blacks, the good news is that millions of blacks benefited from that legislation and from the civil rights movement. Three cheers for us as a society. Well, maybe make that two cheers. Studies by William Julius Wilson at the University of Chicago and by others now show that one of the unintended consequences of that great civil rights success is that thousands of middle- or upper-middle-class blacks who once lived side by side or near very poor blacks in big-city ghettos have now, thanks to their new civil rights, moved out of those ghettos, leaving the impoverished residents behind to fend for themselves without the kind of role models they had when blacks were segregated together. And the subsequent hardening of the so-called underclass has spawned a host of social problems that seem much more difficult to solve than the original problem of public accommodation. We simply did not anticipate this turn of events as being an offshoot of the civil rights movement. We did not know what we were doing.

Anyone who grew up reading newspaper exposés of insane asylums and poorhouses had to cheer the pharmaceutical developments that enabled people to take pills to treat their mental distresses rather than be locked up in huge, dirty, inhumane asylums. The de-institutionalization of America was a great achievement. Three cheers for wonder drugs, halfway houses, social welfare agencies and the decentralization of institutions dealing with the mentally ill, the addicted and the otherwise distressed among us. Well, maybe two cheers. Now we learn that the de-institutionalization of America may contribute significantly to the development of that phenomenon called homelessness in America. The people who are now out on the streets apparently once were inside institutions. We simply did not anticipate that development in doing the "good" we did in tearing down the monster asylums. We didn't know what we were doing.

We spent trillions of dollars to fight the Communists and win the Cold War. Only it turns out that much of what we spent, for example, on intelligence (hundreds of billions), was invested in intelligence that was hugely mistaken about Soviet economic and military strength. And we will debate for many years whether or not it was Ronald Reagan's defense build-up or simply the internal weight of the Soviet military establishment on the Soviet economy that led to the collapse of the USSR, a collapse that almost no one predicted (I attended two different high-level conferences at

224

THE THING OF IT IS

the University of Chicago in the early and mid-1980s and when the experts were asked how long it would take for the Soviet empire to unravel, most predicted one hundred years and one fearless soul suggested fifty years). And we certainly, in most instances, did not anticipate the messy consequences of the end of the Cold War, with all of the ethnic, religious and nationalist turmoil and fighting that have erupted (John Mearsheimer of the University of Chicago was a lonely voice predicting this turmoil). And so to acknowledge that we lack a coherent policy to deal with the hundreds of complexities that accompany the end of the Cold War is to face the humbling truth. I was pleased to see an October, 1993 story on the front page of the *New York Times* that suggested that many other nations in the world are just as confused in their foreign policy formulations as the U.S. is. Under these circumstances of global change and complexity, we do not know what we are doing.

The Congress was proud of its 1986 tax simplification legislation. Not only have we now turned our back on that legislation, but even at the time we passed it, it took thousands of pages of rules to explain that "simplification."

We did away with back-room politics and the big-city boss system and we were proud of our progressive change. Women and minorities at last could participate fully in the electoral process. But now we hear that the national political parties have become irrelevant; that there is little party discipline; that anyone can and does run for office in a television and primary elections free-for-all; and that the level of our politics has, thus, diminished. Apparently we didn't anticipate what we would lose en route to "improving" our political system. Perhaps we didn't know what we were doing.

The list goes on. Savings and loan deregulation. Welfare policy. Immigration policy. The legal system. The space program. *Roe v. Wade*. Going off the gold standard and thus taking the lid off international currency trading. I am sure you have your own list of failed policies that enrage you. The point is that we do what we feel is right and what we feel we must do under the circumstances and challenges of the times, but often we act under extreme political pressure, or the threat of war or the perception of the need for great social need and when we act under pressure and when we act quickly we generate run-away costs and unintended consequences we could not or would not anticipate. I think many people finally are aware of this as they grapple with President Clinton's ambitious health security proposals. However that debate is settled, no one can ever say that we, as a nation, weren't warned about a host of possible unintended costs and consequences. Should we create a Secretary of Unintended Consequences?

If the formulation of sound, broad public policy is so difficult today why don't our politicians behave at the same level of professionalism as our best scientists and specialists? Why does the professional politician indulge in poll-taking, crowd-pleasing rhetoric or quick-fix legislation? Why do these political hacks accept money from the very interests they need to view with independence? Why do they act so differently from the vast majority of professionals who, in medicine, hue to the line of science as closely as possible or who, in engineering, do whatever it takes professionally to make sure that buildings don't topple? Why does the average professional play it so much straighter than the average politician in the Problem Society?

My theory is that aside from any psychological deviancy that might attract certain persons to politics (sadism or videotropism), many who go into politics think they really can help people. And because there is such a huge gap between the rational policies that are needed to deal with complex public policy questions such as race, crime, education and health, and because there is such a cry for immediate action from the public to deal with those problems, anyone who enters this field soon gets caught up in its short-term, quick-fix demands.

A young person who goes into politics thinking he or she can help people by forging good, fair, generalist social and economic policies is very much like the sensitive, gifted, young person who thinks journalism is a field in which one's deeper writing and thinking skills will be appreciated and efficiently utilized. In most daily journalism, one is so busy trying to chase the ambulances that the notion of having the time or concern to achieve a sense of larger truths often is laughable.

Today, the search for "truth" is pretty much in the domain of the specialist. And those tend to be small "truths." And so, the generalist politician finds himself chasing after the latest political demand from constituents who are fed a daily dose of mostly uncontexted, unrelated horror stories from journalists (and their short-term, profit-oriented corporate owners and managers) who end up pandering to unformed and uninformed public opinion. Throw in a few truly evil opportunists in both politics and journalism along the way and you create huge problems of raised and then unfulfilled expectations. Not to mention, a ton of bad public policy. The specialists who tend to know their stuff are filled with nothing but disdain for these "whores" in politics and journalism. The generalist politicians and daily journalists feel equal disdain for the specialists, who are perceived as never needing to emerge from their snug ivory towers to deal with impatient mobs at the polls or tendentious guests on radio talk shows.

C. P. Snow wrote of "Two Cultures"—the scientific and the liberal arts. He, in my view, missed the number of cultures in our society by a few thousand. Each is highly specialized and each becomes more insular. That is often a negative. George Bush, through his speech writer Peggy Noonan, spoke of "a thousand points of light." He was referring to those who, on a volunteer basis, do good in our society. He, in my view, also missed the number—by a few million. There is so much individualized do-gooding in our society that we cannot, in any measurable way, feel or give credit to ourselves for what we do. When we, as Bush-Noonan did, try to make something of the good we do, our motives are suspect as being political. Or, if we in journalism try to write or speak about the good that people do, those stories most often come off as patronizing. And it's not just a problem facing politicians and journalists. We individual citizens seldom stop to think about looking at our pay stubs and analyzing the good that the deductions to government programs or charities have achieved.

So much of the good that we are proud of in this world is the product of the work of specialists. In the Problem Society, the specialist is able to point to millions of incremental, Point A to Point B, successes. Buildings are built, planes fly, crops are grown, people are fed, etc. And all of these specialists make up what are known generally as "the special interests." We think of them as "them." But in truth, they are we. We the people. And those specialties were born of honest science, relatively free speech and relatively free markets (with lots of help from Uncle Sam).

And ask yourself this question: what would happen if we ever came to the day when every campaign finance reform you can think of was enacted? What would happen if all of the undue influence, illegal campaign contributions and inappropriate lobbying was eliminated? I'll tell you what would happen—the problem of the special interests would continue and might even worsen. Why? *Because it is the sincerity of so many of those interests that will remain and will continue to clog the arteries of government.* Thousands of honest do-good special interests can gridlock the government every bit as effectively as the back-room deal boys. When I talk of "sincere" special interests I think of the public television lobbyist who, when he or she gets up in the morning does not say, "Oh, I wonder how I can contribute to governmental gridlock and make a selfish, unfair request for governmental funding of quality children's programming." No, that lobbyist sincerely thinks that if the government increases funding for public television children's programming that more children will learn to read and the republic will be well served. Multiply that kind of "sincere" do-gooding by tens of thousands of well-intentioned special interests and you may long for the day when the powerful back room boys made payoffs and got something done, just as some long for the day when political parties had clout and could name who they wanted to run for public office. I'm not arguing against campaign finance reform, I just want us to think about some of the consequences that might accompany the "cleaning up" of Washington politics. I repeat, the clean, sincere advocacy of special interests will gridlock government every bit as much if not more than the present clout-heavy system does. These sincere special interests will continue to compete with this bulging list of other sincere interests for the time, money and other resources made available by the generalist leadership of our society.

And because that generalist leadership does not and cannot know what the specialists know, and because general social policy tends to spawn unintended consequences when the needs of special interests are mixed, the generalists (the president and the Congress) tend to be the fall guys and gals in the Problem Society.

We can only hope that those generalists know that they can't know. And if *we* know that, given the complexity of all they can't know, we can still beat up on them, criticize them, expose them and throw them out. But at least we shouldn't burden ourselves with the kind of cynicism most of us have been carrying because we thought our political leaders could solve most of the problems of the Problem Society. The miracle under these complex circumstances is that we do as well as we do.

52

⁓

The Problem Century

The temperature is 70 degrees below zero and with a wind of more than 100 miles per hour the wind-chill reading is minus 175. It is January 20 and the sun hasn't been seen for 66 days.

The per capita income of the people who live here is an astounding $90,000 but the government lists them as officially impoverished. Prices are so high—fresh milk, $6 a gallon; corn flakes, $7 a box—that families with six-figure incomes qualify for food stamps.

The sale, consumption and possession of alcoholic beverages are prohibited by law, but one third of the population is alcoholic and the remaining two thirds must live with their alcoholism. Bootleggers thrive. A case of beer or a fifth of cheap whiskey goes for about $100.

This is the picture author Tom Rose paints of Barrow, Alaska, "the largest and most important Eskimo village in the world," in his book *Freeing the Whales*. Rose first discovered the tragic, depressing world of the Barrow Inupiat Eskimos during his assignment by a Japanese television network to cover the freeing of the three whales in the Arctic ice near Barrow in October, 1988. After being a part of the sensationalist, worldwide coverage of the trapped whales, Rose returned to Barrow to investigate, among other things, the history and culture of the Inupiat of Barrow.

He paints a picture of 25,000 years of nomadic tribes living and whaling in complete isolation. And then the British Arctic explorer Thomas Elson arrives and things are never the same. The white man brings disease and liquor. It is just a matter of time until the Eskimos are destroyed. Rose cites the rise of commercial whaling and the Eskimo leaders' offer to give the American sailors the "servitude of their best whalers if the Americans would agree to give the Eskimos the molasses they needed to make their own liquor. Their fate was sealed."

With the discovery of the huge Atlantic Richfield natural gas field in 1968, the Eskimos in Barrow were hit with a new problem—Americanized gas and oil wealth. Rose writes, "In less than a decade, Barrow went from being one of the poorest towns in North America to its absolute richest." He adds, "Barrow's sudden material wealth resulted in a monumental cultural meltdown. The Inupiat were collapsing under the weight of their own riches. The elders, who embodied Eskimo culture, were shunted aside by Barrow's new white masters. Their talents no longer necessary for their people's survival, the Inupiat elite fell into despair. Alcohol, already a severe problem, now afflicted everyone."

I submit to you that if I took you and Anthony Lewis of the *New York Times* and Bill Moyers of PBS and a plane full of other moralists to Barrow and we all were able to see for ourselves the wreckage of that culture, we would not be moralistic about the Inupiat. Lewis, I am sure, would not write a column castigating the leadership of the Inupiat for their irresponsible decision to accept liquor from the first British explorers. He would not criticize those Inupiat who later traded whaling skill for molasses from the American sailors. He would not take the present-day leaders of Barrow to task because their community has one of America's highest rates of murder, rape, suicide and physical abuse of spouses and children.

He and Moyers and the other moralists, I am sure, would write and broadcast the tragic facts. They would point to how a once thriving, isolated whaling community had been done in first by alcohol and then by oil riches. Surely they would criticize those who had corrupted the Inupiat, but they would express empathy with the Inupiat and they would correctly point out that maybe with the passage of a great deal of time and with the help of the best modern social and medical science and perhaps with a great deal of intervention by the Holy Spirit, these good Inupiat might someday come to a better life.

But these astute commentators and moralists would be quite conservative, I think, in their expectations for change for these badly battered and abused Inupiat. Expect no quick fixes, they would caution. And yet these and other commentators have no hesitation in castigating the leadership of modern industrial nations that have been hit not only with the consequences of alcohol addiction in their populations but also with dozens of other cataclysmic agents of change that make alcohol alone look like an easy problem. I argue that the thousands of special problems with which we wrestle daily are overwhelming the ability and capacity of the few remaining generalists to handle, but it needs to be made clear that these thousands of problems are being presented on a stage of recent historical change that is simply too much for most of us even to begin to acknowledge or internalize.

Suppose it was just a relatively quiet period in modern history and there were only ten or twelve little wars raging and some nice things were being invented and some better ways were being discovered to bury the dead from all of the diseases making their way through the continents and God said, "Well, you're doing reasonably well down there on earth. But I'm getting kind of bored up here and I want to throw a little twist into the narrative."

"Okay, God, what is it?"

"Well, I've decided not to give you much warning and suddenly I am going to arrange things so that women, who have been treated like property and slaves for centuries, are going to demand and obtain some measure of equality of opportunity and some measure of parity of achievement, income and justice. And all of this is going to explode in a time span of very few years, compared with the centuries and centuries of abuse that women have suffered up until this time."

"O God," we reply, "don't hit us with all of that in this one generation! Isn't it enough just to get through the day with all these wars and all these diseases, God? How can we get through all this and at the same time deal the emancipation of women? Have you no mercy? Do you realize how complicated and unendingly vexing such a development will be in our lives, God? Don't you know that such a revolution will affect every minute of every day in every corner of our globe and in every room of our homes and every floor of our workplace and on every page of our stories and poems and every canvas of our paintings and every chord of our music? Do you know what you are doing, God! Do you realize what will happen when women get the vote? Do you realize what will happen if women even begin to be treated as equals under the law and in areas of commerce and trade? Do you realize what that will do to the patriarchy? To the law? To politics? To family? To intimacy? Do you, God?"

Now that would be a reasonable lament by the men who controlled things at that time, would it not? Of course it would. We could wrestle morning, noon and night with change of that depth and scope for decades, if not centuries.

But guess what? The women's revolution is just one of dozens of equally stupendous, epoch-shattering developments which we have been blessed with in the past fifty years or so. Oh, I know that many of the developments I am going to mention developed their roots long before this generation, but I am prepared to argue that most if not all of them burst into full force in the last generation or two.

So what else are we talking about here? We're talking about television. Yes, you know that television has entered our lives and has changed our lives; don't lecture us about television, Callaway, we know all about that. No, we don't know all about it. You don't know. I don't know. We don't know. We don't even begin to know. At this point in our understanding of television we are still very much in the stage of the title of the speech I was asked to give— the very first words I ever spoke on radio—at Magnolia High School in New Martinsville, West Virginia, in 1953: "Do the Bad Influences of the Movies Overbalance the Good?"

Yes, we know that we watch too much television. Yes, we know that our kids don't read as much because they watch too much television. Yes, we know that commercials on television denigrate our culture. Yes, we know that watching television makes us less tolerant of war, revolutions and other events which we see via television. Yes, we know that our attention spans are shorter because we watch so much television. Yes, we know that television is watched in the average American household for more than seven hours a day (or at least it is on for more than seven hours a day). Yes, we know that the day of the networks is over and that with the development of hundreds of two-way channels that television's new computerized face will be unendingly multi-dimensional and specialized. Yes, we know that television has cheapened political discourse in the United States and throughout the world. Yes, we know that television is a more potent lure for youngsters than the droning of their classroom teachers. Yes, we know that television has the capacity to link us globally in what we could never previously have imagined.

We know and don't know all of the above because all of the above are in contention. And, aside from the root questions Marshall McLuhan raised about television, we are hard pressed to ask the right questions about television because we are so busy watching it and being absorbed by it that we don't have a clue yet as to what its impact is or will be. We lament that our children don't read the way they used to or that politicians don't debate the way they used to but we spend little time thinking about the reality that we are undergoing—the kind of deep-dish change with the

development of what certain social scientists call "the visualization of knowledge" that our ancestors went through with the development of the printed word. We are too busy moralizing about
some of the short-term discomfort caused by television to take
the time to figure out what it means to our lives.

And one of the reasons we moralize is that it is a way of con-
necting with the past. McLuhan was on to that form of denial. He
reminded us that the British called the radio "the wireless." And
I can tell you that I refer to my television program sometimes as
a special "edition" of "Chicago Tonight." Not only do we not know
what television is about in our lives as a direct force, but we also
are profoundly ignorant of what its changing compound is when
mixed in with all the other scientific and social and political change
I am about to remind us of.

Remember, you don't believe what I just told you. You are
walking around thinking you have a generally good feel for what
you know and don't know about television. You don't worry for
a minute about how it interacts with a thousand other changes.
You don't worry about it because you can't worry about it because
it is entirely too complicated for any of us to worry about or we
would all go bonkers. But be kind enough, thank you, to put television on our little list of little changes we're all living through as
we move on now.

Well, let's just skip on over to the telephone. Nothing too complicated about that. Pick it up, dial or punch up some numbers
and talk. That means you don't have to hang around the house or
the farmstead forever, do you? You can get out there on Eisenhower's lovely interstate system or get to one of those nice regional
airports LBJ's people had built and get the heck away to Eugene,
Oregon, and phone in the latest to the folks back in Philadelphia
or Boston.

Well, I tell you, families don't have the kind of continuity they
used to, do they? We're just an awful bunch of selfish sinners in
this country, aren't we? Worse than those drunken Inupiat up there

in Barrow. Give a kid a car, a national highway system, a plane, and a phone and there's no holding him back. Never writes. No one writes anymore. Lazy, selfish buggers. Just picks up a phone and expects us to be there. Inconsiderate, unkind, runaway lout. And if he thinks I'm getting a fax machine so I can receive his homemade Christmas messages or if he thinks I'm going to buy a computer so we can exchange cuddly little messages, he'd better think again. I want my Hallmark cards or nothing. Don't even try any of that do-gooder UNESCO stuff on me.

Radio? That's so old it doesn't even qualify for this discussion and, of course, we know all about radio and how it has affected our lives so I won't bore you with that little scientific detail.

Calm down. Let's recapitulate here for a minute. We've got the women's revolution thing, we've got television and the telephone and cars and the national highway system and an ever so brief mention of faxes, computers and radio. That's a halfway decent list of changes, but we can handle that, can't we? What else have you got? I'm getting drowsy.

How about a nice wake-up call with nuclear weapons? Doesn't it blow your mind or did you just tuck that one away along with some of the other major denial items on our list? Did you give it an all-out panic during the Cuban missile crisis in 1962 and then decide that if you didn't pack it in then you weren't going to worry about it for the rest of your natural or unnatural life? That's okay. That's how most of us have handled nukes. How could they have invented those things without asking us? We didn't even get to vote on them. What does living with nuclear bombs mean to our lives? To our children? How, God? Well, thank you. At least you didn't pretend you knew all about nukes the way you pretend you know all about TV and radio and telephones.

What's next? Let's dip down into the barrel and see what we pull out. Oh, great. The American civil rights revolution. Remember when they had "whites only" signs over the rest rooms and fountains down south and blacks couldn't eat in most of the restaurants in big cities and small towns and blacks got on the back of buses and blacks got lynched with a regularity that matched the rising of the sun and blacks couldn't vote and blacks went to separate schools, etc., etc., etc.?

Remember that? That was in our lifetimes, friends. And now blacks can vote and blacks can become mayor and governor and blacks can run for president and blacks can be so middle-class successful in such numbers that they leave the ghettos to a hardcore unemployed, uneducated, crime-besotted, drug-infested, single-parent-child-bearing culture that threatens to take us with them on their trip of drugs, despair, crime and violence. Now those of you who live in big cities with big ghettos might agree with those who say that one single problem might do us in, right? But look back and see how far in on the list of cataclysmic events we are and be warned that we're only getting started and then try to put the black underclass problem in perspective. Vietnam is coming up. That's not a bad segué because it was what happened to Martin Luther King, Jr. He moved from the issue of black racial justice to the issue of justice for all Americans who found themselves caught up in the racial and economic and class injustices of Vietnam. Think about it, wouldn't the Vietnam mess be enough of a tragedy, enough of a global and domestic political change for one generation? Wasn't that a foreign and civil war all at the same time? What would Lincoln have done had he fought a war in downtown Africa at the time he presided over the preservation of the Union? But, heck, don't think too much about Vietnam. Just tuck it away with alcohol, the women's revolution, television, telephones, computers, faxes, radio, the national highway system, the American racial revolution and class warfare.

And it wasn't just Vietnam. What we were experiencing was the end of global colonialism as we had known it for several centuries. It was ending on our shift, in our times. And it left some pretty incredible political, social and religious vacuums which have been filled with everything from tyranny to torture to famine to nationalism to ethnic fighting to reform. Just thought I'd mention it here, the end of global colonialism.

Now, let's not forget the Baby Boom. Did you know that the Baby Boom—the birthing of all those millions and millions of kids after GIs returned home from World War II— resulted in a generation which had more adolescents than the entire previous century and a half in America? Isn't that astounding? (Just think about all those kids crammed with all those hormones running in our streets at a time when the rest of what I've been listing has been happening.) A record bunch of adolescents among us just when we're hit with TV, the women's revolution, the racial justice revolution, Vietnam, the total spread of automobiles and highways and the rest of it!

And the rest of it, of course, included rock 'n' roll music. Forget what I said about nuclear arms. We did pretty well with nukes. Think about rock 'n' roll. Think that only a couple of years before the Beatles you and I were going to movie houses which featured Ginger Rogers and Gene Kelly dancing to the music of George Gershwin and Cole Porter. Think about culture and civilization up to that moment and then think about rock 'n' roll. It's like being fire-bombed in your own hearse on your way to your own burial. Rock 'n' roll was to those who didn't dig it simply a rejection of everything civilized and decent that had ever been achieved in the culture.

But when you think about the pace of change that the progenitors of rock encountered in their adolescence, it is no wonder that they reacted with an explosion of noisy, violent instrumentation that screamed, as critic Leslie Fielder coined the term, "no, in thunder." In fairness, the same indictment can be leveled against those who created atonal modern symphonic music. To my ear, Easley Blackwood's work is the symphonic equivalent of rock, but it may be the perfect music for the twentieth century, given the impossible complexity and confusions of this century. Why should post-modern abstract art contain traditional elegance, form and beauty when the world of the post-modern abstract artist is filled with undigestible confusion, change and anguish?

And then there was the pill. How is that for a little social change footnote? And don't forget that while we were inventing and marketing the pill we also revised our social values so that pornography became available in every convenience store and on millions of videos. Did I leave out videos and VCRs, which enabled us to become our own programmers? Sorry.

And then there were those marvelous breakthroughs like in vitro fertilization and laser surgery and genetic implants and all the other futuristic medico-scientific stuff that made us feel as if we were God. And we went to the moon. And we sprinkled the skies with satellites that could spy and show us tomorrow's weather.

And amid of all this wonderful progress God said, "Slow down a bit, friends, and deal with this one—AIDS." And so there we were with all our newfound freedom to screw around and we get hit with AIDS. Thanks so much, God.

I forgot to mention, didn't I, that homosexuals and lesbians finally came out of the closet in this generation, didn't they? Just another tidbit of social change we are asked to absorb nonchalantly.

Just as we were asked to absorb millions and millions of immigrants from all over the world in the second largest wave of immigration in U.S. history—at the exact time we're dealing with everything else I have listed and will list.

So, where are we? Did I forget anything? Oh, my god, I forgot drugs. How could I ever have separated drugs from rock or rock from drugs? Don't they go together? But you understood that, didn't you? When I put rock on my list of unfathomable changes in the twentieth century, you immediately included drugs in your own assimilation of rock, didn't you? Thank you. Now, for those historians among you who look with displeasure on inappropriate claims of disasters for any one generation, I want to acknowledge that we've had drugs and lots of drugs in previous generations. But I submit that, with the record number of adolescents running around in our streets, the current drug craze deserves to be listed along with television, women's rights, the civil rights revolution, rock music and the rest. I know that a previous generation was besotted with alcohol but this generation took to drugs and clung to alcohol at the same time. I submit that this generation makes Hemingway's alcoholic generation look like sweet brandy-drinking innocents.

Well, all right, so we suffered through a lot of change. At least we had inspired leadership, didn't we? "President Kennedy said today . . ." Wham! November 22, 1963, and it's over. Now every generation has a tragic assassination and we had JFK. But then we had 1968. Remember 1968? We had a nice century that year. Martin Luther King gunned down in Memphis. Bobby Kennedy shot in the hotel kitchen in L.A. The Prague Spring crushed by Soviet tanks. The tear-gas and billy club festival that passed for the Democratic National Convention in Chicago. The decision by LBJ not to run again. The Days of Rage riots in Chicago in October. The election of Richard M. Nixon as president of the United States.

Well, with a nice, square, middle-of-the-road Republican like Nixon, things would quiet down, wouldn't they? Not quite. Accused of lying in his 1968 campaign about a "plan" to end the Vietnam War, he became desperate enough to bomb Cambodia and set off a sequence of civil disobedience and campus rioting and police and military actions against the campus rioting. His lasting legacy of Watergate may be not so much the disgrace of being the first president in American history to resign in office under threat of impeachment as the torrent of free-wheeling, investigative journalistic opportunism and congressional political opportunism which continue this day to erode not only the power of the presidency but the ability of generalists anywhere in any setting to command the trust they need to function. That institutional power was coming apart anyway—Nixon's performance just accelerated things. Boy, that's what we really needed at that point in the twentieth century—acceleration of change. Things were so quiet until then.

But then Gerry Ford came into office and this time we really had a nice, square, middle-of-the-road Republican. Things would quiet down. They did. For about a month. And then gracious Gerry pardoned Nixon and we all went berserk again.

This is all happening too fast. We need a break. Even planets need vacations. We don't get one.

Carter is elected. He bets on the shah of Iran and loses.

He bets on Bert Lance and loses and so does everyone else who had faith that Carter would restore "integrity in the White House."

The American embassy in Tehran is overrun and the hostage crisis is on for days and nights.

OPEC hits hard and we find ourselves yelling obscenities at each other in gasoline lines.

Interest rates and inflation hit double-digit rates.

Three Mile Island confirmed our worst fears about the unpredictable consequences of "scientific progress."

Carter, Begin and Sadat achieve the stunning success of the Israeli-Egyptian Peace Treaty at Camp David but Sadat is assassinated.

Things are so bad we turn to ... Ronald Reagan!

Ronald Reagan is president of the United States! I rank that right up there with nuclear bombs, the civil rights revolution, Vietnam, the development of television and the rest of my little list of life-changing events. And I don't mean to be cute or even necessarily critical of Reagan when I say that, although I do mean to take note of some things he did which we'll all be paying for for the rest of our lives and our children's lives. Reagan coopted the Democrats and pushed the federal income tax reduction program and the defense build-up spending spree which guaranteed that we were well on our way to:

- A national debt which many believe to be out of control.
- A relocation of political power in this country associated with the consequences of what happens when responsibility for programs retreats to the states and cities.
- A savings and loan crisis fueled by errors in legislation, con-

gressional malfeasance and regulators who couldn't keep
up with all the political and entrepreneurial greed.

- A hands-off approach to government which guaranteed
  that just as the low-tax, deregulation policies would open
  up new business opportunities, those opportunities would
  be accompanied by such an absence of governmental over-
  sight that the savings and loan and FDIC crisis would hit
  with hundreds of billions of dollars of shortages.
- An investment in defense spending and Star Wars defense
  planning that actually helped bring the Soviets to their knees
  and thus helped end the Cold War.

And so the Berlin Wall comes down.

Poland and all the other Eastern European nations throw off
the yoke of communism because Gorbachev knows he can't finance
the continuation of the enslavement.

And then Gorbachev himself is overthrown in a coup, only to
be rescued three days later by Boris Yeltsin, who, in return, over-
throws Gorbachev as general secretary of the Communist party
of the USSR. Yeltsin then overcomes a coup aimed at him.

And remember, while all of this incredible change was going
on these other tidbits were happening:

- Fourteen million refugees are caught up in civil wars and
  regional conflicts.
- The Roman Catholic church worldwide is torn by controversy over reproductive rights, the role of women and
  the desire of priests to marry (what priests are left).
- Apartheid in South Africa cracks and multi-party power-
  sharing begins. Mandela and DeKlerk receive the Nobel
  Peace Prize.
- The Iran-Iraq war ends after eight years only to be
  followed by one of the most curious and perhaps significant episodes in the history of warfare—the U.S.-U.N.–
  led Persian Gulf initiative which ousted Saddam Hussein

from Kuwait but which allowed him to remain in power in Baghdad.

- The incredible rise and then decline of the Japanese economy worldwide, and the equally incredible rise and then weakening of the German economic machine.
- The change of China from an agrarian to a more urban society, following the development of some free enterprise, followed by the student democratic uprising, followed by the brutal suppression of that uprising by the government at Tienneman Square.
- Another decade of war and turmoil in Latin America.
- The Palestinian intifada against Israeli rule in the West Bank and Gaza Strip, followed by the historic Middle East peace agreement signed in Washington in 1993.
- The unraveling of Yugoslavia and the rape of Bosnia's Muslims.
- The starvation and war in Somalia.
- The struggle for justice and democracy in Haiti.
- The ongoing political upheaval in India, Pakistan, Sri Lanka and more than thirty other countries around the world.

Do you know what all this means? Do you know the capitals of all of the nations involved? Can you find all of these countries on a blank map? Could you tell us the dates of each of these events? Do you know who the Tamil Tigers are? Do you know who runs agriculture in China? Do you know how many persons were killed in the Afghan war? Do you know the pre-1967 Israeli borders? Do you know who owns more property in the United States than the Japanese? Are you ready for a vacation in Baghdad? Are the Holiday Inns ready yet in Da Nang?

We're supposed to know all of this. We're supposed to be sensitive to it. And we're supposed to know who wrote *Little Women* and know what the Sixth Amendment to the Constitution is and be able to write an essay on the *Dred Scott* decision and all that other good stuff in the humanities polls about what we don't know and why we are an intellectual disgrace to ourselves and to history.

And we're supposed to be computer-savvy and capable of human intimacy and competitive but at the same time be cooperative and not forget our father's religious values but be open to all the world's religious values and not eat too much and don't smoke or drink but still be carefree and kind of zany in a friendly sort of way and be aware of the latest study on how decaf coffee causes an increase in "bad" cholesterol and help find money to invest in Eastern Europe and simultaneously give time and money to inner-city causes and root for the Fighting Irish but be aware of how corrupting college football is to the youth who play it and don't use makeup that causes cancer and don't forget to put the answering machine on and why can't our neighborhood recycle all its garbage and don't watch too much television and drink lots of water if you run in weather that's hot but make sure it's bottled water except that some bottled water isn't safe anymore and find a home for the homeless and don't forget to attend your adult-children-of- alcoholics meeting on Thursday and bring back classical music in big-city AM radio and pray and learn and watch and pray and wait and demand and expect everything NOW NOW NOW NOW NOW NOW NOW NOW NOW NOW NOW NOW NOW NOW NOWNOWNOWNOWNOWNOW!

So, it's okay for the Inupiat to be brought down by alcohol. That one big change that did them in is a tragic shame and we grieve for them and feel compassion for them.

But as for our society with all the two-bit changes I've had the gall to list, we're above all the stress and confusion of those changes, those events, those discoveries, those responsibilities. No excuses, kids. All together now. We can do it all. We can do it all and we can do it now because we are proud citizens of the Problem Society.

53

~

The Problem Presidency

Pretend for a minute that you are attending a lecture and the speaker begins with an audience-feedback proposition. He says, "Please applaud if you agree with the following statement: 'However we have arranged it, by whatever means it came to be, somehow, someway, we have devised a system or process in this country by which the very finest among us rise to the very highest offices of the land.'"

There is utter silence in the hall, followed by sarcastic whispers and nervous giggles.

Our speaker continues. "All right, so much for that thought. Let me ask you to think about just one more. Please applaud if you generally agree with this next statement: 'Acknowledging all of our faults and shortcomings and acknowledging how far we have to go, this still is either the greatest nation in the world or surely it's *one* of the greatest in the world.'"

That proposition is greeted with enthusiastic, sincere and sustained applause. The speaker waits until the applause dies down and then asks his audience, "If you agree that this is such a great country, why do you have such a poor opinion of its leadership? How can you reconcile one with the other?"

There is a kind of quiet murmuring in the audience as people think over the apparent conflict in their responses.

The speaker then goes on to suggest that the reason people don't agree that we have devised a system that ensures that the very finest among us will rise to the highest positions of leadership is that (1) we haven't devised such a system and (2) many of us carry around with us a kind of schoolboy or schoolgirl idealism about political leadership. The standard of great leadership for many of us is Washington or Jefferson or Lincoln. We know our leaders aren't in the same ballpark with those greats.

Then the speaker says, "I want you to imagine that an artist has created a collage which represents the sum total of all of the knowledge that existed in Thomas Jefferson's day. And the collage was about this big." And with that the speaker makes a circle with his arms outstretched.

"And let us imagine that Jefferson had a pretty good grasp of a great deal of the knowledge that existed in the late seventeenth and early eighteenth centuries; that he knew a great deal about world history; that he had a more than adequate understanding of theology and philosophy and what was known at that time about geography, astronomy, mathematics, medicine and anatomy, natural history and chemistry, mechanics and architecture, trade and commerce; that he was a voracious reader and collector of books and conversant with most, if not all, of the pertinent issues of the day. In other words, here was a true intellectual and public man whose grasp of his times and his world represents the kind of renaissance man we so dearly miss in our leadership today.

"Now let's turn from Thomas Jefferson's day to George Bush's or Bill Clinton's times. And let's advise that artist about how large his collage needs to be in order proportionally to represent the sum total of all of the knowledge that exists today. How tall and wide do you suppose that collage should be? As tall and wide as this lecture hall? As tall as the Sears Tower and as wide as this telephone area code? Probably closer to the latter, don't you suppose? With the amount of information in this world doubling every five years now and doubling every four years in the near future, that collage is going to be a gargantuan construction.

"Now let's go back and examine the size of Thomas Jefferson's brain and compare it with the size of George Bush's or Bill Clinton's brain." This always generates mocking laughter in the audience.

"The brain sizes are pretty much the same but we think of Jefferson as being the really brilliant man and we think of Bush or Clinton or other contemporary political leaders as being perhaps even very smart but lightweights compared with Jefferson.

"But if you begin to think about the policy expectations and political demands of Bush's and Clinton's day and compare them with the policy and politics of Jefferson's time, you should begin to ask yourself if it is fair to expect that today's leadership, which must contend with thousands upon thousands of strands of science, policy advocacy and problem solving, can possibly master any—much less most—of those endless expectations which wash over the modern presidency.

"You should ask yourself if it isn't true that the democratization of presidential politics means that the good news is that just about anyone in the United States can run for the presidency today and that the bad news is that just about anyone in the United States can run for the presidency today. Isn't it true that this democratization process which took presidential politics out of the back rooms of the kingmakers and into the clear view of modern televised presidential primary contests guarantees by its very nature that the kind of candidates who finally emerge will not be the most thoughtful and scholarly and brilliant among us?

"Isn't it true that the most thoughtful and scholarly among us will not submit themselves to the demeaning and corrupting campaign fund raising? Isn't it true that the most thoughtful and scholarly among us tend to be specialists who would never presume for a minute to try to be the kind of 'all things to all men and women' candidate modern presidential politics demands?"

As you may have gathered by now, I am that speaker and I will now stop quoting myself and simply get on with my sense of what the problem presidency is. I have told you about the speech because this series of problem society essays began with my talks on the subject of the complexities facing the presidency and because so many people who heard those talks encouraged me to put them in writing.

I want to acknowledge that it is true that not everyone walks around with a Jeffersonian presidency in mind. For some, FDR or even Ike would be good enough, not to mention those who dearly wish Adlai Stevenson could have made it to the White House. But I am reminded of a political cartoon reprinted in the "Week-in-Review" section of the *Sunday New York Times* of November 24, 1991, in which cartoonist Mike Shelton of the *Orange County Register* depicts an average Joe voter sitting on a couch with his hair-in-her-curlers wife. He's taking a telephone call and says, "It's a presidential poll. Who's that Democrat we like better than Bush?" She replies, "Thomas Jefferson."

We aren't the only generation that has had a hang-up with the Thomas Jefferson or founding-father ideal of leadership. Jefferson hadn't been dead for more than ten years when Alexis de Tocqueville wrote, in *Democracy in America*, "In the United States the most outstanding men are seldom called on to direct public affairs.... Why, in America, men of distinction often deliberately avoid a political career."

Tocqueville, writing in 1835, sounds wonderfully like today's government bashers: "When I arrived in the United States I discovered with astonishment that good qualities were common among the governed but rare among the rulers. In our day it is a constant fact that the most outstanding Americans are seldom summoned to public office, and it must be recognized that this tendency has increased as democracy has gone beyond its previous limits. It is clear that during the last fifty years the race of American statesmen has strangely shrunk." Clearly, Tocqueville missed the leadership of Thomas Jefferson and those other chaps who started our republic. Their successors had fouled the founding fathers' political and governmental nests.

Those first presidents presided over a governmental operation that would equal that of a large city today. In *The Jeffersonians,* one of the few books that give us good insight into governmental process in the early nineteenth century, Leonard D. White reports: "Expenditures charged against ordinary receipts averaged from 1801 to 1810 about 9 million dollars ... The principal public service maintained by the federal government was the post office. In 1800 there were 903 post offices.... In 1800 mail was transported over 20,000 miles of post road.... In 1800 the business (of the post office) was conducted with a chief clerk and five clerks...."

Referring to the early bureaucracy of the early presidents, White writes, "The President's task was heavier because no one of them had proper assistance. *Congress allowed 'a private secretary and no more.'*" (Italics mine.) He writes of Jefferson's management of the presidency, "To an astonishing degree, the President personally participated in matters large and small.... Thus we find Jefferson instructing Gideon Granger on the problems of the postroad crossings in the western wilderness. 'I would suppose that all streams under 40.f width not fordable at their common winter tide, shall be bridged; & over all streams not bridged, a tree should be laid across if their breadth does not exceed the extent of a single tree.'"

Contrast White's writings about the administrative burdens of Jefferson's presidency with former presidential assistant Bradley H. Patterson, Jr.'s reporting on the modern presidency in his remarkable book *The Ring of Power.* This is a random selection from Patterson's findings and statistics on the executive branch of the federal government and those among us who wish to exercise an impact on the executive branch:

> Sixty-six permanent full-time agencies, thirty-six of which are independent, leaving thirty departments and agencies under the control of the president.

Twenty-four different and separate personnel systems of the executive branch.

1,074 separate domestic-assistance programs.

Endless specialized bureaus, divisions and units—3,137 of them in the Department of Health and Human Services alone.

Relations with 150 foreign nations, relations with incredibly complex military, economic and cultural ramifications.

Responsibility for enforcement of more than 20,000 federal laws.

Responsibility for 4.2 million military and civilian assistants who help the president execute the 20,000 plus laws.

[On the receiving end of a filtered information system that begins each day with] some five hundred thousand cables ... generated each day ... to or from Washington and the U.S. embassies or posts abroad. Eventually, daily, some three thousand messages flow through the White House filters.

Recipient of daily news summaries which, in Richard Nixon's 67 months in office totalled some 15,000 pages.

Twenty-seven hundred executive and judicial presidential appointments, fifteen hundred of whom will be subject to scrutiny and confirmation by the Senate.

In addition to responsibility for relating to all of the above, Patterson reminds us that the modern president is:

Commander-in-Chief of America's military forces ... Chief diplomat ... Chief budget officer and chief economist ... Setter of policy for America's participation in the world's international monetary machine ... [During the long Cold War] chief nuclear negotiator ... Overseer of the Central Intelligence Agency ... National Security Council leader ... Overseas information-propaganda machinery leader ... Overseer of his own White House diplomatic-military operations center ... Chief trade negotiator ... Chief scientist for the Executive Branch ... Priority setter for more than one trillion dollars in expenditures.

And, according to Patterson, when the president finishes tidying up around these executive branch complexities, he can look out the window and see relationships, problems and opportunities "with 50 state governments, under which have been created 3,041 county governments, 19,205 city governments, 16,691 townships, 14,692 school districts and 29,487 special districts—a total of 83,166 to which must be added 506 recognized Indian tribes and groups."

And if that doesn't keep him occupied, he can contemplate the demands which will be made upon him by some or all of the 929,415 tax-exempt organizations, among which are 19,000 who act through some 11,000 Washington representatives, writes Patterson. And remember, those figures are a few years old!

As Richard Neustadt put it in his book *Presidential Power,* "Everybody expects the man inside the White House to do something about everything."

That is to say, we expect the president of the United States to be:

- Honest.
- Brilliant.
- Not bad looking.
- An eloquent speaker.
- A charming presence, a forceful presence, particularly on television.
- A good father. A loving husband. A loyal friend to thouands of friends. A man of good humor. A man who is something of an athlete. A man of great global, political and social vision.
- A man who not only can gracefully handle sixteen-hour days in the White House but also is capable of loving intimacy with his family.
- A political leader who can fight fiercely, but fairly. A man who believes in law and order, civil and human rights, old-fashioned family values, new world consciousness values,

Christian values, Hebraic values, the rights of people everywhere.

- A man who is impeccable in his selection of hundreds of key advisers, cabinet members, Supreme Court justices and military leaders.
- A man who has risen through years of governmental and political assignments but who has an excellent feel for the realities of labor and business.
- A man who knows what the ordinary American is feeling and thinking but who is comfortable in the presence of kings, queens, world leaders, diplomats, artists, scientists, great athletes, prelates and various other personalities.
- A man who has read the great books, is up to date on everything in the current literature of public affairs and life in general but who still finds time to read good mysteries and maybe even a poem or two.
- A man who really knows what the farmer needs, and what the teacher needs, and what the soldier needs, and what the scientist needs, and what the trucker needs, and what the doctor needs, and what the nurse needs, and what the steelworker needs, and what the real estate salesman needs, and what the employee needs, and what the businessman needs, and what the laborer needs, and what the artist needs, and what the clergy need, and what the lawyers need.
- A man who really possesses a keen understanding of the needs of the poor, the lonely, the sick, the old, the young, the dispossessed.
- A man who understands the complexity of global finance, Wall Street manipulations, central banking history, computerized futures trading, currency fluctuations, market theory and practice and governmental regulation and its limits.
- A man who is at ease with any of the problems of the more than 150 nations around the world his administration is asked to interact with.

- A man whose gift of language is so great that he has an innate ability to meet with leaders of any nation, whose cultural sensitivity is so rich that he is comfortable anywhere on the globe.
- A man who knows that your own will and self-discipline are essentials for responsible citizenship and good living, but who also is sensitive to the behavioral knowledge imparted by modern psychology and psychiatry.
- A man who believes in God, attends church regularly, but who doesn't wear his religion on his sleeve.
- A leader who is so knowledgeable and experienced that he is at ease with and competent about almost any issue presented to him, but who has the good sense to delegate significant amounts of work to his associates and to the bureaucracy.
- A man who served in the military, preferably decorated for heroism in combat, but who knows that war is hell and that over-reliance on the military is folly.
- A man who has worked hard enough to prosper enough that he is independently wealthy, but who isn't so rich that he doesn't know what a hard-earned dollar means.
- A man who has a record of having marched in civil rights demonstrations and fought decades for minority rights, but who knows the worst thing one can do to minorities is patronize them and give them unequal opportunity in the work place.
- A man who has worked the precincts and built up a tremendous political network and following over the years, but who is independent of political bosses, PACs, or special interests.
- A man who respects women's rights to make choices of their own, but who also respects the sanctity of life at its earliest formation.
- A man who is sensitive to the destruction of this planet by environmental abuse, but whose common sense balances

that sensitivity with the knowledge that economic growth requires less than perfect environmental standards and enforcement.

- A man whose personal eating habits are admired by all, but who is not so nutritionally correct that he cannot be seen, from time to time, downing a beer and a burger.
- A man who is driven enough by ego and ambition to raise the money, gather the political forces necessary to win campaigns and to be strong enough politically to sustain himself in office but whose ambition is not so great that he would do anything dishonorable, unfair or illegal in order to maintain political advantage.

This not only is what we expect in presidents, but also is what we want to be, if we are little boys, when we grow up. And it is who little girls want to marry when they grow up. Reverse the sexes, if you please, for future reference.

Oh, and we want a man whose family is well educated, interestingly employed, devoid of human blemishes such as alcohol or drug addiction, free of business debts or disabilities and motivated to serve mankind in some noble manner.

Oh, you say, I don't expect all of that in my president. And I know *you* don't, but again, the accumulation of all the yous out there *does* expect that of our president.

And the scary thing is that the modern presidential press imagery machine does its damndest to project the president as all of those things, not all of those things at the same time, but most of those things in small dosages for selected audiences at select times. This isn't necessarily manufactured cynically. Often it is produced defensively so as to protect the president from whichever special problem interest threatens to pierce his image armor today or tomorrow or the next day. This public relations all-things-to-all-men and-women-and-children imagery is best seen as a kind of computer game with incoming special problem interest missiles or unforeseen event missiles to be countered with the correct images, if not programs.

And in the Problem Presidency there are stages and seasons, as predictable as the day following the night.

Fair-Haired Boy: Isn't he wonderful? His cabinet appointments are some of the best we've ever seen. He seems to have a real sense of what he wants to do and where he is going. We haven't seen a president like this in much too long. The American people show once again that they know what they are doing. Not bad, really, not bad at all.

The Honeymoon Is Over: He is much too isolated. Can't get to him through his power-mad chief of staff and those cronies of his. What a mediocre do-nothing cabinet! He really doesn't know how to deal with Congress. Are we ever going to get this country moving again?

The Crisis: We're behind you, big guy. You may be mediocre, but you surely are trying your best on this one and we're with you. My president, right or wrong. Isn't America great?

The Scandal: I told you he was a hypocrite. Look at the scoundrels around him. We've got the best government money can buy. Didn't anyone check these guys out? Why doesn't he get rid of them? How many more guys like this are hiding under the White House rocks? This may destroy his presidency. Me oh my.

Riding Out the Storm: Why is he traveling so much overseas? Did the Russians elect him or did we? Does he really think that another trip to London will make us forget that he hasn't done a damn thing at home? Why did he marry her? She's telling him everything to do when he isn't listening to his intoxicated brother.

The re-enactment of this ritual is as predictable as adolescent growing pains. If the volume of special problem interests fueled by the flood of scientific discovery and social complexity overwhelms the relatively few generalist journalists, educators, mayors, governors and legislators, then imagine what happens when that sea of expectation and complexity relentlessly washes over the White House.

Yes, we have come a long way since those early days of the Republic when presidents had but one assistant, but there is no way that the thousands of workers in the White House can stick their collective fingers in the dike to stem the unending tide of political and social expectation.

And yet we persist in continuing the Great President Expectation Game: what this country needs is a man at the top with the mind of Jefferson, the integrity of Lincoln and the vision of Franklin Roosevelt. Possessing all of those qualities, our Hero will be able to set this nation on a course of rebirth, moral leadership in a global scale and make demonstrable progress toward the solution of most if not all of our great domestic problems.

And so, in the Problem Society the biggest fall guy is the president of the United States. There is no way he can win. And when he loses—as he inevitably does—we also lose. We lose because our failure to acknowledge modern complexity and our insistence on asking the impossible of the president breed a virus of political cynicism that feeds on itself and ourselves. The burden of modern complexity is great enough without adding the weight of unthinking cynicism to it.

54

~

My Jane Brody Problem

You may not have noticed, but you are dead. And you are diseased and disabled many times over. If you are like me, that is how you feel when you read your morning newspaper. You feel dead, diseased and disabled. Sounds like a Gershwin tune, doesn't it?

If the newspapers wanted to put death, disease and disability neatly in perspective all they would have to do is place a data box somewhere near a popular feature that most readers glance at very day—the horoscope comes to mind—and remind us all that about 2,170,000 Americans die every year. That's one person every 15 seconds, 4 deaths a minute, 248 deaths an hour and 5,945 deaths a day. That sounds reasonable doesn't it? You're not particularly shocked by a little more than two million deaths per year in a nation where nearly four million babies are born every year, a nation of nearly 250 million persons.

And if the newspapers wanted to make that data box just a bit larger and/or longer they could break down those two million deaths into the top categories of killers—you know what they are— heart disease, cancer, strokes, pneumonia, motor vehicle accidents, diabetes, infant mortality and AIDS. And they could always add a footnote to the daily mortality box score if any really newsworthy deviant trend emerged. But it would look pretty much the same, day in and day out, because that's the way life and death pretty much go, day in and day out, a few anomalies aside.

But that's not the way the papers play it. The data dudes and divas are nibbling us to death with a daily diet of death, disease, disability and, yes, depression. They do it one traumatizing statistic at a time. And, boy, does it add up.

- A new study reports that the rate of disability is growing so quickly that "the activities of 1 in every 7 Americans are permanently limited because of health reasons. Between 1966 and 1976, the number of people with health-related disabilities jumped 37 percent to a total of 30.2 million Americans."
- More than a million Americans undergo surgery each year to remove cataracts and replace the clouded lenses with plastic ones.
- The National Centers for Disease Control in Atlanta estimates that "between 400,000 and 4 million Americans will contract salmonella this year." (There's evidential certitude for you.)
- One of every 10 persons at any time is suffering depression.
- Schizophrenia strikes 1 of every 100 Americans. More than 2 million people have it now and each year 100,000 new cases are diagnosed.
- About 80 percent of Americans suffer back pain during their lifetimes. Lower back pain hits about 1 million Americans a day.
- More than 419,000 Americans are dying each year from smoking.
- It used to be that the estimates of the number of Americans suffering from Alzheimer's disease was 2.5 million, but the *Journal of the American Medical Association* upped that figure to 4 million people.
- More than 12 percent of the U.S. adult population have varicose or spider veins, according to the Edgewater Medical Center newsletter in Chicago.

- Fifty million Americans suffer from allergies, according to the *Chicago Sun-Times.*
- Some 25,000 Americans died in drinking-related traffic accidents and 500,000 more suffered serious injuries in alcohol-related vehicle crashes, says the Surgeon General of the United States.
- A urologist at Columbia University's College of Physicians and Surgeons in New York says between 12 and 24 million Americans suffer from urinary incontinence known as "weak bladder."
- Thirty-five million Americans suffer from arthritis, according to the Arthritis Foundation.
- Ann Landers begins a column by reminding us that more than 6 million Americans are alive today who have a history of cancer and that more than 500,000 Americans will die of cancer annually. But the American Institute for Cancer Research reminds us that 1 of every 5 Americans will get cancer.
- *Playboy* magazine reports that more than 25 sexually transmitted diseases infect an estimated 13 million Americans a year.
- Bill Stokes of the *Chicago Tribune* reported: "More than 97 million Americans use public rest rooms at work each day. And more than 20 million have genital herpes which can remain viable on toilet seats up to seven hours."
- The U.S. Consumer Product Safety Commission data show that between 1984 and 1988 some 740 persons died in the U.S. as a result of accidents caused by young children who played with disposable cigarette lighters.
- The *New York Times* reports on studies that show that 70 percent of the American people have felt themselves to be a fraud or an imposter for at least one period of their lives. The studies report that "the conviction that one is a fake may be prevalent in as many as two in every five successful people in all varieties of careers."

- More than 1.2 million Americans will have heart attacks this year and about 500,000 will die of heart disease.
- A study in the *American Journal of Industrial Medicine* reports that there is a sharp increase in the rate of brain cancer among people under age 45.
- The *American Journal of Psychiatry* reports a study which suggests that 5 to 10 percent of the general population may suffer from a dissociative disorder. The *New York Times* reports that the research is "part of a flurry of new findings suggesting that bizarre experiences like the sense of being an automaton, feelings of unreality and amnesia are far more prevalent among otherwise normal people than psychiatrists had believed."
- The Centers for Disease Control reports that each month several thousand people who believe they or their friends or relatives have chronic fatigue syndrome seek advice from the agency. A *Chicago Tribune* story says up to ten million Americans are afflicted by chronic fatigue syndrome.

Are you suffering from chronic problem fatigue yet? Don't fade on me. We're just getting started. We have miles to go before we can sleep and even then, according to the American Medical Association, it won't be easy because there are 30 million Americans who snore, among them an estimated 2.5 million whose snores may be symptomatic of a life-threatening syndrome called "sleep apnea."

- The partners of those who snore may be among the 100 million Americans who are sleep deprived, according to the PBS documentary "Sleep Alert." And for those who use certain long-lasting sleeping pills or powerful tranquilizers to help you get to sleep, there is the danger, if you are elderly, that you will fall and break your hip. This according to a report in the *Journal of the American Medical Association.* The study showed that those who used the long-acting drugs were 70 percent more likely to fall and fracture their hip than those who didn't use the drugs. All in all, about 250,000 Americans fracture their hips each year. And if you're not getting enough sleep, you may be among the millions of Americans who are suffering occupational stress, which, according to the book *Healthy Work,* costs $100 billion to $150 billion a year in medical costs, not to mention the costs of absenteeism and lost productivity.

Is this getting you down? Then you may be among the 9.4 million Americans who suffer clinical depression during any six-month period, according to the American Psychiatric Association. The APA says 1 in 4 women and 1 in 10 men can expect to develop clinical depression during their lifetime.

Do you feel left out? Don't worry. You must be among the 96 percent of Americans who suffer from co-dependency, according to the experts who met at the National Conference on Co-dependency in Scottsdale, Arizona.

- A report says that millions of postmenopausal women who smoke lose "a disproportionate amount of bone mass and face a greater risk of osteoporosis."
- A Public Citizen's Health Research Group report estimates that more than 100,000 Americans are injured or killed in hospitals each year because of doctors' negligence.
- Up to 33 percent of premenopausal women at times suffer with some discomfort before their monthly periods begin and about 10 percent of women report severe disturbances.
- More than 19,000 children four years of age or under required emergency treatment for injuries suffered in grocery store shopping cart accidents in 1992.
- Since 1973, the federal government reports 68 children have been killed and 27,000 injured by motorized garage doors.
- Researchers reported in the *New England Journal of Medicine* that left-handed people tend to live significantly shorter

lives than right-handers. The right-handers studied lived, on average, to be 75. The southpaws, on average, died at age 66. Left-handers got into more accidents.

- Uncle Sam reports that half the 2.5 million people in the United States with lens implants have problems with them. 32 percent of the 1.3 million Americans with artificial joints had trouble with those joints. The survey found that about 11 million Americans have one or more implants. A quarter of the people with cardiac pacemakers have trouble, according to the report. A book, *Adolescent Suicide: Assessment and Intervention,* reports that anywhere from 5,000 to 10,000 Americans between the ages of 15 and 24 commit suicide annually and no one is quite sure why.

Forget the news clips. I've got my own problems.

- I have been hit with laryngitis several times in recent years.
- I used to suffer serious sinus infections three or four times a year.
- My eyesight is deteriorating, more rapidly than I expected. I wear thick lenses.
- For years I endured tonsillitis attacks (my parents, who had no health insurance when I was a boy, did not have my tonsils removed).
- Cold sores break out on or around my lips at least twice a year, causing discomfort physically and mental anguish at the prospect of going on camera with embarrassing sores on my mouth.
- Several of my permanent teeth have been removed and most of my front teeth and some further back are crooked, not to mention yellowish.
- I suffer from a nose bleed at least two or three times a year, particularly if I am under stress in dry, cold conditions.
- I am getting bald. My hair is thin and curls at even a hint of humidity. I can't do a thing with it.

- I suffer from frequent headaches in the spring and summer, particularly when weather systems are moving through the area.
- I experience sleep deprivation at least 50 percent of the time.
- I have gout and take medicine every night to control it. Even then, I am hit once or twice a year with painful gout attacks (my right toe swells up in the middle of the night), particularly if I have been on my feet for hours at a time in the heat (I almost always suffer gout attacks while covering midsummer national political conventions in southern cities).
- I know my prostate gland must be enlarging because I am at that age when I can't sleep through the night without urinating.
- I love rich foods but can't eat them without taking Maalox. My digestive system becomes more sensitive with each passing year.
- I am at least 20 pounds overweight and have been for many years.
- I suffer from diarrhea at least three or four times a year, usually during times of great stress or during foreign travels.
- I experience constipation at least once or twice a year.
- I know that I am allergic to many foods and all sorts of things in the environment, but I refuse to test for allergies because I don't want to stop eating any more things than I already have sacrificed.
- I fell and suffered severe contusions to my right knee in a jogging accident three years ago.
- I have had athlete's foot and jockstrap itch a couple of times.
- As a child, I had bouts of measles, scarlet fever, chicken pox and mumps.
- My parents were alcoholics and so that makes me an adult-child of alcoholics. It also makes me a form of co-dependent.
- I was in several cab accidents in past years and still suffer flare-ups of lower back spasms.

- I constantly fight the problem of calf muscle spasms, particularly during times of great stress and little sleep.
- I have experienced some hemorrhoidal swelling when I overeat certain rich foods or when I suffer several days of diarrhea.
- Several years ago, in a period of great stress, I experienced vertigo.
- My cholesterol level is much too high and I don't even want to think about the thickness of plaque in my heart vessels.

Those, as far as I can remember, are the thirty or so physical and mental ailments or disabilities I have experienced in my first 57 years of life. The interesting thing is that I have missed very few days of work in my 36 years of professional journalism. And the thing is, I am not alone. Thanks to Jane Brody, I am not alone.

Jane Brody is the Diva of Disease, Disability, Depression and Death. In her caring, careful, compassionate weekly personal health column in the *New York Times,* she not only reports on an incredibly wide and varied number of personal health problems, but also takes great care to tell you, the reader, how many other Americans suffer from the same problem.

I do not cough and wheeze and drain alone in my valley of allergies. Ms. Brody reminds me that I am but one of 41 million Americans who have allergicrhintis. The American College of Allergy and Immunology told her so. If someday I learn that one of my allergies is caused by the dust mite (and I'd bet a lot that it is), then I will know, thanks to Jane Brody, that I am but one of 30 million Americans who suffer at the hands or perhaps feet of mites. When my hearing starts to go the way of my eyesight, I will know from Ms. Brody that I am in the company of 15 million other Americans with "significant hearing impairment." If I ever wreck my car because of the sleep deprivation I constantly experience, I will know that I am among the 200,000 to 400,000 Americans who get into traffic accidents in which sleeping at the wheel was a contributing factor. And

I know that "millions of Americans do not get enough sleep" from reading Jane Brody. My athlete's foot does not embarrass me as much as it might because Ms. Brody reminds me that 80 to 90 percent of American men are afflicted at one time or another with foot fungus. I survived my childhood diseases unscathed and with gratitude because Jane Brody reminds me that a million American children are chronically ill and 9 to 10 million have less severe chronic ailments; that 10 to 20 percent of Americans between birth and age 20 "are to a greater or lesser degree chronically ill or disabled."

Thanks to my weekly visit with Jane Brody I am grateful that I am not one of 58 million Americans with high blood pressure (of whom only 20 million are treating it with medication); that I am not one of the seven million Americans with mitral valve prolapse; that I am not one of the "millions" who suffer from a "muted or absent sense of smell"; that I am not one of the 500,000 to 700,000 American children and adults who show "one or more symptoms of cerebral palsy"; that I am not one of the 5 to 10 percent of the population who suffer from Raynaud's syndrome (a circulatory disorder which makes it difficult to keep fingers and toes warm in cold weather); that I am not among the "several hundred thousand men" affected by anorexia and bulimia. My weekly reading of Jane Brody, then, either comforts me with the knowledge that thousands or tens of thousands or hundreds of thousands or millions of Americans share my ailments, or comforts me with reporting on the endless list of physical and mental maladies which I do not yet have to endure.

And I think Ms. Brody would be pleased to know that I am among the millions of Americans who are, partly because of influences like her writing, trying to clean up my act so I can die as healthy as possible. I think she would be pleased to know that I now consume mostly non-alcoholic beer and a glass of wine now and then. I think she would applaud the fact that I have greatly reduced my consumption of fat, thanks to the miracle of the invention of sugarless, no-fat frozen yogurt, which enabled me to shake my Häagen-Dazs habit. I want Ms. Brody to know that when I play golf these days I walk and carry my own clubs most of the time.

But I confess that I will never live up to the standards that Jane Brody lives by in her own life. In her column taking note of her fiftieth birthday she reported that she greeted that occasion "with uninhibited joy." She said that "except for a few nagging wear-and-tear-type problems, I am in better shape at 50 than I was at 15, when I lugged around some extra pounds of flab and most likely would have collapsed before finishing an hour of singles tennis in 90-degree heat." From that column, we learn that Jane Brody is "religious about physical activity," which she does daily "because I enjoy it, not just because it's good for me." She reports that her favorite daily activities include an aerobic walk and a half-mile swim, that she plays singles tennis four or more times a week (or ice skates in the winter) and that if it snows, she cross-country skis. She and her husband like to dance and she uses a bicycle for local transportation. Best of all, her sons gave her a "jazzy" pair of rollerblades on her fiftieth birthday. As for her diet, Ms. Brody reports meals that are low in fat and high in fiber and, I might add, high in good sense and restraint. Whole-grain cereals and fruit for breakfast, homemade soup or casserole or turkey sandwich with whole-grain bread for lunch and large salads with five or six vegetables and a low-fat dressing for a typical dinner. Her coffee, of course, is decaffeinated. Her milk is skim. She drinks eight glasses of water a day and she has replaced her ice cream addiction with low-fat frozen yogurt. No wonder Jane Brody reported that her birthday wish was that "the next 50 years be at least as good as the last ones."

I have met Jane Brody, interviewed her on my television program in Chicago and had her autograph one of her superb cook books for one of my daughters. I read Jane Brody as religiously as some people read their Scriptures. I am a better informed human being and I eat and live more sensibly because of Jane Brody. I may even owe my life to Jane Brody, who knows?

But in all of the hundreds of problem columns and essays Jane Brody has written, she has failed to address one problem and that is what I call the Jane Brody Problem.

What is the Jane Brody Problem? Some would say that the problem with her and all the other diet and nutrition and health specialists is that they tell you something is good one day and then tell you the next day it isn't. Decaffeinated is good for you. No it isn't. Cholesterol will kill you. No it won't. You know the routine—Andy Rooney commentary material. That is not Jane Brody's problem. She is on record about how things change. In a column about the complexities of cholesterol and heart disease, she wrote: "Keep in mind, though, that this information is not carved in stone. Science is constantly evolving, and new information may eventually challenge some advice given today. The best you can do to protect your health is to base your choices on what is now known, and make modifications later if they become scientifically warranted."

You can't find a better, more concise "buyer beware" warning than that. My only complaint is that it isn't included in italicized form at the bottom of every column. No, unsound data and advice are not the Jane Brody Problem.

Others might argue that the Jane Brody Problem is that she is such a goody-two-shoes that she and her ilk take all the fun out of a good alcoholic binge, a good cigar and a thick steak. They argue that the Jane Brodys are reducing the world to a place where you can't be human. But that is not Jane Brody's problem. She is not a prude and she's not a purist. And she knows that the advice that she and the other health and nutrition gurus dispense will be heeded by anything but a majority of citizens and so there is no need to rush out and pass a rash of anti-good health and nutrition laws to protect yourself from the Jane Brodys of this world.

Still others might argue that the Jane Brody Problem is that her writing inspires you to do all of these wonderful things for yourself but it won't do any good because (1) you're going to get hit with lightning on a golf course and die young and thus will have passed up a lot of good times for nothing, or (2) you're not going to get hit with lighting on a golf course and you're going to live so long that you will be a colossal burden on your family and your society, which won't have the resources to pay for all of the needs you're going to have when you just keep on ticking through your eighties and nineties. In my view, that's not the problem with Jane Brody. You shouldn't fault someone for telling you how to make your life a more sensible and comfortable one just because you might live to be a hundred. That's not Jane Brody's responsibility. That is not what I mean by the Jane Brody Problem.

No, the real Jane Brody Problem is that she is right on target with what she thinks and with what she writes. Relentlessly, she identifies one personal health problem after another and addresses it with the latest science and with, I might add, an uncommon amount of common sense. And the Jane Brodys of this nation are, I believe, actually succeeding in changing the behavior of Americans; are actually saving lives and making the lives of millions of us more comfortable and productive. Some problem, huh?

The problem with this success is that it makes people who begin to take control of their own diets, their own drinking habits, their own sexual behavior, their own exercise regimens, their own accident-prevention routines—it makes all of these people expect that this is the way things ought to be done in this world and (this is critically important) it ought to be done NOW. I really believe that among those people who are at the heart of the cause of political cynicism in this country are the Jane Brodys who espouse and live such exemplary lives that they cannot even begin to understand why most people in this country and around the world do not emulate them.

If you know that by changing the way you eat and exercise you actually can reverse heart disease, then you *know* that we can eradicate poverty; we can reform the health care system; we can clean up the environment; we can eliminate ignorance and prejudice and bigotry; we can make all of the schools exemplary; we can make our factories highly productive; we can rebuild the cities; we can make the tax system fair and equitable; we can provide whatever is needed for the rebuilding of Eastern Europe; we can persuade China to be democratic; we can rebuild the infrastructure of America's roads and sewers and bridges; we can eliminate inner-city crime; we can do it all and we can do it NOW.

Well, really! How unfair of me toward Jane Brody. Jane Brody, who we have already acknowledged is a woman of common sense, would not for a minute suggest that all of those social ills can be solved immediately. How unfair to suggest that she would think such a thing. Of course, that is unfair. My point is that the Jane Brodys of this world, who succeed day in and day out in demonstrating the good that applied incremental knowledge can achieve, give all of the specialists who work in the other fields of social and political issues the sense that their problems—schools, crime, productivity, prejudice, whatever—are also susceptible to incremental progress and, who knows, eventual triumph. The very model of health reporting gives this impression. State the problem. State what science or common knowledge is being applied to deal with the problem. State how many Americans suffer from the problem. Give the impression—correctly—that something can be done about each and every one of these health problems.

I am, of course, being unfair to Jane Brody in the sense that it appears that I am trying to state that health reporting is *the* critically important model that all other disciplines mimic in attempting to present a unified, unrelenting march toward the *perfection of mankind.* I can't prove that. But I do submit that the Jane Brody model of health reporting is perfectly representative of what I will call the *New York Times* "Here Is The Problem, Here Is Who Is Affected, Here Is What's Being Done, Here's How The Problem Can Be Solved" approach to reporting which permeates American national journalism today. It is a problem-reporting approach which is so multifarious and which insidiously raises so many expectations simultaneously that it becomes impossible for the few generalists left in our society to prioritize in any politically practical way a few, limited, realistic, carefully considered goals. We are driven to attack all problems on all fronts at all times.

55

⁓

The Parliament of Problems

Sometimes too many facts ruin a good story. The title of P.J. O'Rourke's book about government in the United States is *The Parliament of Whores*. Because that title is so vivid and because it fits the image many citizens are said to have about the United States Congress, O'Rourke's book is cited by columnists, editorial writers and others who have made a living for the past few years taking note of the sad state of affairs on Capitol Hill. They're just a bunch of whores in Congress, insulated from reality, on the take from PACs and insensitive to the needs of ordinary, hard-working Americans. Congressmen, as this lament goes, are a bunch of self-serving know-nothings and do-nothings.

Now it is true that Mr. O'Rourke, one of our more celebrated humorists, begins his chapter on Congress by making fun of the litany of One Minute speeches that opens each day of the House of Representatives. After a couple of pages of lampooning these frequently self-serving little on-camera talks about everything from money laundering to Earth Day, Mr. O'Rourke takes us on the by-now-familiar walk through the House which, as almost always, reveals that very few members are to be seen on the House floor; that "about two hundred regular citizens" are in the visitors' galleries; and that only one member of the press—Mr. O'Rourke—is to be found in the press section. O'Rourke then gives us about three pages of description of the banality of discourse on the floor of the House—H.R. 664 being "a heck of a fine amendment" to the Wild and Scenic Rivers Act, and so on and so forth. This is the kind of material high school humorists find irresistible, as does Mr. O'Rourke.

But then a truly funny thing happens on page 55. Mr. O'Rourke gets himself out of the press gallery of the House and makes his way to where the real work in Congress is done—off the floor and off camera. He introduces us to "a highly respected congressman from a fine political party representing an excellent district of a lovely state (and one who would just as soon not have his name in a book by me)." O'Rourke then spends a day meeting and committee-hopping with this tireless representative. That day began with a political breakfast; followed by a second breakfast for the executive committee of a private club on Capitol Hill; followed by attendance at a Housing and Community Development Subcommittee hearing; followed at 10:00 A.M. by a meeting of the Merchant Marine and Fisheries Committee (which dealt with six different pieces of legislation, two of which involved appropriations of more than one billion dollars); followed by an appearance on the House floor; followed by a 1:00 P.M. meeting back in his congressional district; followed by a 1:15 briefing on the European Bank for Reconstruction and Development; followed by a 2:00 work session with his staff in which pending legislation on everything from a farm bill to a commodities futures trading commission re-authorization bill to a food safety act to a bill to close unnecessary military bases to about fifteen other pieces of legislation.

At this point, Mr. O'Rourke takes note:

> And that, one would think, is about the limit of the human capacity for expertise. To be conversant with twenty-five disparate issues at once is as much as we can ask of a person. However, it is less than 10 percent of what we ask of a congressman. During this same week in 1990, 250 other items were also on the congressional calendar....

And then he goes on to fill more than two pages with the "other items," ranging from the federal budget to paperwork reduction. After exhausting us with list, Mr. O'Rourke notes:

> We expect our congressman to know more about each of these than we know about any of them. We expect him to make wiser decisions than we can about them all. And we expect that congressman to make those wise and knowledgeable decisions without regard for his political or financial self-interest. Then we wonder why it's hard to get first-rate people to run for Congress.

Along about this time, P. J. O'Rourke is putting two and two together and realizing that it doesn't add up to anything in the way of a reasonable expectation: "So here was the congressman I was following, a good and conscientious congressman desperately trying to master all 275 of these issues during the approximately two hours a day when he didn't absolutely have to be somewhere else."

Back to the congressman's day. Next he reviews correspondence and then heads for a 4:00 meeting of his congressional "class" (members of his party elected the same year he was) and then a 5:00 meeting with important members of his party, followed by two different dinners from 5:30 to 9:00 with the National Fire and Emergency Services people on one side of town and the governor of his home state on the other side of town. O'Rourke confesses he was so exhausted that he went home at 7:00 P.M. "leaving the congressman, twenty years my senior, looking as animated and energetic as a full school bus—shaking hands and trading chat with the governor, firemen, ambulance drivers, other congressmen and even, at one point, his own wife."

So much for the congressman as whore. O'Rourke's congressman is "good and conscientious," but tell that to any columnist or editorial writer who hasn't bothered to read O'Rourke's book and has employed O'Rourke's now-famous book title for his own moralistic purposes.

I don't mean to suggest that O'Rourke's book isn't larded with accounts of legislative folly. His skewering of U.S. farm policy is as brilliant a piece of analysis of legislative idiocy as I have ever read and his chapter on the savings and loan fiasco accurately reports on the wholesale buying of legislators in the process of deregulating the savings and loans.

But what the person who has read only the title of O'Rourke's book and not the text will be able to tell you is what O'Rourke finally confesses on page 153—things aren't as simple in Washington, D.C., as the title suggests:

> I spent two and a half years examining the American political process. All that time I was looking for a straightforward issue. But everything I investigated—election campaigns, the budget, lawmaking, the court system, bureaucracy, social policy—turned out to be more complicated than I had thought. There were always angles I hadn't considered, aspects I hadn't weighed, complexities I'd never dreamed of.

Hmmm. Sounds like a congressman, doesn't it? Of course, O'Rourke can't confess to rubbing up against complexity without concluding that the omnibus farm bill was the one simple problem with a simple solution—drag the farm bill behind the barn and "kill it with an ax."

But killing Congress with an ax is what columnists, editorialists, think-tank scholars and many of the rest of us have been doing. In our impatience with the consequences of complexity born of our own special needs, problems, aspirations, discoveries and advocacies, we are chopping away at the very institution we ask so much of and expect so much from.

Well, you might say, "I don't ask Congress for much. Just keep the nation safe from invaders and deliver the mail and leave pretty much the rest well enough alone."

Not me. I'm worried about social security. I'm worried about whether or not the deduction for mortgage interest and real estate taxes will continue. I'm worried that the subsidy for public television will disappear completely and so will my job. I'm worried that the investment necessary to improve air controllers' services won't be forthcoming and that I'll die in a mid-air collision over O'Hare Field. I'm worried that the farm subsidies will be goofed up and the farmers will get mad and I won't have enough fresh vegetables and meat on the table. I'm worried that they won't put enough funding into AIDS research and friends of mine will die because they didn't find an AIDS vaccine. I'm worried that Uncle Sam won't appropriate enough money to provide the former Soviet Republics and Eastern Europe with enough support and that all hell will break loose in that part of the world and we'll end up paying more for putting things back together over there. I'm worried that somehow the government won't find enough money to shore up the FDIC and somehow my own bank will close. I'm worried that my pension fund won't be protected and I'll die impoverished. I'm worried that they'll sink all of their money into highways and not enough into mass transit and that my city's roads will become more clogged and my air more polluted than ever.

I'm worried about lots of other things Congress has its nose in and so are you. Collectively, we are "worried" about thousands of issues, problems and priorities. If it is not my mortgage interest deduction, it is your farm price support. One way or the other, millions and millions of us who, through the wonders of free speech, free enterprise, scientific and social discovery, have created thousands and thousands of diverse activities and approaches to life and the thousands upon thousands of organizations and their representatives to speak for us, now find ourselves asking our representatives in Congress to help us, referee disputes among us and allocate resources for us.

And yet most of us want to deny that we are the problem. They—the congressmen—are the problem.

We want to have it both ways. In the Kettering Foundation's report on how "ordinary citizens" viewed their government, a

Richmond, Virginia, woman represented many who were interviewed in the Kettering focus groups: "I think years ago politics
was different. You could talk to your politician.... Today the population is so big that it has distanced him from you."

But look for a minute at a finding of *U.S. News & World
Report*'s scathing report on Congress in October, 1990: "... fully
two-fifths of the staffs of House members now work back home,
almost double the proportion that did so during the 1970s."

So the politician is distant and remote, but you are able to get
constituent service from the increased staff members in the district offices back home. Congressmen are distant and remote, but
they spend too much money on franking privileges of communication with you through the mail. Congressmen are distant and
remote, but they insist on sending you those questionnaires through
the free mails to know your views on the major issues of the day.
Congressmen are distant and remote, but they work from 8 A.M.
until 9 P.M. and later meet with dozens of groups and constituents,
year in and year out. Congressmen are distant and remote, but are
usually re-elected by citizens who tell pollsters that they like and
respect their congressmen, but not Congress as a whole.

And who turns out to be as good a champion of the unknown
Congressman as can be found? None other than our parliamentary whore master, Mr. P. J. O'Rourke:

> The congressman normally spends three such days a week in
> Washington—Tuesday through Thursday—then flies halfway
> across the nation to his congressional district and spends Friday,
> Saturday and Monday doing more of the same at lectures, din-
> ners, town-hall meetings and his two constituent service offices....

So much for being distant and remote.

And what about the intolerable pay raises these congressional
hacks voted themselves that unleashed the venom of so many radio
talk show hosts and their callers? Mr. P. J. O'Rourke to the defense,
if you please:

He takes one week of vacation in August, one week at Christmas and one week at Easter. And he does all of this for $125,000 per year, which, for all the public's caterwauling over the congressional pay raise, is less than what a shortstop hitting .197 makes.

And what about those huge staffs that insulate the congressman and make them so distant and remote? Mr. P. J. O'Rourke returns to the defense:

> I ... we Americans have struck a remarkable bargain. We pay $566,220 a year—less than a dollar apiece—for a congressman and his staff, and in return they listen to us carp and moan and fume and gripe and ask to be given things for free.

O'Rourke said he read a week of the congressman's mail and that of the more than 700 letters received, "there were exactly two thank-you notes in the pile."

O'Rourke, like most of the rest of us, is having it both ways also. He will be receiving royalties from his best-selling book for years, royalties based on the popular perception that his book confirms what all of us have known all along—that the folks in Congress are a bunch of lazy, overfed, pampered, out-of-touch oafs who ought to be horsewhipped and sent home at once. A memorable title—*Parliament of Whores.* The only trouble is, Mr. O'Rourke bothered to do some homework and some legwork and contradicted that title with a wealth of evidence that many of our congressmen are anything but whores. And yet I promise you that the imprint of his book's title, the cynicism that it breeds, will live long after his text, which apparently a whole host of popularizers either didn't read or chose to ignore.

Those who didn't bother to read or report O'Rourke's real findings on the congressman he portrayed also may have failed to read the conclusion of the book: "Every government is a parliament of whores. The trouble is in a democracy, the whores are us."

That, in my view, is cynicism taken to the extreme. But I know that Mr. O'Rourke is not trying to be cynical when he suggests that we are the whores. If his book leaves us with nothing else it is that we make impossible demands on our legislators and our government in that we demand from them but don't want to pay for our demands. We have seen the enemy and he is we, so to speak.

What P. J. O'Rourke and other moralists will not acknowledge is that long before the special interests came barging into town with their buckets of money and their devious means of gaining access to the "whores" in Congress and elsewhere in government, those representatives of the special interests were in direct contact with the teachers, the truckers, the nurses, the farmers, the scientists, the real estate developers, the hospitals, the banks, the insurance companies, the charitable foundations and the thousands of others they represent and they had sincere communication about real-life needs, expectations and goals. Those leaders of special interests were usually selected by the people they represented in meetings and forums that were democratically organized. Then those leaders selected professional representatives-lobbyists—to help them communicate those real-life needs, expectations and goals. And before we introduce any element of bribery, unfair access to or outright purchase of votes of incumbents, we must acknowledge the presence of the thousands of sincere interests and advocacies. Once we have acknowledged that, we can factor in the corruption factor (which is substantial) and then you've got a fair picture of how serious the problem is of being a legislative generalist trying to referee the demands and needs of thousands of organized constituencies.

56

∾

The Age of Blinding Light

Today there is little mystery left about the origins and nature of the Black Death; a few points remain to be clarified but all the essential facts are known. But in the Middle Ages the plague was not only all-destroying, it was totally incomprehensible. Medieval man was equipped with no form of defense—social, medical or psychological—against a violent epidemic of this magnitude.

—Philip Ziegler,
The Black Death

While Divine punishment was accepted as the plague's source, people in their misery still looked for a human agent upon whom to vent the hostility that could not be vented on God. The Jew, as the eternal stranger, was the most obvious target. The sense of a vanishing future created a kind of dementia of despair.

—Barbara W. Tuchman,
A Distant Mirror

In the Age of Blinding Light,* politicians and other leaders are the new Jews, the victims of the despair, discontent and hostility which are the understandable, if not appropriate, reactions to incomprehensible change and complexity. Where there is guilt, there will be scapegoats. In the fourteenth century, the Jews weren't the only scapegoats, but more than the Christians and Arabs and others who were blamed for the Plague, they were seen as the bad guys.

The Black Plague analogy is, of course, inexact. While Jews, Arabs, Christians and other scapegoats were clearly not responsible for spreading the Black Plague, today's politicians and other leaders must bear part of the responsibility for the inadequacy of our public policy and politics. Modern leaders may face greater complexity than at any time in the past, but that does not excuse them from their demonstrable stupidity, greed, incompetence and sometimes killing brutality which they share with leaders—that is to say humans—of previous ages.

What distinguishes, I believe, the situation today from past history is that the very finest minds we have, the most humane of our leadership class, are just as vulnerable to the problems of "not knowing what we are doing" amid the seas of complexity as are the "bad guys" who have been always among us. It doesn't matter if you are the finest scholar, the hardest worker, the most incorruptible of human beings—you still cannot know what you are doing in this environment of thousands of social and political and scientific interactions. But even if you are among "the best and the brightest" and the most caring, the most humane, the hardest working, etc., believe me, you will find that you are blamed for what goes wrong. It almost seems to be more comforting to be a truly evil leader in this situation—at least you end up deserving the scorn directed at you.

The Black Plague analogy holds up best, I fear, in thinking about when we finally will know what it is we need to come to

---

*I mean light as in information and raw data, not wisdom.

terms with modern complexity and its attendant failures and costs. If we were living in the fourteenth century in Florence and watching our family and friends and strangers dying in their homes, on the streets and everywhere else, we would have the following choices of behavior: (1) we could move the bodies off the paths and streets so that we might go on about our business; (2) we could, upon seeing that all of the persons in a certain home or building had died of the Plague, burn down the home or building and hope we had killed whatever caused the Plague; (3) we could blame the Jews or others we deemed appropriate scapegoats. What we would not have known, as we contemplated or took action on those or other choices, is that we were more than 400 years away from possessing a true understanding of what caused the fatal ailment.

And my question is, are we several decades or centuries away from whatever knowledge it is that we require to deal with the level of complexity that plagues us today? If we are a long way off from devising or discovering the means to deal with complexity, should we ask ourselves to behave in such a way as to acknowledge that we know that we don't know? And if we agree that we should acknowledge that we don't know what we are doing, how should we behave politically, socially, morally?

Surely we do not wish to cease our speaking out on issues. Surely we do not wish to stop identifying problems and working on them. Just because we have established that the rise of specialized science and information gave birth to the rise of special problem interests, we surely do not wish to abandon our pursuit of those special problem interests. Who among us would tell those who are working in the laboratories, lobbying, raising funds and spreading information about a cure for a childhood disease, to stop working in behalf of their noble cause?

There is a theological dimension of the Age of Blinding Light that has to do with the ability to know the truth and to tell the truth at a time when we are evolving from a typographical world

into a world of the "visualization of knowledge." Neil Postman
deals with this in his book: *Amusing Ourselves to Death:*

> In studying the Bible as a young man, I found intimations
> of the idea that forms of media favor particular kinds of con-
> tent and therefore are capable of taking command of a culture.
> I refer specifically to the Decalogue, the Second Commandment
> of which prohibits the Israelites from making concrete images
> of anything. "Thou shalt not make unto thee any graven image,
> or any likeness of anything that is in heaven above, or that is in
> the earth beneath, or that is in the water under the earth." I
> wondered then, as so many others have, as to why the God of
> these people would have included instructions on how they
> were to symbolize, or not symbolize, their experience. It is a
> strange injunction to include as a part of an ethical system *unless
> its author assumed a connection between forms of human com-
> munication and the quality of culture.* We may hazard a guess
> that a people who are asked to embrace an abstract, universal
> deity would be rendered unfit to do so by the habit of drawing
> pictures or making statues or depicting their ideas in any con-
> crete, iconographic form. The God of the Jews was to exist in
> the Word and through the Word, an unprecedented conception
> requiring the highest order of abstract thinking. Iconography
> thus became blasphemy so that a new kind of God could enter
> a culture. People like ourselves who are in the process of con-
> verting their culture from word-centered to image-centered
> might profit by reflecting on this Mosaic injunction. But even
> if I am wrong in these conjectures, it is, I believe, a wise and
> particularly relevant supposition that the media of communi-
> cation available to a culture are a dominant influence on the
> formation of the culture's intellectual and social preoccupations.

In this world of thousands of images clamoring for our attention every minute of every day, it is almost embarrassing to give
serious thought to the possibility that the injunction against graven

images has any relevance morally to our lives. We perceive that so much good has accompanied our freedom of political and artistic and commercial expression that the injunction could not possibly apply to us moderns. Aside from using our imagemaking capacities to produce lies, propaganda, appeals to vanity and vulgar consumption and pornography, what is ungodly about so much of our expression of images? It doesn't really seem relevant to our lives at all unless you accept the thesis that we are living in the Age of Blinding Light and that the thousands upon thousands of graven images to be found in our visual, commercial, sexual, political culture are, in the aggregate, leading us away from a life of possible faith in and commitment to God. And when you think about it that way, it isn't such an embarrassment to give the graven image injunction some serious thought.

I have argued that the freedom of expression which is the political oxygen of the capitalistic free market system contains within it the kind of reforming power which can be utilized to combat the evil excesses that capitalism almost always experiences in its various stages in a given industry.

I have argued with only a bit of tongue-in-cheek that if we acknowledge that capitalism in its earliest Western epochs condoned and encouraged slavery, child-labor, smoke-stack pollution, unfair trading practices, colonial imperialism and union busting, then we have no right to expect that, for example, the relatively young capitalization of the means of electronic communication should be denied its period of child abuse, among other sins.

But I have also argued that because the free speech which accompanies capitalism has built into it the reformist possibility, we should not think that television's abuse of children will always be permitted. But I do not mean, by pointing out that freedom of expression has the seeds of political, social and cultural reform in it, that in the end it will necessarily succeed in striking some kind of humane balance. It may very well be that the cacophony of images exploding from our television sets, our radios, our billboards, our junk mail, our telephones, our satellites, our faxes and all of our other forms of communication may do more harm to our spiritual capacities than the political consequences—the cynicism, that grows out of larger public policies which either don't work the way they were intended or have costs associated with them which are backbreakingly higher than anyone ever expected.

Combine the cacophony of images with the explosion of science and God-playing and it may add up to an uncontrollable self-defeating din, a madness which makes the Tower of Babel seem innocent by comparison.

Well, you say, are we to become Amish? Well, I say that may very well be the point of the discussion. Well, you say, why not some sane balance instead of total abstinence of images? Well, I say, I would prefer some sane balance, but you tell me who regulates that balance, who creates it. I would prefer not to think about these extremes, but I cannot face the religious implications of an Age of Blinding Light and ignore them.

Genesis 11:1–9:

And the whole earth was of one language, and of one speech. And it came to pass, as they journeyed from the east, that they found a plain in the land of Shinar; and they dwelt there. And they said one to another, Go to, let us make brick, and burn them thoroughly. And they had brick for stone, and slime had they for mortar. And they said, Go to, let us build us a city and a tower, whose top may reach unto heaven; and let us make us a name, lest we be scattered abroad upon the face of the whole earth. And the LORD came down to see the city and the tower, which the children of men builded. And the LORD said, Behold, the people is one, and they have all one language; and this they begin to do: and now nothing will be restrained from them, which they have imagined to do. Go to, let us go down, and there confound their language, that they may not understand one another's speech. So the LORD scattered them abroad from thence upon the face of all the earth; and they left off to build the city. Therefore is the name of it called Babel because the LORD did there confound the language of all the earth: and from thence did the LORD scatter them abroad upon the face of all the earth; and they left off to build the city.

Is it silly to think about the Tower of Babel in the context of the Age of Blinding Light? Not if you believe in the Bible. Not if you believe that man's secular quest for knowledge can sweep him away from the one thing he can't successfully live and die without: a humbling faith in God. Apparently the Lord's scattering of them and his confounding of their speech did not stop mankind from achieving the incredible knowledge that has led to today's marvels of science and social "progress."

We may have experienced in the course of this great scientific and secular progress a new form of a Tower of Babel. It may be, indeed, an Age of Blinding Light. It may be a time when the pain of our inability to interweave the specialized knowledge we possess with the spiritual needs we have is reflected in the costs, frustrations and futilities experienced in the possession of so much knowledge, knowledge that seems somehow to rise up and bite us in our state of blindness.

There may be a message in this pain, in this frustration, in this futility. We may be deaf to the real message that is upon us: that we cannot live without prayer, without humility, without faith. We may attach deep religious motivation to the pursuits of humane social policy, economic policy and all kinds of other secular policies; we may even give our lives over to those pursuits in the name of Christ or some other deity, but we may in the course of those pursuits be ignoring the underlying, yes, fundamental, need for utter, uncompromising faith. My own view is that those fortunate

enough to be blessed with fundamental faith are better prepared
to navigate in the Age of Blinding Light than those without it. And
those who join together in some kind of community of faith are
able to make their way in an Age of Blinding Light better than
those who try to go it alone.

Thus, the rise of religious fundamentalism should be seen as
a natural response to this age of complexity even if it is seen (usually mistakenly) by most in the Western secular world as a dangerous, reactionary, know-nothing, violence-prone, fanatical
response. My own quarrel with the most brutal of the fundamentalists is that they have little or no compassion for the travails
of those of us who try to make our way through the blinding light
armed only with the very thing that got us into this state of things
in the first place, our secular, scientific knowledge. But maybe they
are the representatives on earth of an angry God who wants to
shake us into an understanding that our secular ways are not the
way. It may not be the task of the religious fundamentalists to sym-
pathize or understand the scientific secularist; it may be only, as
the late literary critic Leslie Fiedler so eloquently put it, "say NO
in thunder."

Think about it. Doesn't it have truly understandable biblical
overtones—this notion that man's rationality will prevail? *Isn't it
quite apparent that we have built a super-scientific manifest complexity that defies the very essence of the humble existence the great
religious texts suggest we should live?* Isn't the picture of all of the
hustle and bustle and trading and exchanging and researching and
financing and bombing and spying a picture of secular desperation?

I think millions of people in this world feel that sense of desperation, and, even if they live basically secular lives, they try to
hold onto something they call the church community and they
continue to struggle for faith and with their faith. I think that struggle is one of the reasons that all of the change which has beset us
has not totally destroyed us. It is why I think we have succeeded
over incredible odds in maintaining, however badly shaken, a foun-

dation of a community of faith. It is why we have not been done in totally by all of the diversions, the entertainments, the conceits of modern electronic communications and the rest of the accoutrements of modernity. The enchantments, the addictions, the seductions of the modern ways of life are so powerful, so pervasive that it, to me, is a miracle that so many millions of people even make a stab at continuing a life of faith, of witnessing to the need for God, to the need for redemption. Surely, it must be the felt pain of all of this scientific and secular achievement—it's ultimate hollowness, it's ultimate futility—which enables even the most distracted, the most consumed among us to know that it is not enough.

My plea is that, while we take that painful trip toward the knowledge of the necessity of faith, that we don't get sidetracked into the very attractive interim moralistic approach of casting stones at our leaders. We are they. They are we. We walk blinded in this Age of Blinding Light together. Sometimes we will lead them, sometimes we will follow, but we should not despise them or permit ourselves to be cynical about them. We are the blind leading the blind in this Age of Blinding Light.

I do not possess that faith. I know I need it. I wish I could find it, because I know that if it is to be found, one is blessed. In a peculiar way, these essays about our problem society may be an exercise, an attempt at working my way toward a faith in God, a faith in salvation, redemption. I love my secular interests and passions, but they are not enough. In the end there is an emptiness, a purposelessness which is so abundantly present in my life, and in the lives of most people I know, that it is pitiful. And yet I feel a certain humble strength in the fact that I have not lost the power to pray; that I have not lost the capacity to feel the pain and despair of faithlessness; that I have not lost the deeply felt understanding that the life of the spirit is the only lasting life; and that I have not lost the capacity to know that I am living in a state of sin, a state of the absence of grace. I have not lost faith in the knowledge that I must find faith.

Does this confession mean that I hope we can all turn our backs on scientific "progress"? No, I don't mean that. I think the challenge is to accumulate over many decades and centuries, an understanding of what the real costs of progress are and to begin to factor those costs into community decisions (world community, regional community, local community, church community, etc.) about the kinds of lives we need to live. It is not enough to have the Clean Air Act and the Clean Water Act. It is not enough to state the needs of "children at risk" in terms of dollars of productivity lost if we don't invest in those children earlier. Economic models will not suffice. Environmental models will not suffice, although human economics and environmentalism can be a part of a larger spiritual consideration required to live lives of reasonable secular success and lives of deep spiritual and religious conviction.

57

⌒

What to Do in the Problem Society

"So, what do we do about it?"
Some people who have listened to the talk I give which presents the main themes of these essays ask that question immediately upon the conclusion of the talk. They ask it with a certain impatience as if to say, "Okay, if you're so smart about describing the problem problem, then solve it. Now."

Their do-it-now expectation is a perfect representation of the problem problem I have been describing. Their attitude, to some extent, is the problem.

I have said the Age of Blinding Light is the modern equivalent of the Black Plague and in some ways I feel that we are just as many years removed from "an answer" to our complexity syndrome as the people in the fourteenth century were removed from the microbiological knowledge they needed to cope with the plague. I'm not saying it necessarily will take us centuries to begin to deal with the problem problem (although it could), but I'm suggesting that it might take a lot longer than our "do it, solve it now" attitude will tolerate.

The other big response to my problem problem talks goes something like, "Thank you for putting politics in perspective. Never again will I take the president for granted. I'll still criticize the president but I will never again criticize him without knowing what the larger context is." I find that response most gratifying because it is the one thing I hope to achieve with these essays and that is to raise our consciousness about the complexity and texture of modern political and social life. We simply must learn to embrace paradox and to be more comfortable with carrying competing truths in our minds. For someone who wants to take the message of this book the wrong way, it will be very tempting to say that complexity excuses incompetence or laziness or greed or malfeasance in public life. It is very easy to use Freudian theory to excuse criminal or anti-social behavior. I think it is important for society to demand of itself and its leaders a level of behavior that meets reasonable standards of public need and accountability. That is, I don't want my complexity message to be used as a cop-out any more than any of us want to excuse criminal behavior because someone had an unhappy childhood. It may be intellectually and morally important to understand that an unhappy childhood may contribute to criminal or anti-social behavior and our understanding of that might make us a more intelligent observer of the human condition and a more compassionate citizen who pays attention to such issues as nutrition, early childhood education, child-abuse prevention and the like, but when the criminal strikes, we can't respond with a seminar on childhood unhappiness.

And so I say to the reformers and the do-gooders and the investigative reporters and the stand-up comedians and the angry citizens, by all means continue to stand on your soapboxes, beat your breast, write and broadcast your exposés, and raise all kinds of Cain about the things you think aren't right in our society. Complexity does not excuse (1) rank stupidity, (2) venality, (3) abject incompetence, (4) criminal malfeasance, (5) gross insensitivity to public need, (6) blind ambition which leads to achieving public office with lack of experience, (7) enactment of policies which deprive people of their basic rights and (8) any other behavior that grossly betrays the public trust and a reasonable standard of public policy achievement. There is so much of this behavior in political and corporate life that all of the moralists and critics should enjoy a long and busy life in watchdogging the scoundrels among us.

But this I do ask of the reformers, the do-gooders, the moralists, the investigators and others who spend so much of their waking hours telling us what is wrong with our leaders and with our society: try to understand that the level of complexity encountered by the relatively few generalists in our leadership makes it almost certain that their attempts at formulating large social policy in this Age of Blinding Light will most frequently either fail or succeed for reasons and events which will be beyond their honest strivings or understanding. Understand that they and you and I simply don't know what we're doing at this level of political and social activity. And I also say to those reformers, moralists et al., that they should remember that they must help referee the psychological battle between those in our society who excel at their specialties and who thus become very impatient, and those generalist leaders among us who don't excel at their tasks. They should also help those of us who have become cynical about our generalist leaders to understand that some of our cynicism may be most self-defeating and counterproductive.

To the generalist political, social, corporate, religious or labor leader who feels overwhelmed by special problem interests, overwhelmed by complexity and by public and journalistic criticism and cynicism, I would counsel a decent amount of non-self-pitying candor about your feelings. One of the most refreshing trends in my interviews with politicians in recent years is their increasing willingness to say, "John, I don't know." It was refreshing to hear President Clinton acknowledge, in his October, 1993, speech to Congress, that there simply were aspects of his 240,000-word, 1,342-page proposed Health Security Act that could not be known in advance.

I would only add that I think it might be useful for politicians, when saying that they don't know, to take another minute and explain why they don't know. If they find themselves roped into voting on a 1,700-page "omnibus" bill at the last minute of a legislative session and have to answer for it later to the press and public, I think they ought to explain in as much detail as possible how that came to be.

To the specialists who are down on generalist politicians, administrators and journalists who simply don't know their specialty and will never know their specialty the way they, the specialists, do, I would advise the investment in education efforts for the leaders they are trying to reach. It is all too easy to say, "Oh, they'll never understand. They won't get it right. They'll just screw it up worse." The fact that they will probably not understand and won't get it right and will just screw it up should not stop you for a minute in making a good-faith effort somehow to translate the language of your specialty to larger leadership and lay audiences. All specialists who know that their findings must eventually seep one way or the other into the larger body politic and society have an intellectual, social, political and moral responsibility to do a better job of communicating and translating their knowledge. You can't retreat to your scientific laboratories, your special problem interest caves, and then complain about the leaders and lay public who don't understand you or your special knowledge. If you don't learn to share your knowledge and translate it successfully to leaders and larger publics, you'll boil in your own special oil of lonely knowledge.

To the universities that try to educate youngsters in a general way, I would plead that you take urgent note of the crisis of generalists in our society and establish well-funded, cross-disciplinary committees or institutes which will begin to utilize every resource at your disposal to begin to acknowledge and deal with the stupefying challenge of preparing generalist leaders to deal with thousands upon thousands of specialists. I would ask that those colleges, universities and laboratories which turn out specialist scholars make sure that there is built into every component of the specialists' education a requirement of several units of study of how that specialty can be better communicated publicly.

If you have stopped voting in general elections because you find the generalist politicians are not worthy of your vote, I hope you'll rethink your position. I hope that you will understand that even the best of men and women under current conditions are going to look like fools because they can't know how complex social and political issues are going to combust once they enter by the hundreds and thousands into the body politic. By all means, don't vote for the scoundrels, the crooks and others you know to be venal, utterly without care or competence. But give yourself permission, please, to consider voting for the generalist who is reasonably bright, but who finds himself or herself dealing with a world that no reasonable person can master. In other words, don't let cynicism prevent you from playing the political game even though we're all playing that game blinded by the light of modern complexity.

My own view is that under the circumstances I have described in this book, we are doing better than we have any right to expect. Go back and read "The Problem Century" and then ask yourself why any of us should enjoy rich family life under those circumstances of incredible social and political upheaval, technological change and the assault on "traditional" values. The fact that many marriages don't make it under these circumstances is not, in my view, big news. The big story is that under this unrelenting assault of change any marriages survive. I know we're supposed to weep and moan and weep and moan about how our children can't read, but given the seductive, narcotic power of television, isn't the real news that as many of our kids read as do?

I'm not being optimistic when I put it in this perspective. For all I know we truly are in the midst of the decline and fall of this civilization. That is very possible. All I am trying to do is point out that what with the hurricane level of change being thrust at us, it is a miracle that we aren't more like the Inupiat of Barrow,

Alaska, who have been reduced almost totally to an alcoholic stupor and dependency.

Perhaps my friend, Leonard Reiffel, a nuclear physicist, has it right. After hearing my thesis of the Problem Society he said the reason we aren't like the Barrow Inupiat is that they had the misfortune to be hit by one major change, alcohol, whereas we have been hit by so many from so many sides that our civilization looks something like a huge rugby scrum—all of us standing, holding together, battered and beaten by change, but still standing from the uplift caused by being hit from all sides, not just one side.

And finally, please, God, give faith to those of us who lack it and help preserve the faith of those who are blessed with it.